Contents

Understanding Data and Information Systems for Recordkeeping

Philip C. Bantin

Neal-Schuman Publishers, Inc.

New York   London

Published by Neal-Schuman Publishers, Inc.
100 William St., Suite 2004
New York, NY 10038

Printed and bound in the United States of America.

The paper used in this publication meets the minimum requirements of American National Standard for Information Sciences—Permanence of Paper for Printed Library Materials, ANSI Z39.48–1992.

Library of Congress Cataloging-in-Publication Data
Bantin, Philip C.
    Understanding data and information systems for recordkeeping / by Philip C. Bantin.
       pp. cm. — (The archives & record manager's bookshelf ; 2)
       Includes bibliographical references and index.
       ISBN 978–1–55570–580–0 (alk. paper)
       1. Records—Management. 2. Electronic information resources. 3. Database management. 4. Business records—Management—Data processing. I. Title.

HF5736.B25 2008
651.50285—dc22

                                                          2008034855

List of Figures

Foreword

Philip Bantin's *Understanding Data and Information Systems for Recordkeeping* is an important book for the archives and records management professional. As the author points out in his introduction, archivists and records managers need to understand the information systems that create and manage contemporary records. This understanding is necessary to communicate our needs and concerns to the information technology professionals responsible for systems and the records they contain. This book goes far to bridge the gap between professional perspectives.

After discussing the development of digital information systems since the Second World War, Bantin summarizes archival theory and practice about the nature of recordkeeping systems. Taken together, these first two chapters present a foundation for discussions among information and recordkeeping professionals.

In chapters 3–6, Bantin presents a structured approach for understanding the most common information systems and applying recordkeeping principles to them. He covers in depth: transaction processing systems (TPS) constructed on the relational database model, enterprise document management, and content management systems; decision support systems and data warehouses; and e-mail management systems. Throughout these chapters, Bantin's central principle is that archivists and records managers need to understand the technology in order to manage the records that flow from each technology. Bantin makes this information accessible to technophobes as well as technophiles.

Chapter 7 recognizes that the information and recordkeeping environments are affected by larger legal and regulatory concerns. Because organizations rely on digital systems for their mission-critical activities, the information systems often are part of legal and regulatory proceedings. Archivists and records managers increasingly are finding themselves part of compliance teams, either permanently or on an ad hoc basis. Understanding the legal system has become as important as understanding the information system itself. This book helps with both levels of understanding.

As series editor, I am pleased that *Understanding Data and Information Systems for Recordkeeping* is part of the Archives and Record Manager's Bookshelf. This is precisely the kind of book that Neal-Schuman and I envisioned when establishing the series—a book that recognizes the commonality of interest among archivists and records managers and facilitates communication between these closely related professions. Philip Bantin has been a leader in the management of digital records for the last two decades. In this book he summarizes much of what he has learned from being in both the trenches and the classroom. Countless archivists and records managers will benefit from his generosity in undertaking this daunting task.

Gregory S. Hunter, Ph.D., CA, CRM
Long Island University
Series Editor

Preface

The automation of records has caused a revolution in archives and records management. Fifty years ago, an organization would create and archive vital business documents such as annual budgets and long-range plans entirely in paper form. Fifteen years ago, the same organization might have created a budget or plan on the computer, but would print it out as a report and file it physically for long-term access. Today, organizations use automated electronic systems to create, store, and manage many of their most important, mission-critical records.

In order to be effective in this new world of electronic records management, archivists and records management professionals require two types of knowledge. First, they must understand the design features and existing functionality of the information systems commonly used by their institutions. Second, they must define the functional requirements for the type of system they want to build. Existing literature doesn't address these issues adequately. IT literature has discussed the first point in great detail—and usually in very technical language. Rarely does IT literature analyze the functionality of these information systems in terms of their impact on recordkeeping. Records management and archives literature, on the other hand, has done a good job of defining recordkeeping requirements, but has rarely described and analyzed information systems in any detail.

In *Understanding Data and Information Systems for Recordkeeping*, I attempt to provide a bridge between the theoretical discussions about recordkeeping requirements and specifications that have taken place in our field and the general technical facts available elsewhere. Using largely non-technical language, I discuss how information systems capture, store, and manage data. I also examine how to adapt these systems for use as recordkeeping systems, which are special information systems that manage and preserve the records that provide evidence of business transactions or of personal activities. I have tried to address the concerns of archivists and records managers in both the public and private sectors. I hope that the basic content will also be useful for others involved in the process, including IT staff, auditors, risk managers, and lawyers.

My discussion of commonly used information systems, such as relational databases, data warehouses, decision support systems, and document management and content management systems, is organized around four objectives. First, I provide information on how these systems are designed and how to identify which types of functionality are primary and which are secondary. Second, I review the basic architecture of these systems to provide readers with a more detailed analysis of how data, information, and records are processed and managed. A third objective is to use the design features and functionality to analyze how the information systems function as recordkeeping systems. To achieve this goal, I compare the known functionality of the system under review with the functional requirements and metadata specifications that have been established for recordkeeping systems. Fourth, I analyze the strengths and weaknesses of the information systems as recordkeeping applications. As part of this analysis, I recommend some options and strategies for transforming these systems into better, more functional recordkeeping systems.

Understanding Data and Information Systems for Recordkeeping reflects the reality that in most cases, you will not be designing a new structure from scratch. Most projects will involve critiquing what currently exists and building future strategies around and through these information systems. Simply knowing what you want to achieve will not get you where you want to go. To reach your goals, you must understand the present and existing environment and fit your requirements and specifications into that framework.

ORGANIZATION

Chapter 1, "The Impact of Change on the Management of Electronic Records," examines the outside forces that have impacted how records are created and managed. Questions that are addressed in the chapter include: What changes have occurred in the business environment? How has computer technology developed? How are these changes in organizational structure and in technology transforming archives and records management theory and practice?

Chapter 2, "Recordkeeping Systems," reviews the definitions of records, recordkeeping systems, and metadata. Functional requirements statements, metadata specifications, and the characteristics that should be considered essential and fundamental for any such system are discussed.

Chapter 3, "Transaction Processing Systems Constructed on the Relational Database Model," details the design features and functionality of these systems. Issues covered include data model construction, structural components of relational databases, the ways in which a database preserves historical information, and strategies for making transaction processing systems better for recordkeeping.

Chapter 4, "Enterprise Document Management and Content Management Systems," discusses the evolution of document management systems from the mid 1990s to the present. It describes the changes of the past few years, current functionality, and the recordkeeping capabilities of content management systems.

Chapter 5, "Decision Support Systems and Data Warehouses," explains these applications, how they are structured, and how they capture, integrate, and transform data. The types of metadata typically found in the warehouse and the changes warehouses may undergo in the near future are also covered. The chapter concludes by examining whether data warehouses can be transformed into effective recordkeeping systems.

Chapter 6, "E-mail Management," outlines strategies for handling e-mail as a business record. It examines relevant court cases and litigation, pinpointing specific challenges in managing e-mail and actions that can be taken to overcome these challenges.

Chapter 7, "Laws, Regulations, and Best Practices Relating to Electronic Records Management," evaluates the most relevant legislation and requirements from the United States, Canada, and the United Kingdom. It also identifies lessons to be learned from these laws, regulations, and best practices as they relate to recordkeeping.

Chapter 8, "Conclusion," suggests reasons to be both optimistic and pessimistic about the future of electronic records management.

Developing effective electronic recordkeeping systems requires a thorough understanding of existing information systems. *Understanding Data and Information Systems for Recordkeeping* is dedicated to providing archivists and records managers with essential knowledge on how commonly used systems process data and information so that our professions can make a real and significant impact on how records are managed within our institutions.

1

The Impact of Change on the Management of Electronic Records

Records and records management strategies are not created in a vacuum. Records are products of events occurring in the physical world, and they are managed by systems (people, technology, etc.) within environments that are always changing. In particular, there are two primary and interrelated developments that have had a major impact on how records are created and managed: changes in technology and transformations in how institutions are structured and in how they organize their workflow.

CHANGES IN TECHNOLOGY

GENERATIONS OF AUTOMATION

Scholars of technology typically classify the history of computers into various generations of automation based largely on the types of processing hardware. (For description of these technology changes, see Campbell-Kelly and Aspray [1996]; Shurkin [1996]; Tapscott and Caston [1993].)

First Generation Computers (1937–1956)

The first generation of computers used vacuum tubes to store and process information. These tubes consumed a great deal of power and had to be replaced frequently. First generation computers were very large and had extremely limited memory and processing capability. They were used primarily for very limited scientific and engineering work. Software technology during this period was also very primitive and consisted of machine code and later a symbolic notation, known as assembly language. The first general purpose programmable electronic computer, the Electronic Numerical Integrator and Computer (ENIAC), was built in 1943.

Second Generation Computers (1957–1963)

The second generation saw several important developments at all levels of computer system design. The most important development was the commercial use of transistors for storing and processing information. Transistors were much more stable and reliable than vacuum tubes, generated less heat, and consumed less power. The enhanced processing power and memory of second generation computers enabled them to be used more widely for scientific work and for such business tasks as automating payroll and billing. The computer language Common Business Oriented Language (COBOL) was defined in 1959, and in 1961, Fairchild Semiconductor distributed the first available integrated circuits, which were first used in Air Force computers and in the Minuteman Missile in 1962.

Third Generation Computers (1964–1970)

The major breakthrough in this period was the widespread use of integrated circuits, which were made by printing hundreds and later thousands of tiny transistors on small silicon chips. These devices were called semiconductors. As a result, microcomputers and workstations were introduced and became viable alternatives to mainframe computers. This period also saw the development of ASCII (American Standard Code for Information Interchange) as a standard code for data transfer, BASIC (Beginners All-purpose Symbolic Instruction Language), and UNIX, which became the dominant operating system of high-end microcomputers.

Fourth Generation Computers (1971–1979)

The next generation of computer systems saw the use of large scale integration (1,000 devices per chip) and very large scale integration (100,000 devices per chip) in the construction of computing elements. The boost to processing power made it possible to develop special software called operating systems, which could be used by people without extensive technical training. Intel introduced the world's first single chip microprocessor. In 1973, the Scelbi Computer Consulting Company offered the first computer kit in the U.S. that used a microprocessor.

Fifth Generation Computers (1980-present)

Computers in this period used very large scale integrated circuits, which were packed with millions of circuits per chip. Semiconductor memories became standard on all computers.

1981: IBM introduced the "Personal Computer" complete with a brand new operating system from Microsoft called MS-DOS 1.0. The first IBM PC ran on a 4.77 MHz Intel 8088 microprocessor and came equipped with 16 kilobytes of memory, expandable to 256k, one or two 160k floppy disk drives, and an optional color monitor. The price tag started at $1,565, which would be nearly $4,000 today.
1982: Commodore introduced the Commodore 64. An estimated 22 million units were sold. The Commodore 64 was the first cheap computer to have 64 Kb of RAM and an audio synthesizer chip.
1984: Apple introduced the Macintosh computer. The introduction of Apple's Macintosh computer generated even more excitement than the IBM PC had three years earlier.
1984: IBM introduced the PC AT (Advanced Technology) computer.
1984: The Tandy 1000 personal computer became the #1 selling IBM PC-compatible computer in its first year.
1984: Satellite Software International introduced Word Perfect, a powerful new word processor for the IBM PC. Word Perfect soon became the dominant word processor for the PC market.
1991: Notebook PCs were introduced by most PC vendors.
1991: Wide Area Information Servers (WAIS) were introduced.
1991: World-Wide Web (WWW) was released by CERN; Tim Berners-Lee was the developer.
1993: The Intel Pentium processor began to be shipped and swept through the PC industry faster than any of Intel's previous processors.

| 1995: Java script development was announced by Netscape. |
| 1995: WWW increased to 100,000 sites. |
| 1997: WWW increased to 1 million sites and 71,618 newsgroups. |

TECHNOLOGY SHIFTS

Another way of viewing the development of computing technology is provided by Tapscott and Caston in their excellent book *Paradigm Shift*. They identified seven critical technology shifts in the last twenty-five years (Tapscott and Caston, 1993: 18–26):

1) "From Traditional Semiconductors to Microprocessor-Based Systems." The creation of the microprocessor made possible the transition to the modern era of computing by allowing users to work directly with the technology through personal computers.

2) "From Host-Based to Network-Based Systems," and from personal work to group computing. The 1980s witnessed the transition from host mainframe or minicomputers attached to a network of dumb, local or remote terminals to hosts that were accessed through PCs that could emulate such terminals. These stand alone computers offered tremendous benefits for users by allowing the worker to break free of the centralized control of data processing departments. However, workers were still limited by the fact that the systems were not integrated. Users essentially functioned as individuals working on their own computer with their own software and files. Modern computing began in earnest in the 1990s with the emergence of networked and group computing that featured client/server architecture and local area networks (LANs). In this architecture the workstation became a client platform that requested information and processing services from servers connected to local and wide area networks. This new approach allowed users to access a wide range of data and applications without worrying about where they were located or how they were connected. More importantly through the use of local area networks, the new technology allowed users to work effectively in groups. The implications for information management and recordkeeping of the dramatic changes in workflow and ready access to tools and resources were immense.

3) "From Vendor Proprietary Software to Open Software Standards," based on industry standards that were not controlled by one vendor. The benefits of open systems include reduced risk of vendor dependence, easier migration of new technology, architectural flexibility and scalability, and software integration. In short, standard operating systems, user interfaces, networking, database tools, and programming languages made it easier to integrate applications across a heterogeneous environment. Again, the implications of these changes for sharing and managing information cannot be overestimated.

4) "From Single to Multi-Media—Data, Text, Voice, and Image." In the past these formats were separate, each with separate technologies to manage them. With the new technologies, the various formats could be integrated into one system.

5) "Software Development—From Craft to Factory." In the early days of computing each software package was unique and difficult to fix or modify. In the new era, software has undergone a re-engineering process and now can be more quickly created, is less expensive, is easier to modify, and can be reused from previously developed modules. The advantages for users of these developments are obvious. However, the rapid development of software creates problems for managers of these systems and of the information these systems produce.

6) "From Alphanumeric to Graphical, Multiform User Interface." In the first era of computing, user interfaces were normally not user friendly; graphical user interfaces have changed this. Workers can now use computers much more easily and quickly.

7) "From Stand-Alone to Integrated Software Applications." Software programs are becoming more modular, interchangeable, and integrated. The modern age of computing has witnessed a transformation from islands of technology to integrated systems characterized most prominently by the new enterprise systems being offered by companies such as SAP, Oracle, and PeopleSoft. These enterprise systems include collections of application modules. SAP, for example, has twelve modules for such activities as financial management, human resource management, and management of the physical plant. These application modules

   communicate with each other by means of common central databases, which are typically relational databases offered by leading vendors such as Oracle and Sybase. These integrated systems provide opportunities as well as challenges to managers of information and records.

To the list created by Tapscott and Caston one must add an eighth obvious development, the growth of the Internet and the World Wide Web. The Web has and continues to revolutionize the way businesses and individuals work, communicate, and market products and ideas. Managing information and digital objects in a dynamic, ever-changing environment like the Web presents real challenges for information and records managers.

Figure 1.1 illustrates some of the major differences between paradigms of the first and second eras of computing.

The impact of these technological changes on recordkeeping extends to all stages of the record life cycle. Developments in automation have had a dramatic impact on how records are created and captured; how they are updated, revised, and deleted; how they are used, distributed, and shared; how they are stored and preserved; how they are structured and assembled; and ultimately how they must be managed.

CHANGES IN ORGANIZATIONAL STRUCTURE AND WORKFLOW

Organizational transformations and workflow changes are the result of many complex developments. Nonetheless, we can identify two primary forces responsible for organizational change.

The first of these has occurred in the business environment and the marketplace. The last several decades have witnessed the emergence of the global economy and the opening of world markets. As the noted consultant Thomas Davenport (1997:193) writes: "All companies have to be informed about the outside world: what customers need, what customers are trying to accomplish, what regulators insist we must do. Much of a company's internal information, in fact, describes the outside world of business." The result of this globalization is a more highly competitive economic environment. New businesses enter into the market as a result of the removal of barriers to previously untapped markets. At the same time, globalization is also fostering greater economic interdependence and collaboration. As one scholar has noted: "The overall picture as a consequence of globaliza-

Figure 1.1
Technology Shifts

	Era I	Era II
Network Computing		
Processing	Traditional semiconductor	Microprocessors
System	Host-based	Network-based
Open Systems		
Software standards	Vendor-proprietary	Vendor-neutral
Information forms	Separate data, text, voice, image	Multi-media
Vendor-customer relationships	Account control	Multi-vendor Partnerships
Industrial Revolution in Software		
Software development	Craft	Engineered
User interface	Alphanumeric character set	Graphical
Applications	Stand-alone	Integrated

Source: *Paradigm Shift: The New Promise of Information Technology* by Don Tapscott and Art Caston, 1993, p. 19. Reprinted with permission of McGraw-Hill Education.

tion is one of turbulence and uncertainty, in which a variety of contradictory processes present a wide range of both opportunities and threats that defy the established ways of doing business and working in organizations" (Helms, 2006). In this environment, it is imperative that businesses be able to respond quickly and decisively to changing market conditions and demand.

The other major force in transforming organizations was technology. While it is certainly true that organizational culture and business strategies shape the way information technology is used in organizations, it is equally true that IT affects how businesses function and organize themselves. Most of these transformations occur gradually. "Contrary to the conventional (and expensive) wisdom of many futurists, technology gurus, and strategy consultants, organizational transformations—at least those tied to IT—seem not to be carefully orchestrated events, quick and sure leaps into a glorious future, or even terribly jarring disruptions of taken-for-granted practices" (Yates and Van Maanen, 2001: xiii). Transformation is often "slow, halting, incremental, and often ironic. Moreover, it is occurring all the time but in almost imperceptible ways" (Yates and Van Maanen, 2001: xiii). Consequently, it is difficult to generalize about these transformations; they are the result of numerous forces over time. (For descriptions of the changing work environment and how technology has altered the workplace, see Davenport [1997]; Davenport [1993]; Hammer and Champy [1994]; Martin [1996]; Tapscott and Caston [1993]; Yates and Van Maanen [2001]; Yates and Benjamin [1991]; Hesselbein, Goldsmith and Beckhard [1997].)

ORGANIZATIONAL MODELS

Many of the changes that occurred in the structure of organizations and workflows are identified with what has come to be called the networked business environment. Traditionally, organizations have aligned themselves into variations and combinations of two basic organizational forms—hierarchies and bureaucracies. Hierarchies are organized around levels of authority and power, and are divided into the governors and the governed, the managers and the workers. It is useful to visualize a pyramid shaped power structure with those at the top having more power than those at the bottom. In this structure, information flows down a vertical chain of command that ranks people in terms of status, compensation, authority, and influence. Communication in hierarchies is typically characterized as a "command and control" environment in which top-down instructions from the president and directors are transmitted through the middle managers to the rank and file. Hierarchical structures present some advantages to a business, primarily due to their tight, centralized control (for descriptions of hierarchical structures, see McGee and Prusak [1993]; Tapscott and Caston [1993]).

Bureaucracies exist alongside and often in conjunction with hierarchies. Bureaucracies are based on defined roles and specialized functions. More specifically they incorporate some or all of the following traits: formal behavior bounded by rules and regulations; a division of labor based on functional specialization; communication by means of standardized forms, structured rules, and defined communication paths; employment based on merit and not status; promotion based on technical competence; and positions organized into a hierarchy of authority based on the importance of the responsibilities and functions and not on the person in the position. While bureaucracies have proven to have many strengths, critics have identified numerous weaknesses including a tendency to promote overspecialization and to create rigidity and inflexibility making decision making slow and delaying change (Laudon and Laudon, 1995).

Hierarchies and bureaucracies have proven to be ineffective organizational models in the new global economy. As a result, businesses have gradually restructured their organizational frameworks and altered workflow and communication patterns. The new enterprise has often been characterized as networked environments. A network consists of nodes and links. A node is made up of individual people, teams, or organizational units. Members of a network may be small groups, hierarchies, bureaucracies, or other networks. Links are the coordination and agreement mechanisms or the communication pathways. These links can be formal or informal and are usually reciprocal. In effect, networked organizations utilize distributed information and communication systems to replace the often inflexible hierarchical controls.

Among the most prominent transformations resulting from the creation of networked environments has been the breakdown of the multi-layered hierarchical structure and the emergence of less centralized communication patterns, of more horizontal communication outside of the traditional bureaucratic channels, and of collaborative, self-managed team projects. In the networked environment people and teams communicate across traditional borders, and management is based more upon mutual responsibility rather than command and control.

These transformations also resulted in a shift from capital to human and information resources. In the words of several commentators, the new enterprise was becoming information-based. Authority was no longer based solely or even primarily on where one was positioned in the hierarchy, but also on individual knowledge and skills. The ultimate goal was to maximize the knowledge base of the organization and to tap into whatever expertise was required to do the job. The result of all these transformations was the creation of more resilient, responsive, flexible and innovative institutions. In short, the networked environment became a strategy for creating the more outward-looking and dynamic institution that could adjust quickly to changing market conditions (Lucas, 2005; Tapscott and Caston, 1993).

The networked organization differs from a traditional hierarchy in ways that affect even the lowest levels of the organization. A summary of the contrasts between a closed hierarchy and an open networked organization can be seen in Figure 1.2.

Technology in the form of the personal computer, client-server architectures, and distributed computing gradually and sometimes imperceptibly made possible the transformation of business structures into networked environments by providing access to the information and tools required to support the new strategies. The new technology was able to tie together the people, processes, and units in the networked environment so that they could communicate quickly and collect and analyze the information needed to make decisions.

THE EFFECT OF CHANGE ON RECORDS MANAGEMENT

(Please note that for the purposes of this book, we will be using the terms "records management" and "recordkeeping" interchangeably.) In the early decades of computing, archivists and records managers relied heavily upon conversion of computer data to paper documentation to do their work. The prevailing recordkeeping methodology of the time was to generate printouts of computer files—so-called "data dumps"—as a means of appraising the value of the data. For records with primary value to the institution, it was common practice to print to paper and store the record in established filing systems, and to summarize the data and produce various standard reference reports (the annual budget, the biweekly payroll, etc.). Some files, particularly research files, were retained in electronic form. However, research files at this time were fairly simple in structure and could be converted into so-called flat files, which could be reconstructed using a standard social science software package. For these records, the general rule was to retain the files on computer tapes in tape libraries and develop descriptive finding aids to facilitate access to the tapes. In practice this was not a dramatic departure from strategies employed for paper records.

In this period, managing data and not records was the objective, and archivists dealing with this information were known as data ar-

Figure 1.2
Networked Organizations

	Closed Hierarchy	**Open Networked Organization**
Structure	Hierarchical	Networked
Scope	Internal/Closed	External/Open
Resource/Focus	Capital	Human, Information
State	Static, Stable	Dynamic, Changing
Personnel/Focus	Managers	Professionals
Key Drivers	Reward and Punishment	Commitment
Direction	Management Commands	Self-Management
Basis of Action	Control	Empowerment to Act
Individual Motivation	Satisfy Superiors	Achieve Team Goals
Learning	Specific Skills	Broader Competencies
Basis for Compensation	Position in Hierarchy	Accomplishment, Competence Level
Relationships	Competitive (my turf)	Cooperative (our challenge)
Employee Attitude	Detachment (it's a job)	Identification (it's my company)
Dominant Requirements	Sound Management	Leadership

Source: *Paradigm Shift: The New Promise of Information Technology* by Don Tapscott and Art Caston, 1993, p. 11. Reprinted with permission of McGraw-Hill Education.

chivists. Overall, recordkeeping practices in the early decades of automation were not radically different from techniques employed for paper records. In a system where the basic strategy was to convert paper forms to an automated environment, where paper file management systems predominated, and where systems were characterized by functional units creating and managing their own files in isolation from other applications, it was possible to devise a records management strategy based on capturing screen views or forms and converting them to paper documents. In this environment, methodologies designed for the management of papers systems still had relevance (Cook, 1991).

However, the emergence of a new generation of technology and of transformations in organizational structure and workflow in the last two to three decades have prompted the archival profession to reexamine some of its most basic archival theories and concepts, such as provenance, original order, the nature of a record and the life cycle concept. The result has been spirited debates about whether traditional methodologies and procedures developed for paper records would be effective in the world of electronic records, and about what changes in traditional concepts and practices might need to be made. In short, throughout the 1990s and into the twenty-first century, archivists and records managers have been asking themselves the question, "What are the principles and criteria that will guide the development of international, national, and organizational strategies, policies, and standards for the long-term preservation of authentic and reliable electronic records?" (For analyses of the impact of automation on archival concepts and theories, see Bantin [1998]; Bearman [1994]; Bearman and Hedstrom [1993]; Cook [1994]; Cook [1997]; Yakel [1996].)

RECORDS APPRAISAL

Traditional appraisal theory, particularly in North America, focuses primarily on the analysis of two factors: the provenance of the record, defined as the office or person responsible for creating the records, and the secondary, research value of the records based largely on the analysis of content. The value of this appraisal strategy is predicated upon the presence of two prominent characteristics of records: 1) they are created in hierarchical and bureaucratic organizations where most mission critical documents are located at the top of the business structure (often characterized as a pyramid); and 2) the records are stored in systems and in a format that can easily be reviewed or browsed visually so as to discover content and uncover relationships. In other words, it is an appraisal methodology based upon an older organizational framework and built around paper record systems (for a classic statement of traditional appraisal theory see Schellenberg [1975]).

In the last two decades, some archivists have advocated a different type of appraisal methodology that they claim better fits the modern world of recordkeeping. This approach has come to be known as a functional appraisal model. Archivists who advocate this model, like Terry Cook and Helen Samuels, point to three basic reasons to support the argument that content and structure are not the best sources for determining value. First, they argue that in a business environment characterized by a flattening of the organizational structure and a more decentralized approach, structure and setting will have much less relevance in understanding the nature and significance of records than they did in the more traditional, hierarchical business environment. Ultimately, business functions and not organizational structure will define provenance and will guide appraisal decisions. Second, in the modern world of high volume documentation and of electronic records that exist as logical and not physical entities, archivists can no longer hope to focus on a strategy that requires reviewing records to conduct content analysis. Finally, they assert that in the search for evidence, the most accurate and complete documentation will be provided by examining the function, activity, and transaction that generated the record, rather than the record itself.

Advocates of this model assert that the traditional appraisal model is a flawed and essentially backwards approach which employs a "bottom-up" approach to appraisal, that is, value is established by moving upwards from analysis of the record, to the examination of the transactions and activities, and finally to identification of the functions and administrative structure. Supporters of a new model maintain that a more rational and productive appraisal process would employ a "top-down" approach. For proponents of the functional appraisal model, the process begins with an analysis of business functions and structure or of the archival fonds, and of the interaction between function and structure, then moves downward to an analysis of the activities and transactional processes, and finally arrives at an examination of the record, if necessary. In this process, two appraisal assessments would be made: of the most important record creating entities and of the critical functions and transactions. These units and functions then become the targets of record collecting activities by the archives. In short, supporters of functional appraisal argue that the context and not the content of the record must be the starting point in the search for evidence. (For descriptions of the functional appraisal model, see Cook [1997]; Samuels [1992]; Samuels [1991]; Cook [1994]; Hedstrom [1995]; Booms [1991]; O'Shea [1994]; Bearman [1994]; Dollar [1992]; Wickman [1999]; Orr [2006]. For applications of the functional model, see Bailey [1997]; Beaven [1999]; Suderman [1997].)

Most archivists agree that in the world of electronic records the profession must make some significant changes in the way records have been traditionally described. Critics of employing traditional strategies for describing electronic records identify three major reasons for adopting other methods. First, they argue that documentation of business processes cannot be postponed until the point when records become inactive. To be effective, description must take place over the life of the record so that archivists can document business transactions throughout their life cycle.

Second, it is argued that traditional prose narratives and descriptions of data structures cannot possibly describe the multitude of record linkages or reflect the relationships between and among transactions in automated systems. To properly describe these complex record systems, they recommend that much more dynamic and interactive documentation strategies be employed. In a related argument, critics claim that traditional descriptive methodologies that depend upon physically reviewing records, files, and series to identify content and context are not viable in the world of electronic records. Unlike paper documents, where content and physical form are united in a medium that provides the record of the transaction, and where relationships among documents can be observed, electronic records are not physical but are logically constructed and often "virtual" entities. Consequently, electronic documents cannot be viewed in the same way as paper records, where so much of the content, context and structural metadata is embedded in or is part of the record. (For our purposes, metadata is defined as "structured or semi-structured information that documents the creation, management, and use of records through time and across domains" [European Commission, 2002: 13].) In automated systems, the vital metadata, if it exists at all, may or may not be physically associated with the content data. Vital links between metadata and the record content data may exist only in computer software programs. In some cases, the metadata may actually not be a part of the automated system at all, but may exist only as a paper document totally disassociated from the records it is describing. Therefore, it is argued, efforts to document business transactions based on an examination of "views" or of automated forms will fail to reveal the nature of the business transactions.

Finally, proponents of this position of change argue that a viable system of documenting electronic records already exists in the form of system metadata. It is routine for systems designers and programmers to generate documentation on the content and structure of the systems and programs they create. Why not, it is suggested, make this metadata system the basis for describing electronic records? Why not consider a shift from creating descriptive information to capturing, managing, and adding value to system metadata? (For discussions of this strategy for documenting electronic records, see Wallace [1995]; Hedstrom [1993]; Bearman [1992]; Reed [1997]; Hurley [2005]).

RECORDS PRESERVATION

Clearly, the many strategies for preserving paper records will not work in the world of automated records. The problems or challenges of preserving automated records fall into three categories: hardware obsolescence, software dependence, and storage medium deterioration. While all three are eventually lethal to the long-term survival of digital objects, most experts agree that it is software dependence or "the fact that digital documents are in general dependent on application software to make them accessible and meaningful" that presents the greatest challenge (Rothenberg, 1999).

There is widespread agreement that unlike paper records, digital objects cannot remain neglected and unmanaged at any point in the life cycle. Digital records must be actively monitored and managed to ensure that they continue to be readable or can be processed on a computer system or device other than the one that initially created them or on which they are currently stored and are intelligible or comprehensible to a human being (Garrett and Waters, 1996; Hunter, 2000).

RECORDS MANAGEMENT AND STORAGE

Where are electronic records to be physically housed, and who will manage them? In response to these questions, archivists have developed two possible strategies: 1) Centralized Archival Custody Approach—"Archives as a Place"; and 2) Non-Custody, "Post Custody," or "Distributed Custody" Approach.

Centralized Custody Approach

Supporters of the centralized custody model argue that the authenticity over time of inactive, archival records can be ensured only when their custody is entrusted to professional archivists. According to Luciana Duranti (1996: 252), "The life cycle of the managerial activity directed to the preservation of the integrity of electronic records may be divided into two phases: one aimed at the control of the creation of reliable records and to the maintenance of authentic active and semi-active records, and the other aimed at the preservation of authentic inactive records." The position of the proponents of this argument can be characterized as a centralized archival custody approach, or "Archives as a Place," where there must exist an "archival threshold" or "space beyond which no alteration or permutation is possible, and where every written act can be treated as evidence and memory" (Duranti, 1996: 252). More specifically, proponents of this position identify five reasons inactive records should be transferred to an archival repository and not left in the custody of the record creators:

1) Mission and Competencies: It is not part of the mission of the creating agency, nor does its staff possess the necessary skills to safeguard the authenticity of non-current, archival records.
2) Ability to Monitor Compliance: There are not enough trained archivists available to monitor or audit records in a distributed custody environment.
3) Cost to Monitor Compliance: Costs to manage records in a distributed environment are as yet unknown and untested, but it may likely be more costly to monitor recordkeeping practices than to assume custody of the records.
4) Changes in Work Environment: Changes in staffing and in departmental priorities can place records left with creating offices at great risk.
5) Vested Interests: Inactive records must be taken from those who have a vested interest in either corrupting or in neglecting the records (Duranti, 1996; Duranti and MacNeil, 1996; Eastwood, 1996; Thibodeau, 1991).

For all these reasons, supporters of the "Archives as Place" argument conclude "that the routine transfer of records to a neutral third party, that is, to a competent archival body . . . is an essential requirement for ensuring their authenticity over time" (Duranti and MacNeil, 1996: 60).

Distributed Custody Approach

As opposed to the "Archives as a Place" position, archivists who support a less centralized custody model portray their strategy regarding custody and use as a "Post-Custody" or "Distributed Custody" approach. In this strategy, the transfer of inactive records to an archives may be delayed or deferred for much longer periods than in the past; indeed, in some cases, the records may actually remain indefinitely in the custody of the originating office. The basic premise supporting this position is that in the electronic environment archival institutions can fulfill their responsibilities without assuming physical custody of the records. To achieve these goals, however, archivists must develop new methodologies and techniques for managing records in a distributed custody environment. Proponents of this strategy identify four arguments to support their position of distributed custody and access:

1) Costs: It would be enormously expensive and a massive waste of resources to attempt to duplicate within the archival setting the technological environments already in place within the creating offices.
2) Changes in Technology: Rapid technological change and reluctance of manufacturers to support old hardware make it extremely difficult for a centralized repository to manage an institution's electronic records.
3) Skills Required: It would be difficult, if not impossible, for an archives staff to learn the skills and provide the expertise needed to access and preserve the wide variety of technologies and formats in use.
4) Loss of Records: Insisting on custody will result in some cases in leaving important records outside the recordkeeping boundary.

(For descriptions of the "Distributed Custody" approach and articulation of arguments for implementing this strategy, see Bearman [1991]; O'Shea and Roberts [1996]; Cunningham [1996b]; and Dollar [1992].)

In the words of one advocate of this position, "archivists cannot afford—politically, professionally, economically, or culturally—to acquire records except as a last resort. . . . Indeed, the evidence indicates that acquisition of records and the maintenance of the archives as a repository, gets in the way of achieving archival objectives and that this dysfunction will increase dramatically with the spread of electronic communications" (Bearman, 1991: 14).

As some archivists have argued, however, the primary issue may not be custody, but rather ensuring that a viable and widely accepted system for managing electronic records is in place. This means establishing policies and procedures that ensure that no matter where the records are housed they will be managed according to well-established standards. More specifically, a distributed strategy for custody necessitates the creation of legally binding agreements with offices, reliable means of auditing records, an extensive network of training programs, and other mechanisms designed to ensure that custodians of records understand their responsibilities and are living up to those expectations. An Australian archivist sums up this position when he writes: "The real issue is not custody, but the control of records and the archivist's role in this. . . . What archivists should have been talking to their clients about is not custody, but good recordkeeping practices which make it possible for archivists to exercise the necessary control" (Cunningham 1996a).

MODELS FOR MANAGING ELECTRONIC RECORDS

These real and potential changes in archival theory and methodology have inspired two new, overarching models that better define how electronic records will be managed. The first of these is the development of a new model for visualizing the records management process.

THE LIFE CYCLE MODEL VERSUS THE RECORDS CONTINUUM MODEL

Archivists and records managers have traditionally defined the records management process in terms of a "life cycle model." The life cycle model for managing records, as articulated by Theodore Schellenberg and others, has been the prominent model for North American archivists and records managers since at least the 1960s. This model portrays a record going sequentially through various stages or periods, much like a living organism. In stage one, the record is created, presumably for a legitimate reason and according to certain standards. In the second stage, the record goes through an active period when it has maximum primary value and is used or referred to frequently by the creating office and others involved in decision making processes. During this time the record is stored on-site in the active or current files of the creating office. At the end of stage two the record may be reviewed and determined to have no further value, at which point it is destroyed, or the record can enter stage three, where it is relegated to a semi-active status, which means it still has value, but is not needed for day-to-day decision making. Because the record need not be consulted regularly, it is often stored in an off-site storage center. At the end of stage three, another review occurs, at which point a determination is made to destroy or send the record to stage four, which is reserved for inactive records with long-term, indefinite, archival value. This small percentage of records (normally estimated at approximately five percent of the total documentation) is sent to an archival repository, where specific activities are undertaken to preserve and describe the records.

The life cycle model not only describes what will happen to a record, it also defines who will manage the record during each stage. During the creation and active periods, the record creators have primary responsibility for managing the record, although records managers may well be involved to various degrees. In the semi-active stage, it is the records manager who takes center stage and assumes major responsibility for managing the records. Finally, in the inactive stage, the archivist takes the lead in preserving, describing, and providing access to the archival record (for a summary of the life cycle concept, see Penn, Pennix and Coulson [1994]). The life cycle model has contributed, particularly in North America, to the creation of a fairly strict demarcation of responsibilities between the archives and records management professions. Among archivists it has resulted in a tendency to view the life of a record in terms of pre-archival and archival and active and inactive, and to regard the stage when the archivist intervenes in the cycle as occurring sometime towards the end of the life cycle when the record becomes inactive and archival.

Criticisms of the life cycle model as means of managing records have surfaced at times in the past. The emergence of electronic records has turned this into a very spirited debate. This dialogue has resulted in not only a critique of the model but in the definition of an alternate model or framework. This alternate model is most commonly referred to as the records continuum model. Discussions of strategies for better integrating the activities of archivists and records managers date back at least several decades. However, it was not until the 1990s that a more formally constructed model emerged for viewing records management as a continuous process from the moment of creation, in which archivists and records managers are actively involved at all points in the continuum. The primary motivation in formulating and supporting this model was a concern that lacking a strategy for active and early intervention by the archivist in the records management process, electronic records documenting vital transactions may never be created, fully documented, or survive. Perhaps the most basic difference between the continuum model and the life cycle approach is that while the life cycle model proposes a strict separation of records management responsibilities, the continuum model is based upon an integration of the responsibilities and accountabilities associated with the management of records. The Australian records management standard, which has adopted the continuum model, defines the integrated nature of the record continuum in the following terms: the record continuum is "the whole extent of a record's existence." It "refers to a consistent and coherent regime of management processes from the time of creation of records (and before creation, in the design of recordkeeping systems) through to the preservation and use of records as archives" (Australian Standard, AS 4390.1–1996F: General, Clause 4.6). A noted Australian archivist Ann Pederson describes the differences between the life cycle and continuum models in the following manner: "The life cycle relates to records and information . . . records have a life cycle . . . The continuum is not about records. It is about a regime for recordkeeping. The continuum is a model of management that relates to the recordkeeping regime," which is "continuous, dynamic and ongoing without any distinct breaks or phases" (Pederson, message to listserv, 1999).

Viewing records management as a continuum undercuts and destroys the distinction between active and inactive, and archival and non-archival records, and blurs or wipes out the defined set of responsibilities associated with managing records at each stage. This viewpoint propels archivists and archival functions forward in the records management process. Strategies and methodologies for appraising, describing, and preserving records are implemented early in the records management process, preferably at the design stage, and not at the end of the life cycle. However, much research and testing needs to be completed to determine just how this strategy will be implemented and how archivists will interact with other records management partners.

The primary proponents of the continuum model have been Australian archivists. (For descriptions of the records continuum model, see Upward [1996]; Upward [1997]; Cunningham [1996b]; Bearman [1996]; Upward [2004]; Piggott and McKemmish [2002].)

CONCEPTUAL MODELS

A second strategy that incorporates many of the changes in archival theory and practice is the wider use of conceptual models to represent records and systems. The modern era of computers has presented many new and difficult challenges for capturing, accessing, and describing records. In the paper world, much of our methodology and decision making relies heavily on physically reviewing records and file systems. However, in many automated systems, such as relational databases, records are not stored as physical entities; rather records are logically constructed entities, created by combining and reusing data stored as discrete data elements organized in relational tables. Moreover, many of these systems are very large and very complex. To effectively access and use them requires a great deal of instruction and experience, and each system and application has its own rules and logic. In short, with the emergence of database views, dynamic and virtual documents, complex software linkages, hypermedia documents, and multi-layered geographical information systems, the differences in the way paper and electronic records are created and used has been accentuated and can no longer be ignored. Eventually, archivists and records managers recognized that they were dealing with systems that could not be easily be reviewed on-site to identify records, to uncover relationships between records, and to discover the content of the records.

Over time archivists and records managers have arrived at the conclusion that like our IT brethren, the professions must be able to construct and manage systems based on conceptual models and documentary evidence. Models are a representation of some reality, in this case an automated system. Conceptual models show what this system does or must do. They are implementation independent models, i.e., they depict the system independent of any technical implementation. In other words, these conceptual models depict the functionality of the system before it is ever built (Whitten and Bentley, 1998).

A particularly important type of conceptual model for archivists and records is the business process model. This form of analysis has been defined as "a process-centered technique that is used to model business requirements for a system. The models are structured pictures that illustrate the processes, inputs, outputs, and files required to respond to business events" (Whitten and Bentley, 1998: 122). The value of business models for archivists is that they can depict precisely when, where, and how record creation occurs. They provide the archivist with a conceptual model based on depiction of real-life activities of the context for creation, and consequently provide the information needed to precisely describe and define for system designers what pieces of data need to be captured as evidence of the business transaction.

We will examine conceptual models in more detail in later chapters, especially chapter 3. In the next chapter, we will review core concepts related to recordkeeping and take a detailed look at the functional requirements for recordkeeping systems.

REFERENCES

Australian Standard AS 4390.1–1996.

Bailey, Catherine. 1997. "From the Top Down: The Practice of Macro-Appraisal." *Archivaria* 43 (Spring): 89–128.

Bantin, Philip. 1998. "Strategies for Managing Electronic Records: A New Archival Paradigm? An Affirmation of Our Archival Traditions?" *Archival Issues: Journal of the Midwest Archives Conference* 23, no. 1: 17–34.

Bearman, David, ed. 1991. *Archival Management of Electronic Records.* Archives and Museum Informatics Technical Report No. 13. Pittsburgh, PA: Archives and Museum Informatics.

Bearman, David. 1992. "Documenting Documentation," *Archivaria* 34 (Summer): 33–49.

Bearman, David. 1996. "Item Level Control and Electronic Recordkeeping." *Cultural Heritage Informatics Quarterly* 10, no. 3: 195–245.

Bearman, David, and Margaret Hedstrom. 1993. "Reinventing Archives for Electronic Records: Alternative Service Delivery Options." In *Electronic Records Management Program Strategies,* edited by Margaret Hedstrom. Pittsburgh, PA: Archives and Museum Informatics.

Beaven, Brian P. N. 1999. "Macro-Appraisal: From Theory to Practice." *Archivaria* 48 (Fall): 154–198.

Booms, Hans. 1991. "Uberlieferungsbildung: Keeping Archives as a Social and Political Activity." *Archivaria* 33 (Winter): 25–33.

Cook, Terry. 1991. "Easy to Byte, Harder to Chew: The Second Generation of Electronic Records Archives." *Archivaria* 33 (Winter): 202–216.

Cook, Terry. 1994. "Electronic Records, Paper Minds: The Revolution in Information Management and Archives in the Post-Custodial and Post-Modernist Era." *Archives and Manuscripts* 22 (November): 300–328.

Cook, Terry. 1997. "What is Past is Prologue: A History of Archival Ideas Since 1898, and the Future Paradigm Shift." *Archivaria* 43 (Spring): 17–63.

Cunningham, Adrian. 1996a. "Ensuring Essential Evidence." *National Library of Australia News* (November). Available: www.nla.gov.au/nla/staffpaper/acunning5.html

Cunningham, Adrian. 1996b. "Journey to the End of Night: Custody and the Dawning of a New Era on the Archival Threshold." *Archives and Manuscripts* 24, no. 2 (November): 312–321.

Davenport, Thomas. 1993. *Process Innovation: Reengineering Work through Information Technology.* Boston: Harvard Business School Press.

Davenport, Thomas. 1997. *Information Ecology: Mastering the Information and Knowledge Environment.* New York: Oxford University Press.

Dollar, Charles. 1992. *Archival Theory and Information Technologies: The Impact of Information Technologies on Archival Principles and Methods.* Macerata, Italy: University of Macerata.

Duranti, Luciana. 1996. "Archives as a Place." *Archives and Manuscripts* 24, no. 2 (November): 252.

Duranti, Luciana, and Heather MacNeil. 1996. "The Protection of the Integrity of Records: An Overview of the UBC-MAS Research Project." *Archivaria* 42 (Fall): 46–67.

Eastwood, Terry. 1996. "Should Creating Agencies Keep Electronic Records Indefinitely?" *Archives and Manuscripts* 24, no. 2 (November): 256–267.

European Commission. 2002. *Model Requirements for the Management of Electronic Records (MoReqs).* Available: www.cornwell.co.uk/edrm/moreq.asp

Garrett, John, and Donald Waters. 1996. *Preserving Digital Information: Report of the Task Force on Archiving Digital Information*, section on "The Challenge of Archiving Digital Information." Washington, DC: Commission on Preservation and Access and Research Libraries Group. Available: http://clir.org/pubs/Abstract/pub63/html

Hammer, Michael, and James Champy. 1994. *Reengineering the Corporation: A Manifesto for Business Revolution.* New York: Harper Business.

Hedstrom, Margaret. 1993. "Descriptive Practices for Electronic

Records: Deciding What Is Essential and Imagining What Is Possible." *Archivaria* 36 (Autumn): 53–63.

Hedstrom, Margaret. 1995. "Electronic Archives: Integrity and Access in the Network Environment." *American Archivist* 58, no. 3 (Summer): 312–324.

Helms, Marilyn M., ed. 2006. *Encyclopedia of Management*. Farmington Hills, MI: Thomson-Gale. Available: http://business.enotes.com/management-encyclopedia/trends-organizational-change.

Hunter, Gregory S. 2000. *Preserving Digital Information*. New York: Neal-Schuman.

Hurley, Chris. 2005. "Parallel Provenance: (1) What If Anything Is Archival Description?" *Archives and Manuscripts*, Vol. 33, no. 1: 110–145.

Laudon, Kenneth C., and Jane P. Laudon. 1995. *Essentials of Management Systems*. Englewood Cliffs, NJ: Prentice Hall.

Lucas, Henry C., Jr. 2005. *Information Technology: Strategic Decision Making for Managers*. Hoboken, NJ: John Wiley and Sons.

Martin, James. 1996. *Cybercorp: The New Business Revolution*. New York: AMACOM.

McGee, James, and Laurence Prusak. 1993. *Managing Information Strategically*. New York: John Wiley and Sons.

Orr, Stuart. 2006. "Functions-Based Classification of Records: Is It Functional?" *Archives and Manuscripts*, Vol. 34, no. 1: 44–96.

O'Shea, Greg, and David Roberts. 1996. "Living in a Digital World." *Archives and Manuscripts* 24, no. 2 (November): 286–311.

Pederson, Ann. 1999. In an e-mail message to the Australian Archivists listserv, February 17, 1999.

Penn, Ira A., Gail Pennix, and Jim Coulson. 1994. *Records Management Handbook*. 2nd ed. Hampshire, UK: Gower Publishing.

Piggott, Michael, and Sue McKemmish. 2002. "Recordkeeping, Reconciliation, and Political Reality." Society of Archivists Annual Conference, Sydney, Australia. Available: www.sims.monash.edu.au/research/rcrg/publications/piggottmckemmish2002.pdf

Polsson, Ken. "Chronology of Personal Computers." Available: www.islandnet.com/~kpolsson/comphist/

Reed, Barbara. "Metadata: Core Record or Core Business." Available: www.sims.monash.edu.au/research/rcrg/publications/recordscontinuum/brep1.html

Rothenberg, Jeff. 1999. "Avoiding Technological Quicksand: Finding a Viable Technological Foundation for Digital Preservation." Washington, DC: Council on Library and Information Resources. Available: www.clir.org/cpa/reports/rothenberg/contents.html

Samuels, Helen Willia. 1992. *Varsity Letters: Documenting Modern Colleges and Universities*. Metuchen, NJ: The Society of American Archivists and Scarecrow Press.

Schellenberg, T. R. 1975. *Modern Archives: Principles and Techniques*. Midway reprint. Chicago: University of Chicago Press.

Shurkin, Joel. 1996. *Engines of the Mind: The Evolution of the Computer from Mainframes to Microprocessors*. New York: W.W. Norton.

Suderman, Jim. 1997. "Appraising Records of the Expenditure Management Function: An Exercise in Functional Analysis." *Archivaria* 43 (Spring): 129–142.

Tapscott, Don, and Art Caston. 1993. *Paradigm Shift: The New Promise of Information Technology*. New York: McGraw-Hill.

Thibodeau, Ken. 1991. "To Be Or Not To Be: Archive Methods for Electronic Records" in *Archival Management of Electronic Records*. Archives and Museum Informatics Technical Report, No. 13, edited by David Bearman. Pittsburgh, PA: Archives and Museum Informatics.

Upward, Frank. 1996. "Structuring the Records Continuum: Part One, Post-custodial Principles and Properties." *Archives and Manuscripts* 24, no. 2 (November): 268–285.

Upward, Frank. 1997. "Structuring the Records Continuum: Part Two, Structuration Theory and Recordkeeping." *Archives and Manuscripts* 25, no. 1 (May): 10–35.

Upward, Frank. 2004. "The Records Continuum Concept of an End Product." *Archives and Manuscripts*, Vol. 32, no. 1: 40–63.

Wallace, David A. 1995. "Managing the Present: Metadata as Archival Description." *Archivaria* 36 (Spring): 11–21.

Whitten, Jeffrey L., and Lonnie D. Bentley. 1998. *Systems Analysis and Design Methods*. 4th ed. Boston: McGraw-Hill.

Wickman, Danielle. 1999. "What's New? Functional Analysis in Life Cycle and Continuum Environments." *Archives and Manuscripts*, Vol. 27, no. 1: 114–127.

Yakel, Elizabeth. 1996. "The Way Things Work: Procedures, Processes, and Institutional Records." *American Archivist* 59, no. 4 (Fall): 454–464.

Yates, Joanne, and John Van Maanen, eds. 2001. *Information Technology and Organizational Transformation: History, Rhetoric, and Practice*. Thousand Oaks, CA: Sage Publications.

Yates, Joanne, and R. I. Benjamin. 1991. "The Past and Present as Windows on the Future." In *The Corporation of the 1990s: Information Technology and Organization Transformation*, edited by M. S. Scott Morton. New York: Oxford University Press.

2

Recordkeeping Systems

WHAT ARE RECORDS?

What are records, and how do they differ from other types of information? There is growing support for the basic definition of a record found in the ISO International Standard 15489–1: Information and Documentation-Records Management. This standard defines records as: "Recorded information produced or received in the initiation, conduct or completion of an institutional or individual activity and that comprises content, context, and structure sufficient to provide evidence of that activity" (ISO, 2001, sec. 3: 3).

This definition identifies two distinguishing characteristics of records. First of all, records reflect business processes or individual activities; a record is not just a collection of data, but is the consequence or product of an event. This is not a new concept; older definitions identify records with a process or an activity. What is new is the emphasis on defining more precisely and conceptually when the record is created by the business event or personal activity. What this means in practice is a much greater emphasis on understanding functions and processes and on precisely linking the records to the events that created them.

The other part of the definition of a record stresses that records provide evidence of these transactions or activities. Recorded documentation cannot qualify as a record, or at least as an authentic and reliable record, unless this evidence is present and available. It is this concept of evidence that largely differentiates records from other types of information. Again, this is not exactly a new concept. However, newer definitions provide much more detail than ever before on the type and exact nature of this evidence. Later in this chapter we will review the nature of this evidence in some detail. For now let it be simply stated that this evidence consists of the content of the record plus a defined set of recordkeeping metadata that documents and defines the record in terms of three elements: 1) content—metadata that defines the words, symbols, sounds, or images that constitute the primary message of the record; 2) context—metadata that defines the organizational, functional, and operational circumstances surrounding the record's creation, storage, use, or management over time; and 3) structure—metadata that defines the record's physical characteristics and the internal organization of its contents. By stating that the existence of a reliable and authentic record is dependent upon content *plus* a defined set of metadata, record professionals have created a type of information object, the record, that has its own unique set of characteristics. Moreover, a record is an information object or concept that can be conceptually defined, and consequently can be identified, captured, and managed as either a discrete body of bytes in a database or as an object in a document management system. These more detailed descriptions of records will allow archivists and records managers to define a record with enough precision to inform systems designers when records are created and what kind of data needs to be captured. (For a good discussion of evidence, see David Bearman [1994]. For discussions of the concept of the record, see Cox [1994]; Cox [1996]; Roberts [1994]; Ackland [1992]; McKimmish and Piggott [1994]; Bearman [1994]; Bearman [1996]; Dollar [1992].)

Mention should be made of the active and spirited debates on the possible shortcomings of the "records as evidence" concept. The dialogue on this issue is sometimes framed in terms of describing "Records as Evidence" and "Records as Memory." (For good summaries of this debate, see Greene [2002] and Nesmith [2002].) Canadian archivist and educator Terry Cook has characterized the debate in the following terms: "There seems little space in this new discourse that is dominated by talk of business transactions, evidence, accountability, metadata, electronic records and distributed custody of archives, for the *traditional* discourse of archivists centered around history, heritage, culture, research, social memory and the curatorial custody of archives. . . . Record-keeping by archivists, some assert, is a business activity, not a cultural pursuit." Cook claims that what is needed is a "renewed balancing of the two concepts" of evidence and memory (Cook, 2000: 3). Verne Harris, a South African archivist, asserts that the "records as evidence" definition "excludes the possibility that people (individuals, organizations, societies) generate and keep records for reasons other than 'evidence of process.' It excludes the possibility that qualities, or attributes, or dynamics, other than 'evidence' enjoy equally legitimate claims on the concept of 'record.'" (Harris, 2000: 15). In response to these critiques, advocates of the continuum model have proposed the development of a "fourth dimension" that will "pluralise records-as-individual/group/corporate memory by placing them into an all-encompassing framework that enables them to function as accessible collective memory" (Piggott and McKemmish, 2002: 10). A popular definition of records that attempts to incorporate the value and meaning of records as evidence and as societal memory defines records as "extensions of the human memory, purposefully created to record information, document transactions, communicate thoughts, substantiate claims, advance explanations, offer justifications, and provide lasting evidence of events. Their creation results from a fundamental human need to create and store information, to retrieve and transmit it, and to establish tangible connections with the past" (Dearstyne, 1993: 1).

WHAT IS RECORDS MANAGEMENT?

ISO 15489 defines records management as the "field of management responsible for the efficient and systematic control of the creation, receipt, maintenance, use and disposition of records, including processes for capturing and maintaining evidence of and information about business activities and transactions in the form of records" (ISO, 2001, sec. 3). ISO 15489 identifies several benefits of records management programs including "setting policies and procedures; assigning responsibilities and authorities; establishing and promulgating procedures and guidelines; providing a range of services relating to the management and use of records; designing, implementing and administering specialized systems for managing records; and integrating records management into business systems and processes" (ISO, 2001, sec. 4).

Most of the principles and techniques used in modern records management within the United States originated in the federal government. The establishment of the National Archives in 1934 was a major event in the development of recordkeeping practices. The National Archives developed the records disposal schedule, and its use was authorized by the Records Disposal Act of 1943. Records management in government was given formal status in 1946 as a result of Executive Order 9784. This was followed by recommendations of the so-called Hoover Commission and by the Federal Records Act in 1950, which mandated that agencies develop records management programs and assigned the National Archives with the responsibility of supervising and monitoring records management activities. By June 1952, the National Archives had established records centers throughout the country. They also had drafted and issued regulations on records management and a new set of record schedules (Robek, Brown and Stephens, 1996).

In the 1960s, these government practices worked their way into business and academic institutions. Statistics indicate that over half of the records management programs in existence in the 1980s were organized since 1967. In the early 1980s, a survey indicated that of the 860 members of the Association of Records Managers and Administrators (ARMA) who responded to the survey form, 78 percent worked at institutions that had a formal records management program in place. Every two years since 1999, Cohasset Associates has conducted a detailed and widely distributed survey of records management programs within institutions in the United States. In 1999, surveys conducted by Cohasset Associates revealed that 83 percent of institutions responding had a formal records management program; by 2001, this number had increased to 93 percent (Williams and Ashley, 2005: 5). When comparing the results from the 2003 and 2005 surveys, Cohasset Associates concluded that in those two years records management programs improved their performance on an average of 10 percent to 20 percent in most of the critical categories. Overall the authors conclude that "the improved findings strongly suggest 'the tide is turning.' Many organizations believe they are more effectively and efficiently managing their electronic records. . . . It is the first time since this survey was first conducted in 1999 that such a conclusion is possible" (Williams and Ashley, 2005: 8). They attribute this improvement primarily to new regulations, court cases, technology solutions, and the realization that sound records management is the keystone to compliance and effective governance.

However, if we look more closely at records management programs, the news is not so good. While recognizing that significant progress had been made on many key issues, Cohasset warns that a great deal of improvement is needed in the life cycle management of electronic records. One overwhelming conclusion from the Cohasset's surveys is that most organizations still have not developed strong programs for managing electronic records. For example, according to the 2005 Cohasset survey 35 percent of the institutions do not include electronic records in their records management program, and 43 percent do not have comprehensive records retention schedules for electronic records. In this same survey 49 percent said that if legally challenged they were slightly confident or not at all confident (the two lowest categories) that their business organization could successfully demonstrate that its electronic records were accurate, reliable, and trustworthy. In regard to such a basic management requirement as preservation of records, 68 percent responded that their business does not have in place a formal plan to migrate older electronic records, and 82 percent responded they do not have a specific budget in the organization for record migration (Williams and Ashley, 2005).

Similarly, a 2006 survey on compliance by AIIM discovered that while respondents had a fairly high level of confidence in their organization's strategies for managing paper records, they were not nearly as confident about the corporation's ability to manage electronic records. When asked whether clear policies were in place related to electronic records, only 39.9 percent could "strongly" or "somewhat agree" that there were such policies. Only 34.4 percent of respondents could "strongly" or "somewhat agree" that there was widespread understanding of what electronic records are and how they should be retained (AIIM, 2006: 13). A year later, the situation had not improved. A 2007 survey by AIIM found that 33 percent of participating organizations gave a poor rating to the overall effectiveness of their electronic information management practices. Overall participants in the AIIM survey gave their electronic information management programs a 5.43 rating on a 10 point scale, which AIIM concluded was "hardly a ringing endorsement" (Mancini, 2007: 11).

PRIMARY FUNCTIONAL REQUIREMENTS FOR RECORDKEEPING SYSTEMS

Newer definitions of records management have focused on the evaluation of the processes that created the records and management of the systems that maintain the records. These systems have come to be known as electronic records management systems (ERMS), records management applications (RMA), electronic recordkeeping systems (ERKS), and trusted or trustworthy systems.

A recordkeeping system differs from other types of systems, such as transaction processing and document/content management systems. It can be defined as a special kind of information system that manages and preserves the records that provide evidence of business transactions or of personal activities. The International Council on Archives defines a recordkeeping system as "an information system that has been developed for the purpose of storing and retrieving records, and is organized to control the specific functions of creating, storing, and accessing records to safeguard their authenticity and reliability" (International Council on Archives, 2005: 14). The ISO Records Management Standard 15489 defines a records system as an "information system which captures, manages and provides access to records through time" (ISO, 2001, sec. 3). In this context, the term "system" is used in its broadest sense to depict the organizational mission, business processes, policies, procedures, practices, and human and automated mechanisms to bring about desired ends, which in this case is trustworthy recordkeeping.

The ISO Records Management Standard 15489 identifies three primary characteristics of records that must be managed by a recordkeeping system:

- authenticity
- reliability
- integrity

Since these characteristics are so critical to understanding recordkeeping systems, let us review in more detail the meaning of the terms.

AUTHENTICITY

ISO 15489 defines an authentic record as "one that can be proven a) to be what it purports to be; b) to have been created or sent by the person purported to have created or sent it; and c) to have been created or sent at the time purported" (ISO, 2001, sec. 7; other definitions of authenticity can be found in Dollar [1999] and Hunter [2000] and at the International Research on Permanent Authentic Records in Electronic Systems project [InterPARES] Web site). To be authentic there must be assurances that the record has not been modified or corrupted in essential respects. To ensure the authenticity of records, organizations must create and implement policies and procedures which control the creation, receipt, transmission, maintenance, and disposition of records throughout their life cycle. In practice authenticity can only exist if sufficient elements of the other two characteristics of reliability and integrity are present. As such authenticity is an implicit record value that is derived from the existence of explicit or demonstrable characteristics of a record that is reliable and has integrity.

RELIABILITY

Reliability refers to the authority and trustworthiness of records as evidence. A reliable record is "one whose contents can be trusted as a full and accurate representation of the transactions, activities or facts" which they document (ISO, 2001, sec. 7; other definitions of reliability can be found at the International Research on Permanent Authentic Records in Electronic Systems project [InterPARES] Web site at: www.interpares.org and in Hunter [2000]). Reliability maintains the identity of a record, or those attributes, including context and provenance, that uniquely characterize it and distinguish it from other records. In order for the system to capture and manage accurate and complete records it must have tight controls over operational processes, particularly creation and capture, over the entire life cycle. Major requirements for satisfying the requirement for reliability are that records were created and captured as part of a legitimate business process; records creation was carefully managed and the identity and responsibilities of those involved in creation and capture were precisely defined; the system captured the required contextual metadata documenting creation and use of the record and its relationships to other records; and the system managed records over the entire life cycle.

INTEGRITY

"The integrity of a record refers to its being complete and unaltered" (ISO, 2001, sec. 7). Record integrity requires that records are protected from unauthorized and undocumented alteration or deletion. Records created and maintained in electronic form are continually at risk of inadvertent or intentional alteration. These unauthorized and undocumented modifications of the record can occur anytime during the creation, access, transmission, and preservation of the record. In order to confirm that the record is unchanged or that only authorized and appropriate changes have been made, the status of the records and the presence or absence of changes has to be auditable or traceable. In other words, to meet the test of integrity the recordkeeping system must establish controls over the creation, transmission, use, custody, and preservation of the records. One vital type of control is a requirement that only authorized record creators can perform these functions. Other types of controls that define integrity include procedures to prevent, discover, and correct loss or corruption of records; measures to guarantee the continuing identity and integrity of records against media deterioration and across technological change; where multiple copies of records exist, formal procedures for identifying the authoritative record; and where planned and conscious changes were made, such as in the preservation process, the creation of metadata that will reflect how the record was modified and who authorized it.

SPECIFIC REQUIREMENTS FOR RECORDKEEPING SYSTEMS

Articulating recordkeeping only in terms of some broadly defined goals does not achieve the ultimate objective of communicating the requirements of a recordkeeping system. To achieve this, the set of requirements must eventually include enough specificity to allow system designers to understand the various elements of the requirement and ultimately to begin to translate the requirement into a set of automated or executable solutions or strategies. Over the last ten years, a number of institutions have created detailed lists of recordkeeping requirements.

The University of Pittsburgh's School of Information Science conducted the first systematic research on this topic. The Pitt project established a set of functional requirements for recordkeeping that addressed three levels of requirements: the organizational level, the recordkeeping system level, and the record level. Within these levels, they established five categories—conscientious organization, accountable recordkeeping system, captured records, maintained records, and useable records. Within these categories, they established twenty requirements, which they claimed "are identified in law, regulation, and best practices throughout society as the fundamental properties" of evidential records. (Functional requirements for evidence in record-keeping. The Pittsburgh Project Web Site.) Since the creation of the Pittsburgh document, numerous other projects have produced lists of requirements for recordkeeping systems. Among the most prominent requirements are those created by the United States Department of Defense, the National Archives of Australia; the State Archives of Victoria (Australia), the National Archives of the United Kingdom, and the European Commission, and those defined in ISO 15489–1.

Requirements for Recordkeeping Systems on the Web	
United States Department of Defense	http://jitc.fhu.disa.mil/recmgt/standards/html
National Archives of Australia	www.naa.gov.au/records-management/index.aspx
State Archives of Victoria	www.prov.vic.gov.au/vers/standard/version2.htm
National Archives of the United Kingdom	www.nationalarchives.gov.uk/electronicrecords/default.htm
European Commission	http://ec.europa.eu/transparency/archival_policy/moreq/index_en.htm
ISO	*International Standard 15489–1. Information and Documentation-Records Management, Part 1: General*, Section 8—Design and Implementation of a Records System: 8–11

Although these lists differ on some of the details, most of the lists of recordkeeping requirements agree on the basic types or categories of functionality a recordkeeping system must possess. These categories include the following:

Capture records
o The term capture typically represents the processes of: 1) Registering a record with a unique ID and a time and date when the record entered the recordkeeping system; 2) Assigning classification and retention/disposal metadata to the record; 3) Adding additional metadata defining the context, content, structure, and management of the record, and retaining this metadata in a tightly bound relationship to record content; and 4) transferring and storing the record in a recordkeeping repository.

| **Support classification scheme** |
| o The record must organize records according to some well-defined classification scheme. |
| **Capture record metadata** |
| o The recordkeeping system must support the capture and presentation of metadata for electronic records. |
| **Support audit control** |
| o The system must maintain audit trails for all processes that create, update, delete, access and use records, categories or files of records, metadata associated with records, and the classification schemes that manage the records. |
| **Ensure records are usable** |
| o System must ensure that records can be easily accessed and retrieved in a timely manner in the normal course of all business processes or for reference or secondary uses. |
| **Manage security and control** |
| o System must control access to the records according to well-defined criteria. |
| **Schedule records for disposition** |
| o System must provide for the automated retention of records with long-term value in accordance with authorized and approved disposition schedules. |
| o System must provide for the automated destruction of records in accordance with authorized and approved disposition schedules. |
| **Preserve records** |
| o System must ensure that records, including relevant metadata, notes, and attachments, can be converted or migrated to new system hardware, software, and storage media without loss of vital information. |

Within each of these categories, the better, more useful functional requirement statements list numerous mandatory and optional requirements. For example, the European Commission's *Model Requirements for the Management of Electronic Records* (MoReqs) breaks down its requirements in the following manner:

Classification Scheme: 39 requirements, of these 28 are mandatory
Controls and Security: 50 requirements, of these 38 are mandatory
Retention and Disposal: 46 requirements, of these 30 are mandatory
Capture: 27 requirements, of these 18 are mandatory
Referencing (unique identifiers): 7 requirements, of these 4 are mandatory
Searching, Retrieval, and Rendering: 46 requirements, of these 28 are mandatory
Administrative Functions: 30 requirements, of these 21 are mandatory
Other Functionality (non-electronic records, workflow, electronic signatures, encryption, and several other functions): 71 requirements, of these 33 are mandatory
Total: 316 requirements, of these 200 (63 percent) are mandatory.

The Department of Defense 5015.2-STD for records management applications breaks down their requirements in the following manner:

Mandatory Requirements
General Requirements: 5 requirements
Implementing File Plans: 6 requirements
Scheduling Records: 7 requirements, 6 sub-requirements
Declaring and Filing Records: 26 requirements
Filing E-Mail: 3 requirements
Storing Records: 4 requirements
Retention and Vital Records Management: 8 requirements, 47 sub-requirements
Access Controls: 5 requirements, 3 sub-requirements
System Audits: 6 requirements, 7 sub-requirements
System Management Requirements: 6 requirements, 2 sub-requirements
Additional Baseline Requirements: 6 requirements, 3 sub-requirements
Classified Records Requirements: 21 requirements, 8 sub-requirements
Non-Mandatory Requirements: 28 requirements, 15 sub-requirements
Total: 121 Requirements and 91 Sub-requirements for a total of 212 requirements, of these 93 requirements and 76 sub-requirements are mandatory for a total of 169 (80 percent) mandatory requirements

Though some of the requirements in these lists are unique, many of the specifications are common to all or most of the noteworthy requirement statements. Listed below is a summary and paraphrase of some of the most frequently occurring requirements in the Australian, DoD, and European Commission sets of requirements, This list does not constitute a comprehensive set of functional requirements for record-keeping, but it does include the basic, critical requirements that will likely form the foundation for any institution's requirements statement.

CAPTURES RECORDS

This requirement includes three critical activities: capture, registering the record, and assigning classification data and other metadata.

Capture Process

- The system must capture a record for all defined functions and activities. Records may be captured within a system manually or automatically by the system itself either as part of the system's workflow or through a batch process.
- The system must be capable of capturing records from all types of applications including standard office applications, imaging systems, e-mail applications, transaction processing systems and databases.
- The system must allow a compound document to be captured as a single record. Some electronic records, such as Web pages with graphics or e-mail messages with attachments, are composed of more than one component. The system must capture all of these components and maintain them as one record. This means maintaining the relationships between the components to ensure future retrieval, rendering, management, and retention or disposal.
- The system must support versioning. Sometimes, records have more then one version that must be captured. The system must allow either the capture of all versions as one record or the capture of each version as separate records. In the later case, a version number should be added to the metadata.
- The system must ensure the reliability of the capture process. To make a system like this work, the capture process must be reliable as records are migrated from the creating system or stor-

age medium to the recordkeeping system. Records cannot be lost or changed during the capture process.

Registers or Declares a Record

- The system must support the process of declaring or marking a document as a formally recognized electronic record. As part of the declaration process, the system must register the record by assigning it a unique identifier and documenting the date and time when the record entered the recordkeeping system.
- The system must prevent any revisions or alterations to the content of any registered electronic record
- The system must prevent the destruction or deletion of an electronic record unless undertaken in accordance with a formally approved disposition schedule.

Assigns Classification and Other Metadata

- The system must automatically assign appropriate classification metadata and other metadata to records and files and to classes at the point of creation and capture.
- The system must be capable of extracting metadata elements automatically from records when they are captured.
- The system must maintain a logical relationship between the record and the metadata that relates to the record.

Maintains a Classification Scheme

- As part of the metadata structure, the recordkeeping system must support a robust classification scheme. Classification is "the systematic identification and arrangement of records into categories according to logically structured conventions, methods, and procedural rules represented in a classification scheme" (Australian Standard AS ISO 15489, part 1, clause 3.5). The classification scheme, sometimes also called a file plan, is a diagram, table, or other representation categorizing the creator's records, usually by hierarchical classes, and according to a coding system expressed in alphabetical, numerical, or alphanumeric symbols.
- The system must ensure that records are associated with a classification scheme, and are associated with one or more electronic

files. Electronic files can be defined simply as a set of electronic records. A file is a group of records accumulated and kept together because they deal with the same subject, activity, or transaction. In other words, there is some common bond or relationship between records in a file. Electronic files need not have a physical existence; often they are virtual entities and exist because the metadata attributes of the records and the application software allows users to view and manage folders as if they physically contained the records assigned to them.

- The system must support and be compatible with the organization's or the application's classification scheme. When the classification scheme is non-existent or only partially constructed, or when designing a new system, it is strongly recommended that the classification scheme be based upon business processes and the identification of the business transactions that create records. The advantages of a business process classification scheme are to: 1) provide a means of determining that all the right records are captured; 2) create linkages between records related to specific functions and activities; 3) provide metadata on the context of creation; 4) determine appropriate retention periods for classes of records; 5) assist in establishing user permissions for access to records; and 6) define responsibility for managing classes of records over time.
- The system must ensure that the authorization to reclassify, add, delete, or otherwise modify the classification scheme is carefully controlled and monitored.

ASSIGNS METADATA OVER THE LIFE OF THE RECORD

In the context of archives and records management, metadata is "structured or semi-structured information that documents the creation, management, and use of records through time and within and across domains" (European Commission, 2002: 13).

- The system must permit metadata values to be retrieved and captured from lookup tables or from other software applications.
- The system must allow creators of records to enter manually pertinent record metadata that cannot be captured automatically.
- The system must support the validation of metadata that is en-

tered by users, or metadata that is imported from other systems.

- Metadata must be logically linked to the records, files, and classes it documents, so that users can review metadata information when they retrieve records.
- The system must allow for the addition, modification, or reconfiguration of metadata sets, but the authorization to make changes must be restricted.

SUPPORTS AUDIT CONTROL

- The system must maintain audit trails for all processes that create, update or modify, delete, access, and use records, categories or files of records, metadata associated with records, and the classification schemes that manage the records. These processes include, but are not limited to, creation, import or export, modifications, transfer, destruction, deletion, and access and use of a record, electronic files, metadata, classification schemes, and disposition schedules.
- At a minimum, the system must track: the action that was implemented; what data or information was accessed, added, deleted, or modified; who performed these functions; and when they were performed.
- The system must automatically capture the audit trail. The system must track events without manual intervention, and automatically store information about these activities in the audit trail.
- The audit trail data must be unalterable. The system must ensure that audit trail data cannot be modified in any way.
- The audit trail must be maintained for as long as required by law or policy or to facilitate continued access to records. At a minimum, the audit trail must be kept until the records it refers to are destroyed. Even after record content is destroyed, however, some audit data should be retained relating to the retention and destruction of the record.
- The audit trail must be logically linked to the records it documents, so that users can review audit information when they retrieve records. This logical relationship must be maintained even when the records and audit are stored in different systems.
- The audit data must be available for inspection or export (without affecting vital audit trail data) by authorized users with little or no experience with the system. This requirement is necessary

to enable users such as internal or external auditors to investigate system activity.

- The system must maintain basic system documentation and audit trails of system modifications as long as they are required to facilitate continued access to records. This includes tracking all changes made to system hardware or software and to administrative parameters such as changing user access rights.
- The system must provide reports for actions taken on the basis of audit trail data. The department or organization will determine what audit trail reports are needed and how they are organized. Possible reports include, but are not limited to, a chronological listing of activities for the entire system; a listing of activities involving an individual record, file, or class; a listing of activities undertaken by a particular user; and a listing of activities completed at a particular workstation.

MANAGES ACCESS AND USE

- The system must ensure that records can be easily accessed and retrieved in a timely manner in the normal course of all business processes or for reference or secondary uses.
- The system must be capable of searching the full-text content of electronic records.
- The system must present an integrated interface for searching both metadata and record content.
- The system must allow searching within an electronic file, across files, and at any level in the classification scheme hierarchy.
- The system must ensure that all components of a record or file, including contents, relevant metadata, notes, attachments, etc., can be accessed, retrieved, and rendered as a discrete unit or group and in a single retrieval process.

MANAGES RETENTION AND DISPOSAL

- The system must provide for the automated retention of records with long-term value in accordance with authorized and approved record retention schedules.
- The system must provide for the automated destruction of records in accordance with authorized and approved records retention schedules.

- The system must be capable of associating a retention schedule with all records, record metadata, files, or classes of a classification scheme.
- The system must automatically notify and get approval of designated personnel in advance of disposition activities.
- The system must ensure that any function to delete records on an ad hoc basis (outside of the disposal process) is restricted to only the highest level of administrator.
- The system must provide for the interruption of disposition activities on records or classes of records that have been or are expected to become the subjects of litigation.
- Within the system, every record in a file or class of records must be governed by the retention schedule associated with that file or class.
- The system must allow the administrator in charge of schedules to change or amend schedules associated with records at any point in the life of the record.

MANAGES SECURITY AND CONTROL

- The system must allow only authorized personnel to create, capture, update, or purge records, metadata associated with records, files of records, classes in classification schemes, and retention schedules.
- The system must control access to the records according to well-defined criteria. A user must never be presented with information that he or she is not permitted to receive. The criteria for access will vary according to the type of data or records contained in the system.

MANAGES PRESERVATION, BACKUPS, AND RECOVERY STRATEGIES

- The system must ensure that records, components of records, audit trails, metadata, links to metadata or to files, and classification schemes can be converted or migrated to new system hardware, software, and storage media without loss of vital information.
- The system must produce a report detailing any failure during a conversion or transfer and identifying records that were not successfully exported.

- The system must retain all records that have been exported until confirmation of a successful transfer process.
- The system must provide automated procedures that allow for the regular backup and recovery of all records, files, metadata, and classification schemes. Back-up procedures must not be regarded as a substitute for a preservation strategy based on procedures for systematically migrating or converting records over time.
- The system must support a capability for separate physical storage of back-up data.

Non-Electronic Records

The system must be capable of classifying and managing non-electronic, physical records and of managing electronic and non-electronic records in an integrated manner. This means the system must be able to classify, create, and retrieve audit information and other metadata; control access and define security; and apply retention and disposal schedules for non-electronic records according to the same requirements that have been defined for electronic records.

Documentation

All system policies and procedures must be defined and documented. This documentation helps to ensure continuing access to records within the system, and can be used to help prove the authenticity of a record.

- System administrators must maintain policy and procedural documentation. The documentation should include at a minimum an overview of the purpose and uses of the system; policies and procedures for system operation and maintenance, quality control, security, testing, and records retention; and software/hardware specifications and operation.
- Documentation must be accurate and up-to-date.
- Documentation must be readily available and accessible.
- Documentation must be retained according to a set retention schedule.

THE IMPORTANCE OF METADATA

As indicated earlier, the concept of evidence is a very critical element within the definition of a record. The essence of a record, and what distinguishes it from other types of digital objects, is the existence of metadata defining content, context, and structure of the record. Without sufficient documentation describing the content of the record and the context of its creation and use, the record loses its value as evidence and in some cases ceases to be a record at all. Archivists also recognize that in many instances metadata is the evidence and proof that a particular functional requirement for recordkeeping has been met. This is particularly true for activities that occur routinely over time, such as disposition scheduling and preservation. Without metadata that is associated with the record content, there would be no way to determine whether certain actions were actually implemented and by whom.

The term metadata comes from the world of information technology, where it is used primarily to describe the structures, characteristics, location, and usage of data, tables, applications, and programs. This information is organized into data dictionaries, which are repositories of information that typically include data on the name of each data element, its definition (size and type), where and how it is used, and its relationship to other data. Metadata is widely used in the library and archives professions as well, although it was not called by that term until recently. Most often this documentation appeared as cataloging information or archival finding aids, and focused largely on describing the content and some of the structure of the original object.

In the last five years, the concept of metadata within the archives and digital management communities has expanded to include considerably more documentation on context of creation and use and on managing the object over the life cycle. In the context of archives and records management, metadata is presently most accurately defined as "structured or semi-structured information that documents the creation, management and use of records through time and within and across domains" (European Commission, 2002: 13). Another good working definition of metadata is provided in the ISO 15489–1 standard: "data describing context, content and structure of records and their management through time" (ISO, 2001, sec. 3).

The emergence of electronic records has created some new problems and challenges for archivists and records managers attempting to preserve evidence or metadata. The primary challenge is associated with the basic but extremely important recognition that unlike paper documents, electronic records are logically constructed and often "virtual" entities. Consequently, electronic documents cannot be viewed in the same way as paper records, where so much of the content, context, and structural metadata is embedded in or is part of the record or is physically available as part of a classification scheme or filing structure. In automated systems, the critical metadata, if it exists at all, may or may not be physically associated with the content data.

Archivists and records managers have also discovered that metadata as typically defined by systems designers and technologists is often not as complete as necessary to describe a record. There seem to be two major reasons for these deficiencies. Most IT metadata specifications are incomplete because they were created primarily for information systems designers and programmers, not for end users and particularly not for future generations of researchers. Consequently, much user related metadata is missing from the typical IT lists of important metadata elements. In addition most IT lists are limited to only simple contextual information; these lists do not routinely capture or manage external or complex contextual metadata. For example, although transaction logs maintained in typical transaction processing systems do contain some critical data on updates and revisions, they do not, on the whole, provide sufficient evidence on the context of creation and use—metadata that addresses the questions of why the record was created, when it was transmitted and received, who were the users of the record, and who had custody of the record. The availability of this contextual metadata, archivists argue, could make the difference between a useful and a useless record, particularly when viewed over longer periods of time.

Another deficiency of typical system metadata is the absence of some critical documentation on the structure of the record. Of particular importance is structural metadata describing how to open and read a record as it was originally created and viewed. Finally, most metadata systems do not include sufficient amounts of metadata to allow administrators to manage the object over time and to convey to future users the types of management decisions made and the consequences of these decisions. Taken as a whole, the absence of critical metadata has meant, as one archivist has noted, that "most collections of electronic data, electronic documents, or information are not records because they cannot qualify as evidence" (Bearman, 1994: 2).

KEY RECORDKEEPING METADATA

The challenge receiving the most attention from archivists and records managers is the determination of which types of metadata are needed to meet requirements for recordkeeping. The first research project designed to identify key recordkeeping metadata was the University of Pittsburgh project discussed earlier in this chapter. One of the products of this project was a set of metadata specifications "designed to satisfy the functional requirements for evidence," and to "guarantee that the data object will be usable over time, be accessible by its creator, and have properties required to be fully trustworthy as evidence and for purposes of executing business" (Bearman and Sochats, 1994: 1). Pitt project personnel identified 67 metadata items organized into six categories or layers (The University of Pittsburgh Electronic Records Project, Metadata Specifications).

Since the emergence of the Pittsburgh metadata specifications, several other institutions or projects have put forward their own set of recordkeeping metadata. Among the most prominent are those proposed by the National Archives of Australia, the State Archives of Victoria (Australia), the United States Department of Defense, the European Commission, and the National Archives of the United Kingdom.

At present, there is no real consensus on a core set of metadata specifications or a set of minimum metadata standards; as yet, there is nothing for recordkeeping that resembles or has been accepted in the way that, say, the Dublin Core Metadata has been embraced by many professional communities (see the Dublin Core Metadata Initiative). However, there is general agreement among archivists and records managers about the categories of recordkeeping metadata that need to be present. Most recordkeeping specifications include documentation on the content and structure of the record, on the context of its creation and use, on the activities performed on the records over the life cycle, and data on how to manage or administer the record over time. (For discussions on the need for metadata documenting context and structure, see Bearman [1994]; Bearman [1996]; Hedstrom [1993].)

The Primary Categories of Recordkeeping Metadata

Identification or Registration Metadata: Metadata uniquely identifying the record and documenting when it entered the recordkeeping system

Content Metadata: Information on the words, numbers, images, and sounds that make up the content of the record.

Contextual Metadata: Metadata on the context of creation and transmission, and information on the relationships between the record and other records, or to files or classes of records.

Audit Trail Metadata: Metadata on activities performed on individual records or on classes or files of records over the life cycle.

Access and Use Metadata: Metadata that defines the terms of access or use, including restrictions such as those related to security classification and intellectual property rights.

Disposition Metadata: Metadata that defines how long the record will be retained and how disposition will be managed over time.

Preservation History Metadata: Metadata that defines how the record will be preserved over time and the impact of preservation activities on the record.

Structural Metadata: Metadata on the record's physical characteristics and internal organization.

History of Use Metadata: Metadata documenting access and use of the record over time.

Within these basic categories, most lists of recordkeeping metadata differ noticeably in the number of metadata elements, the way they are organized, the amount of description they provide on the specifications, and the specific items they list as essential or mandatory. For example, the National Archives of Australia "Recordkeeping Metadata Standard for Commonwealth Agencies" includes 20 primary metadata elements. Eight of these are mandatory: Agent, Rights Management, Title, Date, Aggregation Level, Record Identifier, Management History, and Disposal. The Standard also includes 65 sub-elements, of which 34 (52 percent) are mandatory. Metadata elements with the highest number of sub-elements include agent responsible for some action or use of the record (11 metadata sub-elements), rights management (7 metadata sub-elements), preservation history (5 metadata sub-elements), and mandate (5 metadata sub-elements).

The Model Requirements for the Management of Electronic Records created by the European Commission organizes its metadata elements according to levels of the filing hierarchy (classes, files, and records). The MoReq metadata scheme includes 103 elements, of which 79 (77 percent) are mandatory. Finally, the National Archives of United Kingdom's *Metadata Standard* is divided into 17 metadata elements, of which 10 are mandatory. The standard also includes a total of 56 sub-elements, of which 28 (50 percent) are mandatory. Within the British standard, metadata elements with the highest number of sub-elements include access rights (17 metadata sub-elements), disposal (15 metadata sub-elements), relationships (8 metadata sub-elements), and dates (6 metadata sub-elements).

There are legitimate reasons for these differences. Ultimately, metadata specifications should be defined by the environment and system they are documenting. Factors that will determine the types and amount of metadata collected include security and risk issues and the number of records that have long-term value to the organization. For example, a system managing records in the United States Department of Defense would include much more metadata relating to security and access than would a recordkeeping system within a public university. Similarly, one would expect to find many more metadata elements designed to strictly control and monitor retention of records related to the discovery of new drugs in a pharmaceutical business than in most other types of businesses. This does not mean that a core set of metadata specifications is not appropriate; it does mean, however, that the selection of specific metadata specifications will ultimately be dependent on the particular business environment or automated system being documented.

However, despite these differences in size and organization, most of the primary recordkeeping metadata lists consider the following metadata elements as essential to any system that creates, captures, manages, and preserves authentic records over time.

IDENTIFICATION METADATA

RECORD IDENTIFIER

Definition: A unique identifier for the record

Purpose: To uniquely identify the record and to act as an access point to other data about the record.

DATE/TIME REGISTERED

Definition: The date when the record was entered into the recordkeeping system.

Purpose: To provide system validation of the act of officially "registering" the record, and to provide evidence of the record's authenticity.

LOCATION

Definition: The current (physical or system) location of the record.

Purpose: To keep track of the record, to enable identification of the record's current location, and to facilitate quick retrieval when required.

CONTEXT METADATA

AGENT—ORIGINATOR

Definition: A corporate entity, organizational unit, or an individual responsible for performing some action on a record.

Purpose: To ensure accountability and facilitate access to the record.

AGENT—RECEIVER

Definition: If the record is transmitted, the individual(s), unit(s), or system(s) to whom the record is addressed and/or who receives the record.

Purpose: To ensure accountability and facilitate access to the record.

DATE/TIME—CREATION OF RECORD

Definition: The date and times at which a record is created in the course of business.

Purpose: To provide evidence on the act of creation.

Date/Time—Transmission of Record

Definition: If the record is transmitted, the dates and times when the originator sent the record.

Purpose: To provide evidence of the act of transmitting the record.

Date/Time—Receipt of Record

Definition: If the record is transmitted, the dates and times when the fundamental recordkeeping action of receiving the record occurs.

Purpose: To provide evidence of the act of receiving the record.

Record Relationships—Functions and Activities

Definition: The business functions and activities documented by the record.

Purpose: To provide contextual information for a record by documenting its relationship with the function and activities it documents.

Record Relationships—Related Record(s)

Definition: Other records created by the same business process.

Purpose: To provide contextual information for a record by documenting its relationship with other related records documenting a business process.

Content Metadata

Title

Definition: The name given to the record that is representative of its contents or function.

Purpose: To describe the functions and subjects documented in the record, and to assist in identifying the record.

Subject

Definition: The subject or topic of a record which describes the record's content.

Purpose: To serve as a resource discovery access point at a finer level of detail.

Description

Definition: Description of the content or purpose of the record.

Purpose: To enable additional access points based on keywords describing the record.

COVERAGE
Definition: The jurisdictional, spatial, and/or temporal characteristics of the content of the record.

Purpose: To allow a search to be restricted to records about a certain jurisdiction, place, or time.

LANGUAGE
Definition: The language of the content of the record.

Purpose: To allow searches by the language in which the records were created.

TERMS AND CONDITIONS OF USE METADATA

MANDATE OR WARRANT
Definition: Citations and references to laws, policies, and best practices that impose a requirement to control access to and use of a record.

Purpose: To provide a source or warrant for recordkeeping requirements as they relate to access and use.

ACCESS AND USE TERMS AND CONDITIONS
Definition: The terms under which the record may be accessed and used.

Purpose: To advise users of record restrictions, to protect the privacy of individuals and the business interests of corporate entities, to facilitate effective access and use of the record, and to comply with any legal or policy restrictions.

RESPONSIBILITY
Definition: Identifies who (person, system, organization) is responsible for performing or authorizing access and restrictions or the lifting of restrictions for the record.

Purpose: To facilitate access and use management activities over time.

Disposal Metadata

DISPOSAL AUTHORIZATION OR WARRANT
Definition: Citations or references to laws, policies, and best practices that govern the disposition of the record.

Purpose: To ensure the efficient management of the record, and to comply with laws and regulations relating to the retention and disposal of the record.

DISPOSAL DATE
Definition: Identifies how long the record must be retained and the date when the record should be destroyed.

Purpose: To ensure the efficient management of the record, and to comply with laws and regulations relating to recordkeeping.

DISPOSAL ACTION HISTORY
Definition: Identifies when the record was destroyed and by whom.

Purpose: To ensure that recordkeeping disposition requirements are met and provide for a more accountable system.

Structural Metadata

FILE ENCODING METADATA—DATA FORMAT
Definition: The data format or the logical or file format of the data (e.g., ASCII, UNICODE, XML, TIFF)

Purpose: To enable retrieval and use of the record and facilitate preservation management.

FILE ENCODING METADATA—MEDIA FORMAT
Definition: The type of data representation (e.g., text, image, audio, video) and file types.

Purpose: To enable retrieval and use of the record and facilitate preservation management.

FILE ENCODING METADATA—COMPRESSION/ENCRYPTION
Definition: The method of compression and the algorithms used to compress or encrypt the record.

Purpose: To enable retrieval and use of the record and facilitate preservation management.

FILE RENDERING METADATA—HARDWARE/SOFTWARE DEPENDENCIES

Definition: Any hardware and software the record is dependent upon that will affect how the record can be rendered.

Purpose: To enable retrieval and use of the record and facilitate preservation management.

AGGREGATION LEVEL

Definition: The level at which the record is being described and controlled. Typical levels include record, files or folder, and class or series.

Purpose: To control the management actions which may be taken on the record, and allow searches to be restricted to records at a particular level of aggregation.

EXTENT

Definition: The physical size and/or capacity of the record.

Purpose: To provide information about the size of the record and the amount of storage space that it requires.

PRESERVATION HISTORY METADATA

RESPONSIBILITY

Definition: Identifies who (person, system, organization) is responsible for performing or authorizing preservation activities for the record.

Purpose: To facilitate preservation management activities over time.

ACTIVITY DATE

Definition: Identifies when a preservation action was completed.

Purpose: To provide evidence of activities for preserving the record over time

ACTIVITY TYPE

Definition: Identifies what specific preservation activity was initiated (e.g., backed-up, imaged, medium refreshed, microfilmed, migrated).

Purpose: To provide evidence of activities for preserving the record over time.

IMPACT OF THE PRESERVATION PROCESS

Definition: Identifies the effect of preservation activities on the form, content, accessibility, and use of the record.

Purpose: To provide evidence of activities for preserving the record over time.

NEXT ACTION

Definition: Identifies activity types and date for next preservation action.

Purpose: To facilitate preservation management activities over time.

MEDIUM

Definition: Identifies the physical medium on which the record is stored (e.g., CD-R, hard disk, microfilm, videotape).

Purpose: To track how a record is stored.

HISTORY OF USE METADATA

ACCESS AND USE HISTORY

Definition: Identifies who accessed and used the record, and when this action occurred.

Purpose: To act as a cumulative audit trail of all significant accesses to and uses made of the record over time. This evidence can be used to provide contextual information about the ways in which the record was used over time, and to provide a mechanism by which recordkeeping system security can be monitored.

OAIS MODEL

The Open Archival Information System (OAIS) Reference Model merits special mention (see OASIS Reference Model Web site). It has emerged as the model around which the architecture of many archival or preservation repositories are being built. Visual diagrams of the two components of the OAIS model can be found in figures 2.1 and 2.2.

One of the primary reasons for its popularity is that it defines preservation more broadly than past models. Most definitions of preservation focus exclusively on technology or the hardware and software requirements to preserve the object over time. In other words, the goals of these requirements were to ensure readability (records can be processed on a functioning computer system), and intelligibility (information in the records is comprehensible to a human being).

Obviously, these are critical requirements that the OAIS model also emphasizes. However, the OAIS model recognizes that there is more to preservation than bits and bytes. A preservation system must also ensure that the record is complete and trustworthy and that it can be used over time. In other words, the system must preserve the authenticity of the record and ensure that the record is useable and can be retrieved, manipulated, and transmitted or transported from a repository to sites of research, presentation, and teaching.

To ensure that preservation systems achieve these goals the OAIS model has developed an extensive set of metadata specifications. At the highest level the model divides metadata into content information and preservation description information. Content information is divided into two categories: content data object and representation information.

The content data object is a representation of the bit streams that comprise the digital content being preserved. Representation information is the metadata that translates the bit streams into useful information. It is the information that will later allow an administrator of the system or a user to render/display, understand, and interpret the content data object. The OAIS model divides representation information into two categories of metadata: Content Data Object Description and Environment Description. Content Data Object Description metadata documents the characteristics of the Content Data Object so that it can be rendered and its content can be understood. It consists of thirteen metadata elements, including information on structural type (e.g., image, sound, database, etc.), file description (e.g., GIF image file, resolution, etc.), installation requirements (e.g., object in AIP file), size, access inhibitors (e.g., encryption, password protected), significant properties (e.g., preserving color scheme or format is essential), description of rendered content (e.g., definition and description of data structures), and documentation.

Environment Description metadata describes the technical environment in which the object is stored and is divided into descriptions of the hardware environment and the software environment. Metadata on the hardware includes information or requirements on micropro-

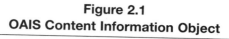

Figure 2.1
OAIS Content Information Object

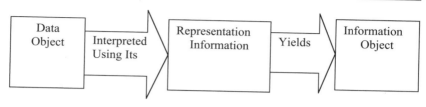

Source: www.ccsds.org/publications/archive/650x0b1.pdf. Consultative Committee for Space Data Systems. *Recommendation for Space Data System Standards: Reference Model for an Open Archival Information System (OAIS).*

cessors and memory, on storage and on any peripherals, such as sound cards, CD-ROM drives, etc. Hardware Environment metadata consists of 8 metadata elements.

Metadata on the software environment is more extensive and consists of 6 metadata elements and 10 sub-elements. It includes information on rendering programs that transform, display, and access the data, and metadata that describes the operating system. The ultimate goal in creating this metadata is to allow users to display the Content Data Object as it exists in the archival repository.

Preservation Description Information is metadata required to manage, interpret, and preserve the content information over time and the entire life cycle. Preservation Description Information is divided into four categories of metadata, as shown in figure 2.2: reference information, context information, provenance information, and fixity information.

Reference Information consists of 3 metadata elements and 8 sub-elements. The primary purpose of this requirement is to provide the object with a unique identifier.

Context Information consists of 3 metadata elements and 5 sub-elements. It is metadata that documents relationships of the content information with its environment, including the reasons for its creation and its relationships to other objects.

Provenance Information is quite extensive; it consists of 10 metadata elements and 30 sub-elements. It includes metadata that essentially documents the history of the management and use of the content information over time. The OAIS model divides the Provenance Information into the collection of metadata at several key points in the life cycle: origin, pre-ingest period, ingest period, archival retention, and rights management. At each of these points in the life cycle, metadata is collected on the activities or events relating to management and use of the record, including designation and description of the event, date it occurred, responsible agency, outcome, and next occurrence.

Fixity Information consists of 1 metadata element and 4 subelements. This is metadata establishing the integrity of the object and ensuring that the content information object has not been altered in an undocumented manner. It achieves this by documenting authenticity verifications on the record throughout its life cycle. Taken as a whole the OAIS model consists of 44 metadata elements and 57 subelements. It is certainly one of the most extensive and influential preservation metadata models in existence.

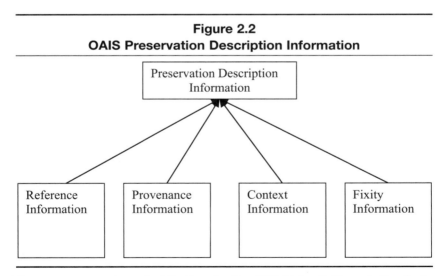

Figure 2.2
OAIS Preservation Description Information

Source: www.ccsds.org/publications/archive/650x0b1.pdf. Consultative Committee for Space Data Systems. *Recommendation for Space Data System Standards: Reference Model for an Open Archival Information System (OAIS).*

OTHER POINTS OF AGREEMENT ABOUT RECORDKEEPING METADATA

Archivists and records managers generally agree on several other characteristics of a recordkeeping metadata strategy.

- To be successful, some, even most, of the metadata must be automatically captured by the system. Most of the documented failures in the application of metadata within records management systems have been due to the requirement for extensive manual entry of metadata elements. Experience has shown that over time users who are asked to manually enter extra metadata elements will simply stop complying, and the system will eventually break down. Any realistic strategy for creating and capturing metadata must begin with the assumption that most metadata elements will be automatically captured or harvested by the system.
- Metadata must be automatically assigned to many records within a classification system. Normally this metadata can be applied at three levels: 1) Class or Record Series, which could be identified with the highest level business process or the business function; 2) File Level, which could correspond to the business transaction; and 3) the individual record or the product of the business event. The primary value of assigning records to various levels is to document and display relationships between records, and to provide a means of more efficiently managing records. Grouping records into classes or files will facilitate decision making on such issues as access rights, disposition, and preservation strategies by allowing administrators to make decisions at the aggregate level, i.e., for files or entire classes of records rather than one record at a time. The idea behind this concept is that records within a classification will share characteristics, such as a retention period, and as a result a single value can be applied, at least as a default, to all the records in that classification.
- One of the most important strategies for creating better recordkeeping systems is to associate information, documents, data in tables, etc., with business functions and processes. The reasons for this are: 1) It provides an effective means of deter-

mining that all the right records are being captured. Modeling of business processes will generate a detailed map to all the records that are created. 2) It identifies all metadata on the context of creation. Building a model for identifying records within and as part of a process is the surest and most direct means of capturing contextual metadata that documents that process. 3) It builds an effective classification structure for managing these records over time. Functional appraisal has been advocated as a viable strategy for a decade or more. This concept claims that the value of the record can best be determined by evaluating the importance of the process that created the record. A number of archivists have advocated a similar strategy for determining retention, preservation, and access strategies. In other words, by associating records with business processes or individual activities, the relative importance of the process can define, at least initially and as a default value, the strategy for appraising, preserving, and restricting access to records.

- Metadata can come from a variety of sources. It can be found within the record itself, in tables associated with the document, or in a metadata repository that stores documentation about the record.

- Metadata continues to accrue during the life of an information object or system. The best examples of this are audit trail, disposition, and management metadata. As action is taken to preserve or manage a record over time, metadata will be added to the documentation about the record.

- To repeat a point made in the functional requirements section, there must be a logical relationship between the metadata elements and the digital object. The system must ensure that all components of a record, including relevant metadata, can be accessed and displayed as a unit or as a complete record of a business transaction. In some cases this will mean providing links to values stored in lookup tables or other software applications.

While there are still different opinions on the nature of specific requirements for recordkeeping and on which requirements are mandatory and which optional, there are enough areas of consensus that records managers can make informed and thoughtful decisions about how their systems can fulfill the required functions and supply the required metadata. Keeping in mind the many requirements that may apply to recordkeeping systems, we can now proceed to examine some specific information systems that may be used for recordkeeping and how they can be adapted to fulfill these requirements.

REFERENCES

Ackland, Glenda. 1992. "Managing the Record Rather Than the Relic." *Archives and Manuscripts* 20, no. 1: 57–63.

AIIM. 2006. *Compliance: It's Real, It's Relevant, and It's More Than Just Records*. Silver Spring, MD: AIIM.

Bearman, David. 1994. *Electronic Evidence: Strategies for Managing Records in Contemporary Organizations*. Pittsburgh, PA: Archives and Museum Informatics.

Bearman, David. 1996. "Item Level Control and Electronic Record-keeping." *Archives and Museum Informatics* 10, no. 3: 211–214.

Bearman, David, and Ken Sochats. "Metadata Requirements for Evidence in Recordkeeping." The Pittsburgh Project (1994). Available: www.archimuse.com/papers/nhprc/BACartic.html

Cook, Terry. 2000. "Beyond the Screen: The Records Continuum and Archival Cultural Heritage." Paper delivered at the Australian Society of Archivists Conference, Melbourne, August 18, 2000. Available: www.mybestdocs.com/cookt-beyondthescreen-000818.htm

Cox, Richard. 1994. "The Record: Is it Evolving?" *The Records and Retrieval Report* 10, no. 3: 1–16.

Cox, Richard. 1996. "The Record in the Information Age: A Progress Report on Research." *The Records and Retrieval Report* 5, no. 1 (January): 1–16.

Dearstyne, Bruce W. 1993. *The Archival Enterprise: Modern Archival Principles, Practices, and Techniques*. Chicago: American Library Association.

Dollar, Charles. 1992. *Archival Theory and Information Technologies: The Impact of Information Technologies on Archival Principles and Methods*. Macerata, Italy: University of Macerata.

Dollar, Charles. 1999. *Authentic Electronic Records: Strategies for Long-Term Access*. Chicago: Cohasset Associates.

"Dublin Core Metadata Initiative." Available: http://dublincore.org/

European Commission. 2002. *Model Requirements for the Management of Electronic Records" (MoReqs)*. Available: http://e.europa.eu/transparency/archival_policy/moreq/index_en.htm

"Functional Requirements for Evidence in Recordkeeping: The Pitts-burgh Project." Available: www.archimuse.com/papers/nhprc

Greene, Mark A. 2002. "The Power of Meaning: The Archival Mission in the Postmodern Age." *American Archivist* 65, no. 1 (Spring/Summer): 42–55.

Harris, Verne. 2000. "Law, Evidence and Electronic Records: A Strategic Perspective from the Global Periphery." Paper presented at the ICA Conference in Seville, August 2000. Available: www.archivists.org.au/sem/misc/harris.pdf

Hedstrom, Margaret. 1993. "Descriptive Standards for Electronic Records: Deciding What Is Essential and Imagining What Is Possible." *Archivaria* 36 (Autumn): 53–63.

Hunter, Gregory. 2000. *Preserving Digital Information*. New York: Neal-Schuman.

International Council on Archives. 2005. *Electronic Records: A WorkBook for Archivists*. ICA Studies 16. Paris: ICA.

"International Research on Permanent Authentic Records in Electronic Systems (InterPARES) Project." Available: www.interpages.org

International Standards Organization (ISO). 2001. *International Standard 15489–1–2001, Part 1: General*. Geneva: ISO.

Mancini, John. 2007. "Scanning and Capture Technologies 2007: Process Integration and ROI Enhancements." *AIIM E-Doc Magazine* (May/June).

McKemmish, Sue, and Michael Piggott, eds. 1994. *The Records Continuum, Ian Maclean and Australian Archives First Fifty Years*. Clayton, Australia: Ancora Press.

Nesmith, Tom. 2002. "Seeing Archives: Postmodernism and the Changing Intellectual Place of Archives." *American Archivist* 65, no. 1 (Spring/Summer): 24–41.

"Open Archival Information System (OAIS) Reference Model." Available: http://public.ccsds.org/publications/archive/650x0b1.pdf

Piggott, Michael, and Sue McKemmish. 2002. "Recordkeeping, Reconciliation, and Political Reality." Paper presented at the Society of Archivists Annual Conference, Sydney, August, 2002. Available: www.sims.monash.edu.au/research/rcrg/publications/piggottmckemmish2002.pdf

Robek, Mary, Gerald Brown, and David Stephens. 1996. *Information and Records Management*. New York: Glencoe.

Roberts, David. 1994. "Defining Electronic Records, Documents and Data," *Archives and Manuscripts* 22, no. 1 (May): 14–26.

"The University of Pittsburgh Electronic Records Project, Metadata Specifications." Available: www.archimuse.com/papers/nhprc/meta96.html

Williams, Robert, and Lori Ashley. 2005. *2005 Electronic Records Management Survey. A Renewed Call to Action.* Chicago: Cohasset Associates. Available: www.cohasset.com/whitepaper_survey2005.html

3

Transaction Processing Systems Constructed on the Relational Database Model

In chapter 2, the functional requirements and metadata specifications for a recordkeeping system were defined. We have defined what we want the system to do, what functions it will perform, and the types of documentation or metadata that must be present to ensure the creation of authentic records. With these tools or models we are ready to define for system designers and analysts the nature of the records they need to capture. We are ready to describe for them when a record should be created, its components (content plus metadata), and how the system should manage these records over time. We have created the blueprints for our recordkeeping system.

If we were designing a new recordkeeping system or purchasing an off-the-shelf application, these blueprints would be all we needed to move forward to design and implementation. However, more often than not archivists and records managers will be seeking to transform existing information systems into better recordkeeping systems. In these cases, defining recordkeeping requirements is only one half of the equation. The other half is an understanding of the design features and existing functionality of the system that is under review. Of particular importance is acquiring a good working knowledge of the most commonly used systems in most institutions: transaction processing systems (TPS), enterprise document or content management systems (EDMS), decision support systems (DSS), electronic mail systems, and Web management systems. Understanding how these data and information systems function and how they manage records throughout their life cycle is one of the starting points in the quest to develop recordkeeping systems. Once this knowledge is obtained, we can begin to compare the results of the analysis to the recordkeeping requirements and metadata specifications, and address the hard questions relating to how well these systems meet the requirements for recordkeeping. Once that review is completed, the discussion of strategies for modifying the existing system can begin.

TECHNOLOGY AND INFORMATION

In his book *Managing Information as a Corporate Resource,* Paul Tom identifies five periods in the progression of technology and information. The first of these is the period of discovery. This is the period when the computer is introduced and is successfully employed to undertake relatively simple tasks. The reaction of management at this stage is one of enthusiasm and high hopes. The second period he describes is one of surprise. It is characterized by delays in implementation and requests for more powerful hardware, and generally by a failure of technology to meet expectations. Management's optimism in this stage has transformed into caution and concern. The third period Tom has labeled as disillusionment. In this period management finds technology is not able to deliver the types of information that are useful and necessary for decision making, and managers begin to seriously question whether the massive investment in technology is justified. In this stage, management and IT are at odds, and neither side accepts responsibility for the problems. However, it is typically the case that too many resources have been invested in technology to turn back the clock. The fourth stage is motivation and signals a breakthrough to the recognition by management that the computer technology has advanced, and that automated systems can indeed be an important enabler of change. The fifth stage is knowledge or dependency, where computers are being used to generate knowledge-based products, and businesses are becoming increasingly dependent on automation. In essence it is a period that incorporates optimism—automation will help address challenges—and pessimism—we are becoming too dependent on automation. This aptly describes the present condition: optimism for the future and yet anxiety whether computers can meet our needs for better and more useful information and knowledge (Tom, 1987).

Technology is not the "silver bullet" that will solve an institution's problems. In an effort to correct what is often perceived as the misplaced dependence on technology, some experts have proclaimed that the primary goal is to manage information rather than technology. It is increasingly understood that "technology used to enable these information processes is considerably less important than the information that systems hold. Information is dynamic, capable of creating great value, and is the glue that holds enterprises together" (McGee and Prusak, 1993: 3). As the scholar Paul Tom (1987: 2) has succinctly stated: "The computer age is over; the information age has begun."

DATA AND INFORMATION

Before we examine the development of information management systems, we need to review definitions of the key terms: data and information.

There are certainly many definitions of information, but a particularly good one is that "information is not just data collected; rather it is data collected, organized, ordered, and imbued with meaning and context. Information must inform, while data has no such mandate. Information must be bounded, while data can be limitless. In order for data to become useful to a decision maker as information, it must be presented in such a way that he or she can relate to it and act upon it" (McGee and Prusak, 1993: 22).

From this definition, one can derive some primary characteristics of information and data. In the first place, information is comprised of data, which has been defined as raw facts about the organization and its business transactions. Most data items have little meaning and use by themselves; they possess little or no context; they are devoid of sequence and often appear in isolation from other related data. (Definitions of data can be found in Bellaver and Lusa [2002]; Davenport [2002]; and Whitten and Bentley [1998].) Unlike data, information has been refined, organized, and processed, and value has been added. Information is data that has some purpose and meaning. To be useful the data must be contextualized so that relationships between data and other information objects are revealed. By adding context to content data, users are able to answer questions such as: Who created the data? Where and when was it created? Why was it created? and How was it used and managed? Adding context also allows one to understand how the information relates to other information on the same subject or business process. As James McGee and Lawrence Prusak (1993: 210) write: "Contextualizing data is where learning occurs." (Other definitions of information can be found in Chaffey and Wood [2005]; Davenport [2002]; Whitten and Bentley [1998]; Bellaver and Lusa [2002].)

INFORMATION MANAGEMENT SYSTEMS

An information system can be defined as a set of interrelated components that collect, process, store and distribute information to support planning, decision making, and control in an organization. An information system is comprised of three main elements: technology (the what), people (the who), and process (the how). Over the past five decades, several major types of information systems have been used by institutions. (General descriptions of information systems can be found at Laudon and Laudon [1999]; and Chaffey and Wood [2005]. General descriptions of the various types of data and information systems can be found at Laudon and Laudon [1999]; Turban [1993]; Stair [2003]; Boddy, Boonstra and Kennedy [2004]; and Whitten and Bentley [1998].)

ELECTRONIC DATA PROCESSING SYSTEMS AND TRANSACTION PROCESSING SYSTEMS

The operational level systems often known as *electronic data processing systems (EDP)* or *transaction processing systems (TPS)* were introduced in the 1950s. These systems were used in only the largest organizations and were employed primarily to handle elementary but fundamental transactions, primarily in the area of finance. In early days of computing the focus was on data and data processing and was about replacing manual tasks with the computer and making these procedures more routine and efficient. In this first decade of automated systems, there was very little emphasis on turning this data into information for management purposes.

MANAGEMENT INFORMATION SYSTEMS

By the 1960s *management information systems (MIS)* were being created in response to manager's requests for more useful information. Generally these systems were independent of the transaction processing systems, although they were dependent on the TPS for data. These early MIS had little analytical capability and were relatively inflexible. Nonetheless these were the first automated systems to provide managers with the types of information they needed for planning and decision making, such as reports, inventories, and other summarized and aggregated summary statements.

DECISION SUPPORT SYSTEMS

More sophisticated information systems known as *decision support systems (DSS)* were introduced in the 1970s. DSS differed from MIS in that they were more flexible and adaptable. DSS allowed users to work directly with the system; there was far less need for assistance from programmers than was the case with MIS. These systems were interactive in the sense that they allowed the user to choose between numerous options and configurations and to customize both inputs and outputs. DSS also used more sophisticated analysis and modeling tools than MIS. Consequently, DSS were capable of creating more complex, more useful information for decision making and planning.

By the 1980s information systems had expanded into custom built decision support systems and early strategic planning systems. The new decision support systems became known as *executive support systems (ESS)*, and, as the name suggests, these systems were designed to serve the strategic needs of senior management. ESS imported data and information from TPS and DSS and from outside sources and presented filtered, summarized information useful for addressing the more complex, unstructured problems managers faced. DSS were designed to deliver information on demand and on a highly interactive basis. Often this information was presented in the most advanced graphics software employing easy to use interfaces.

ELECTRONIC DOCUMENT MANAGEMENT SYSTEMS

Electronic document management systems (EDMS) were also introduced in the 1980s. In the preceding decades the computer industry had focused on data management and on creating a variety of relational databases for managing data in the transaction processing environment. However, the new technology introduced in the 1980s with its workstations and networking systems placed greater emphasis on the creation of electronic documents. Documents are defined as discrete and identifiable information objects that are structured or formatted in a way that is useful and recognizable by users. Examples of documents are reports, correspondence, e-mail, and minutes (Bielawski and Boyle, 1997; Dollar, 1999; and Sutton, 1996). It eventually became apparent that only a relatively small percentage of the institution's information resources were stored in data, perhaps 20 percent or less. Experts estimate that today up to 80 percent of an institution's information resources are stored as documents (Sutton, 1996).

It was also discovered that relational databases of the type used to manage operational data were not the most effective means of storing and managing these objects. The result was the creation of document management systems. The first systems had fairly limited functionality. However, in the last five years these EDMS have added considerable functionality so that now they are capable of managing additional content, such as e-mail, images and video, and can do this successfully over the entire life cycle. Because of this expanded functionality, they have come to be known as Enterprise Document Management Systems.

KNOWLEDGE-BASED SYSTEMS AND STRATEGIC INFORMATION SYSTEMS

Sophisticated knowledge-based systems and *strategic information systems* were developed in the late 1980s and the 1990s. Knowledge is often defined as a higher, more complex form of information; it is information that has been transformed and augmented with organizational and personal insight to create a more useful type of information that is capable of addressing more complex analytical problems. In order to create and manage this knowledge, automated systems required more computing power, more powerful graphics and analytical and integrated software, better communications capabilities and user interfaces, and many more workstations. (Definitions of knowledge can be found in Chaffey and Wood [2005]; Davenport [2002]; Pearlson and Saunders [2005]; Sutton [1996]; Bellaver and Lusa [2002].)

One popular type of knowledge-based system was the *expert system*, based on artificial intelligence techniques. These systems were knowledge intensive programs that solved problems by capturing the expertise of a human. In other words, they performed some of the problem solving work of humans through the use of formally stated rules.

The 1990s witnessed the rapid growth of other knowledge enabling systems, known collectively as *Office Automation Systems (OAS)*. These systems included electronic publishing tools, electronic communications systems, electronic collaboration systems, image processing systems, and office management systems. They included such commonly known technologies as e-mail, word processing, fax, desktop publishing, and image processing. The backbone of these systems was a network, a LAN or internet, that connected everything together. OAS are at the center of most businesses strategies to build knowledge-based systems and to create knowledge workers. These systems are the enablers to allow information to be processed, distributed, used, and reused by workers.

Other newer forms of knowledge management are *Content Management Systems (CMS)*. Initially content management focused on Web content management, which included the ability to update, publish and manage the various content objects on a Web site. It also came to mean the ability to build templates that would enable dynamic content presentation and personalization based on user preferences.

The concept of a content manager has recently become associated with a system that has much more functionality. This system, known as an Enterprise Content Manager, is capable of interacting with and managing many more types of content, including transaction processing systems, desktop applications, e-mail, images, and video. In addition, these systems have the functionality to manage this content effectively over the entire life cycle. The enterprise content management solution has the potential to be the most completely integrated environment for structured and unstructured content within the enterprise.

Another type of knowledge system that emerged in the 1990s is known as *Enterprise Systems (ES)* or *Enterprise Resource Planning (ERP)* systems. These systems, offered by companies such as SAP, Oracle, and PeopleSoft, reflect the transformation from islands of technology to modular, interchangeable, and integrated systems. Enterprise systems include collections of application modules. SAP, for example, has twelve modules for such activities such as financial management, human resource management, and management of the physical plant. These application modules communicate with each other by means of a common central database, which are typically relational databases offered by leading vendors such as Oracle and Sybase. Other enterprise-wide solutions include enterprise document management and content management systems. These integrated systems provided unique opportunities for the creation of knowledge by facilitating the integration of data and information and the building of more useful information to solve complex questions and problems (for a description of ERP systems, see Davenport [2000]).

In the next four chapters, we will look at the functionality of several of these information systems in much more detail. Let us begin this process of reviewing information systems by examining the Transaction Processing Systems, with a primary focus on how the relational database structure, which is at the heart of the TPS, manages data and records.

TRANSACTION PROCESSING SYSTEMS

The most basic business system and the heart of most organizations is the Transaction Processing System (TPS) or as it is sometimes called, On-Line Transactional Processing (OLTP). A transaction processing system is a computerized system that manages the daily routine transactions necessary to the conduct of business, particularly in computing intensive areas, such as in the financial, human resources, and student recordkeeping functional areas. The TPS is the primary organizational resource for current data and information about the enterprise. The primary goals of these systems are to provide consistently fast, often real-time processing (sorting, listing, updating, merging); to create data that is current, up-to-date, accurate, and consistent throughout the system; to reduce clerical costs; and to output the documents required to do business, such as bills, paychecks, orders, detailed inventories, and reports. Until recently, separate systems existed for each functional area of the institution. However, in the last few years enterprise-wide operational systems, from such companies as SAP and Oracle, have integrated into one system the management of data and information created in most of the major functional areas. (For general description of TPS, see Lauden and Lauden [1999] and Williams, Sawyer and Hutchinson [1999].)

Data in transaction processing systems is typically organized and managed in a database structure. A database consists of data and metadata that is organized into structures comprised of tables, defined views, stored procedures and rules, and queries. Implementation and management of the data within the database is controlled by a collection of programs known as a database management system (DBMS) or more recently Enterprise Resource Planning (ERP) software. There are various types of databases, but the most popular by far is the relational model. The key to understanding how transaction systems manage data and ultimately records is learning how databases and database management system software are designed and how they function.

RELATIONAL DATABASES

Database design consists of three major components: 1) Conceptual design, which includes most prominently analyzing the business processes and user needs, and modeling or representing these processes in terms of data entities, attributes, and relationships; 2) the Logical design, which is the translation of the conceptual data model into an internal model designed for a specific database management system (for a relational database manager, the logical design would result in the creation of tables, indexes, views, etc.); 3) Physical design, which is the definition of the physical requirements that will allow the system to function; it includes the selection of the data storage and the data access characteristics of the database (Rob and Coronel, 2002). The relationships between the components of relational database design are shown in figure 3.1.

Design Goals and Data Modeling

Database designers must reconcile three often contradictory requirements: design elegance and performance, processing speed, and information requirements. Most of the design emphasis is on achieving maximum performance and maintaining data integrity. As one DB2 expert writes about designing databases: "Rule of Thumb: Always design for performance . . . If you do not design for performance, then by default you are designing for poor performance" (Yevich and Lawson, 2001: xxxi). The guiding principles are to create data that is current, accurate, and consistent; support current business needs for information; minimize the amount of data stored in the system; improve overall efficiency of the system; remove obsolete data; and provide an organizational resource to current data.

The first task in creating a database is to identify the data and

Figure 3.1
Relational Database Design

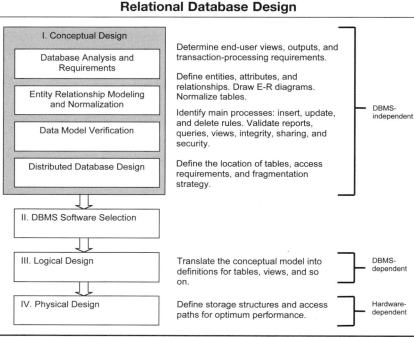

From *Database Systems: Design, Implementation, and Management*, 5th edition, by ROB/CORONEL (p. 332). 2002. Reprinted with permission of Delmar Learning, a division of Thomson Learning: www.thomsonrights.com. Fax 800 730–2215.

information that will be stored. This is achieved by means of a data model. A data model is a description of the processes that are being modeled; it is a representation, usually graphic, of a real world environment. As one expert has written: "A data model is to an information system as an architectural drawing is to a building or as a wiring diagram is to a circuit" (Schmidt, 1999: xxxv). It should be clearly recognized that the data model is a conceptual model; it does not include any reference to the physical layout of the system. The most common methodology for modeling or representing data in the database is the Entity Relationship Data Model (E-R Model). The E-R model was introduced by Peter Chen in 1976. The E-R model divides the environment it is modeling into three main components: entities, attributes and relationships. Let us review how this analysis works. (For more information on data modeling, see Rob and Coronel [2002]; Schmidt [1999]; and Whitten and Bentley [1998].)

Identifying Business Processes

An E-R model is created through an iterative process. For large databases, most designers employ a top-down approach—they first create an overview of the environment being modeled and then work downwards to the creation of entities and the relationships between entities, and eventually to the definition of individual attributes that describe the entity types.

The top-down process begins with a macro level or global view of an organization's data requirements and operations by analyzing actual business processes. The primary goal is to understand the functions and activities the creators of data actually perform. An initial objective of the process is to identify the so-called "Business Rules" established by the organization. Business rules are defined as "brief and precise narrative descriptions of a policy, procedure, or principle within a specific organization's environment" (Rob and Coronel, 2002: 334). Business rules create and enforce actions within a business. The main sources of information on business rules are upper- to mid-level managers and administrators and written documentation such as policy and procedures manuals. Examples of business rules include: A faculty member may teach only three courses. A student may take only sixteen credits in a semester. A course can meet in only one classroom. A faculty member cannot receive overtime pay. Identifying business rules allows designers to begin defining the nature, role, and scope of the database entities and the relationships between and among the entities.

In these preliminary first steps, analysts also seek to understand user needs and requirements—who uses data and information, how is it used, how frequently, and the typical outputs, such as forms and reports. To gather this information, system analysts interview system owners and users; review documentation that defines the types of records that are created; and observe the current system in action. This part of the review provides the end users' perspective on the data environment, and is designed to match the data model with specific business needs and users' requirements and constraints.

This analysis of business processes typically produces functional decomposition lists and diagrams that depict business functions and sub-functions within the primary functional categories. (For more information on process modeling, see Tenner and DeToro [1997]; and Whitten and Bentley [1998].) For example, within a university a common function is "awarding credit with grade to student." Within this larger function there are a number of sub-functions: recognition of course completion, withdrawal from courses, recognition of coursework equivalent, and grade changes. Within these sub-functions there are a number of processes and activities to define. A narrative statement of business activities for the sub-function "recognition of course completion" might read:

> Upon completion of regular semester coursework, the Office of the Registrar produces a set of on-line grade rosters to be used by faculty members for the assignment of grades. Faculty complete grade rosters and submit them electronically to the registrar. The registrar checks to determine whether all grades have been submitted. Faculty who have not submitted grades are notified. Grades (and credit which is determined through a combination of grade and credit hours for which student registered) are posted by the Office of the Registrar. Creation of the grade is under the authority of the instructor assigned to the section of the course which the student completed. Creation of the record in the system is the responsibility of the Office of the Registrar. Potential use of information associated with transaction is controlled by FERPA. Disposition decisions are governed by the official IU schedule for student records.

Identifying Entities

Once this basic analysis of business processes is completed, system designers move into the data modeling process. The first step in this process is the identification of entities, which are the persons, events, places, or things about which data is collected and stored. As entities are discovered they are given meaningful, business oriented names. Entities are nouns and not verbs or adjectives; entities can act or be acted upon (subject or objects of a sentence), are describable and can be uniquely identified. Examples of entities from a university environment include:

People: Students, Faculty, Staff, Administrators
Places: State, City, Registrar's Office
Objects: Buildings, Classrooms, Libraries
Events: Registration, Withdrawal, Scheduling
Concepts: Course, Grade, Account

Returning to the sub-function "recognition of course completion," the entities or objects involved in this process that need to be described include student, class, faculty, grade, grade rosters, credit hours, and Office of the Registrar.

Eventually these entities are identified in the data model. All of the characteristics of the data in the model are consistently depicted by a symbol that is unique to that element. In the commonly used Chen and Crow's Foot models, entities are represented by a rectangle containing the entity's name (Rob and Coronel, 2002).

Identifying Relationships

The next step in the data modeling process is the identification of relationships—associations or logical relationships among data or between two entities. The relationship may represent an event that links the entities or merely a logical affinity that exists between the entities. Relationships are named with an active or passive verb phrase that when combined with entity names form simple business sentences or assertions. For the sub-function "recognition of course completion," the relationship statements would be: 1) Student enrolls in class; 2) Faculty teaches class; 3) Faculty submits grade; 4) Office of Registrar creates grade roster; 5) Office of Registrar assigns credit to student. Defining relationships is extremely important in data modeling. One scholar has called relationships the "transportation network of the database" (Schmidt, 1999: 155), because they provide all the essential connections between the various entities or classes of entities. For recordkeeping, correctly defining relationships is essential because it is the means of pulling together data to form records and to define relationships between records. In the Chen data model, relationships are represented by a diamond shape containing the relationship's name and are connected to the entity rectangle with a line. The Crow's Foot model writes the relationship name above, below, or on the relationship line that connects to the entity rectangle.

Because relationships between entities can be simple or complex, there are numerous ways to express them. Establishing relationships between entities begins by defining the connectivity or relationship, which classifies the relationship into one of three categories: as "one-to-one" (1:1), one-to-many" (1:M), and "many-to-many" (M:N or M:M). As the name implies, a 1:1 relationship means that one entity can be related to only one other entity. An example is a university has only one president. In reality 1:1 relationships are rare. The most common type of relationship is 1:M. In this relationship an entity can be related to many entities. An example is a faculty member teaches many courses. Although not as common as one to many, many to many relationships are also not unusual. In this relationship many entities can be related to many other entities. An example is students who take many courses. In the Chen data model, the relationship type is represented by the symbols 1, M, or N next to the entity rectangle. In the Crow's Foot model the relationships are represented by one bar across the relationship line for the 1:1 relationship and by a three-pronged "Crow's Foot" for the M:M relationship.

Once the relationship is defined, it can be articulated in terms of a variety of other criteria. These include:

Cardinality: This concept expresses the specific number of allowed entity occurrences associated with a single occurrence of the related entity. This is usually defined by the business rules of the organization, and is expressed in the format (x,y) with the first number representing the minimum value and the second the maximum. For example in the Chen model, the Cardinality of (1,3) next to the faculty entity in the relationship defined as faculty teaches class means that faculty teaches at least one but no more than three classes.

Relationship Strength: This quality defines whether an entity is 1) existence dependent, in which case the entity's existence is entirely dependent upon the existence of one or more other entities; this is also known as a weak or non-identifying relationship; or is 2) existence independent, in which case the entity can exist apart or independent from other entities; this is also known as a strong or identifying relationship. In the Crow's Foot model the weak relationship is depicted by a dashed line between the related entities and the strong relationship by a solid line. The Chen model does not make a distinction between weak and strong relationships.

Relationship Participation: An entity participating in a relationship is classified as either mandatory or optional. This classification defines whether an entity does (mandatory) or does not (optional) require a corresponding entity occurrence in a particular relationship. An example of a mandatory relationship might exist for the entity's professor and class, whereby a professor is mandatory to a class (a professor must teach the course), but class is optional to professor (a professor is not required to teach a course). In both the Chen and Crow's Foot models, an optional relationship between entities is represented by drawing a small circle on the line closest to the optional entity. If the relationships are mandatory, no optionality symbol is depicted with the entities.

Relationship Degree: This quality defines the number of entities associated with the relationship. A unary or recursive relationship exists when an association is maintained within a single entity. A binary exists when two entities are associated; the vast majority of relationships are binary. A ternary relationship exists when three entities are associated (additional information on types of relationships can be found in Rob and Coronel [2002] and Schmidt [1999]).

The Entity-Relationship model in Figure 3.2 shows two different ways of expressing various types of entity relationships.

Identifying Attributes

The final important activity in data modeling is identifying attributes that describe the particular characteristics of the entity. "An attribute is any property, quality or characteristic ascribed to a person or thing" (Schmidt, 1999: 199). An entity without any attributes is unknowable and not useful, and attributes themselves are understood only in the context of the associated entity. An attribute operates as an adjective. Examples of the attributes for the entity student would be first name, last name, e-mail address, local phone, local address, gender, and age. Attributes are also defined in terms of the following characteristics:

Domain: A domain is a set of all possible values that an attribute may validly contain. Examples of domains for attributes assigned to the entity Archives Collections would include: Finding Aid (domain value defined as Yes or No), Location (domain values defined as Bryan Hall, Library, and Annex), Containers (domain values defined as record center boxes, document boxes, oversize boxes).

Elemental or simple: A simple attribute is a single characteristic that cannot be subdivided into additional attributes. For example, age, gender, and marital status are simple attributes.

Figure 3.2
Data Models Depicting Entitles and Relationships

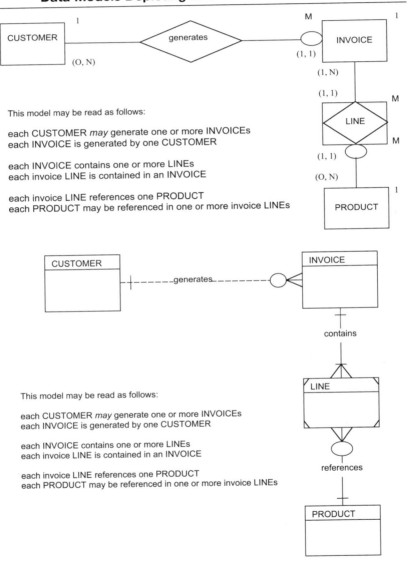

This model may be read as follows:

each CUSTOMER *may* generate one or more INVOICEs
each INVOICE is generated by one CUSTOMER

each INVOICE contains one or more LINEs
each invoice LINE is contained in an INVOICE

each invoice LINE references one PRODUCT
each PRODUCT may be referenced in one or more invoice LINEs

This model may be read as follows:

each CUSTOMER *may* generate one or more INVOICEs
each INVOICE is generated by one CUSTOMER

each INVOICE contains one or more LINEs
each invoice LINE is contained in an INVOICE

each invoice LINE references one PRODUCT
each PRODUCT may be referenced in one or more invoice LINEs

From *Database Systems: Design, Implementation, and Management*, 5th edition, by ROB/CORONEL (p. 148). 2002. Reprinted with permission of Delmar Learning, a division of Thomson Learning: www.thomsonrights.com. Fax 800 730–2215.

Composite: Composite attributes on the other hand can be subdivided into additional characteristics. Examples include an address, which can be subdivided into street, city, state, and zip code.

Derived: A derived attribute is a value created from some logical or arithmetic operation use data from within the system. An example is a derived attribute for total sales for the quarter which is calculated from the values for two simple attributes, sale amounts and sale taxes (Rob and Coronel, 2002; Schmidt, 1999).

In the Chen data model, attributes are displayed as ovals with the attribute name within and are connected to the entity rectangle with a line. This type of data model is shown in figure 3.3. In the Crow's Foot model attributes are written into an attribute box below the entity rectangle.

DATABASE STRUCTURES

The next issue that must be addressed is how transaction systems actually use the relational model to organize or structure data. The pro-

---

Figure 3.3
Data Models Depicting Attributes

Chen Model

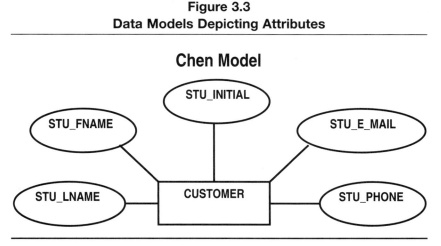

From *Database Systems: Design, Implementation, and Management*, 5th edition, by ROB/CORONEL (p. 120). 2002. Reprinted with permission of Delmar Learning, a division of Thomson Learning: www.thomsonrights.com. Fax 800 730–2215.

cess of defining database structures is called the creation of the Logi-cal Model. Over the decades, there have been a number of different structures for organizing data.

The first automated system was the file management system (Rob and Coronel, 2002; Williams, Sawyer and Hutchinson, 1999; Laudon and Laudon, 1999). This system consisted of software for creating, re-trieving, and manipulating files, one file at a time. It was an approach in which separate and logically unrelated data files were created and stored, much like in a filing structure for paper records. Each of the files in this system used its own application programs, and was owned and managed separately by the departments that created them. A rep-resentation of the file management structure is shown in figure 3.4.

There are a number of problems inherent in the file manage-ment system. The most critical are its data dependence, structural de-pendence, and program dependence. Data dependence is a condition

Figure 3.4
Representation of the File Management Structure

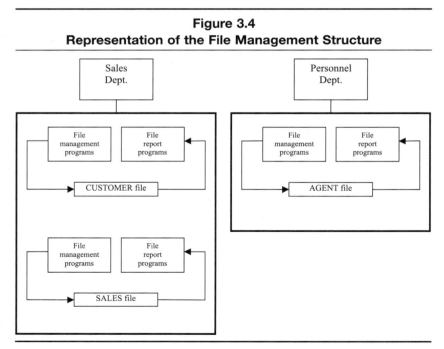

From *Database Systems: Design, Implementation, and Management*, 5th edi-tion, by ROB/CORONEL (p. 13). 2002. Reprinted with permission of Delmar Learning, a division of Thomson Learning: www.thomsonrights.com. Fax 800 730–2215.

in which changes to any of the file's data characteristics require that all programs that update and maintain these files be changed as well. The result is the potential for two types of serious problems. 1) Data redundancy: This is a condition in which the same data fields appear in many different files and often in different formats. An example of this condition is when many student data elements (name, address, phone number) appear in both the course grades file and a billing file. This condition leads to the other major problem. 2) Lack of data integrity: Data integrity means that data is accurate, consistent and up to date. The file system structure, which often duplicates data in different files, makes it more difficult to maintain the integrity of data. Every time an update is made, there is a distinct possibility that the duplicate data in other files may be missed and that mistakes will go undetected. The result is data inconsistency or the existence of data anomalies (modification anomalies, insertion anomalies, and deletion anomalies), a condition where different and conflicting versions of the same data appear in different places.

Structural dependence is a condition in which changes in the structure of the database, such as the addition or deletion of a field, require modifications of all programs accessing that file. These modifications in the database structure can lead to application programs that were operating correctly before the changes were made becoming inoperative. Program dependence means that different files are often written by different programmers using different formats. As a result more time is required to maintain files, and programmers are prevented from writing a single program to access all data in multiple files.

In the 1970s, a new type of system known as a database model was created. Unlike the file system, with its many separate and logically unrelated files, the database model consisted of logically related or integrated files stored in a single data repository. As a consequence many of the problems associated with file systems were addressed. These included:

1) Reduced data redundancy: In the database the vast majority of the data appears just once;
2) Improved data integrity: Reduced redundancy increases integrity because each updating change is made in only one place;
3) More program independence: Program and file formats are the same so less time is needed to maintain the database.

HIERARCHICAL DATABASES

There are four basic types of databases. The first to appear was the hierarchical database. In a hierarchical database, fields or records are arranged in related groups resembling a family tree, with lower level records subordinate to higher level records. These hierarchical relationships are referred to as parent and child, and they are linked to one another by a series of pointers that form chains of related data segments. An example of a hierarchical database model is shown in figure 3.5. The strengths of this model are its ability to depict one-to-many relationships and to quickly update and access fields because relationships have been predefined in the structure. The weakness is its structural dependence. All of the access paths, directories, and indices must be specified in advance. Once defined these paths are not easily changed without a major programming effort. Every time a new field is added to the database the entire structure must be redefined. Consequently the hierarchical database is a programming intensive system that is both difficult to install and, if design errors occur, difficult to redesign. On the whole, hierarchical databases are no longer major players in the database industry, except in industries like banks where many of the relationships remained fixed over time. (Descriptions of the hierarchical database structure can be found in Rob and Coronel [2002]; Williams, Sawyer and Hutchinson [1999]; Lauden and Lauden [1999].)

NETWORK DATABASES

An example of a network database model is shown in figure 3.6. The network structure is similar to the hierarchical structure, but in the network model, each child record can have more than one parent record, and many more relationships can be established between different branches. As a result, the network database can handle more relationship types than the hierarchical database, making the network database more flexible. The network database is employed today primarily on mainframe systems and for high-volume transaction processing applications. It is particularly useful for depicting many-to-many relationships. However, the network database still requires that the structure be defined in advance, and consequently it suffers from the same structural dependence problems as the hierarchical database. In addition, as the number of pointers in the network structures increase,

Figure 3.5
Hierarchical Database Structure

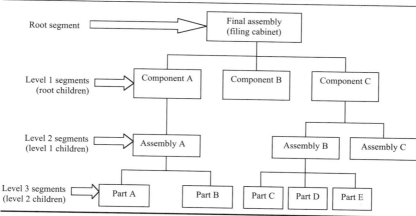

From *Database Systems: Design, Implementation, and Management*, 5th edition, by ROB/CORONEL (p. 26). 2002. Reprinted with permission of Delmar Learning, a division of Thomson Learning: www.thomsonrights.com. Fax 800 730–2215.

Figure 3.6
Network Database Model

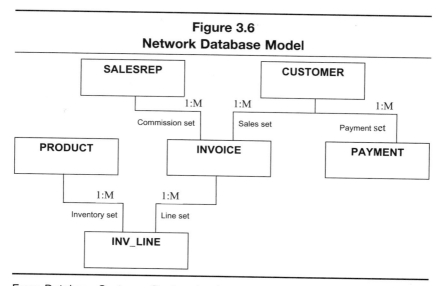

From *Database Systems: Design, Implementation, and Management*, 5th edition, by ROB/CORONEL (p. 30). 2002. Reprinted with permission of Delmar Learning, a division of Thomson Learning: www.thomsonrights.com. Fax 800 730–2215.

the database becomes more and more expensive to manage. (Descriptions of the network database structure can be found in Rob and Coronel [2002]; Williams, Sawyer and Hutchinson [1999]; Laudon and Laudon [1999].)

OBJECT-ORIENTED DATABASES

The most recent database type to emerge is the object-oriented database. One of the primary virtues of the object model is that it can handle new data types. While the other models were designed for structured data, i.e., data that can be neatly classified into fields, rows, and columns, the object model can deal with graphics, audio, and video, as well as text. For example, student information in a relational database would only contain text data such as name and address. In an object-oriented database the object might also contain a photo, some audio, or a video of an interview with the student. Another positive aspect of the object model is that information about objects and procedures for processing the object can be encapsulated or bound with the content data. This additional data could include metadata about the context of creation or other audit trail documentation, or it could include operations or programs that the object could use to process itself—for example on how to display or print a record or to interact with another object. The object model can also represent relationships between objects, in structures called object classes, and relationships between object classes by nesting or encapsulating one object class with another. The advantages of the object-oriented data model have made it an attractive option for some applications. However there are disadvantages to using this model. Chief among these are the lack of standards for the model, and the rather steep learning curve. In addition, potential implementers of the model have to consider the expense to develop and convert all the data presently in relational databases. Consequently, object-oriented databases have been slow to develop. The traditional relational database structure is still by far the most popular model and will likely maintain its dominance for many years. (Descriptions of the object-oriented model can be found in Taylor [1990]; Marshall [2000]; Montgomery [1994].)

RELATIONAL DATABASES

The fourth and by far the most popular database model is the relational database. The relational model was first developed by E.F. Codd in 1970, but it was not widely used until the following decade. The relational database consists of tables related to one another by means of shared and common entity characteristics. However, unlike the pointers in the hierarchical and network model, the table is a purely logical structure; how the data are physically stored in the database is of no consequence to the user or designer. Consequently the relational model, unlike the file, hierarchical, and network models, achieves both complete data and structural independence. Another critical feature of the relational model is the use of a database management system (DBMS) or a set of programs that manages the relational database. These DBMS have created a database that is much easier to use, design, and maintain.

The five primary types of database models are contrasted in figure 3.7, which shows the strengths and weaknesses of each.

BASIC DESIGN FEATURES OF THE RELATIONAL DATABASE

Once the conceptual data model is generated, it must be translated into a physical representation, the Logical Model, that can be implemented using a database management system (Rob and Coronel, 2002). This translation tool is the database schema, which defines the physical layout, the tables and views that will be implemented within the database. In essence, the schema is nothing more than the data model expressed in a language that the database engine can understand and implement.

Tables

The relational database is perceived by the user to be a collection of tables in which data are stored. Each table is a matrix consisting of a series of row/column intersections. Tables, also called relations, are related to each other by sharing a common entity or characteristic. The Entity in the Entity-Relation Model corresponds to a table. Another way of expressing this concept is that a table represents an entity or entity set. For example, in the process of scheduling classes, the entity's faculty, class, and room would be the titles of individual tables or entity sets. Rows within a table are called records, or tuples, and represent a single entity occurrence within the entity set. Each table column represents an attribute that has been assigned to the entity, and each column, sometimes called fields, has a distinct name. Each column and row intersection contains only a single data value. An example of a table in a relational database is showin in Figure 3.8.

Figure 3.8
Example of a Table in a Relational Database

Table name: STUDENT

STU_NUM	STU_LNAME	STU_FNAME	STU_INIT	STU_DOB	STU_HRS	STU_CLASS
321452	Bowser	William	C	Saturday, February 12, 1972	42	So
324257	Smithson	Anne	K	Tuesday, November 15, 1977	81	Jr
324258	Brewer	Juliette		Tuesday, August 23, 1966	36	So
324269	Oblonski	Walter	H	Sunday, September 16, 1973	66	Jr
324273	Smith	John	D	Friday, December 30, 1955	102	Jr
324274	Katinga	Raphael	P	Thursday, October 21, 1976	114	Sr
324291	Robertson	Gerald	T	Wednesday, April 08, 1970	120	Sr
324299	Smith	John	B	Wednesday, November 30, 1983	15	Fr

STUDENT table, cont.

STU_GPA	STU_TRANSFER	DEPT_CODE	STU_PHONE	PROF_NUM
2.84	No	BIOL	2134	205
3.27	Yes	CIS	2256	222
2.26	Yes	ACCT	2256	228
3.09	No	CIS	2114	222
2.11	Yes	ENGL	2231	199
3.15	No	ACCT	2267	228
3.87	No	EDU	2267	311
2.92	No	ACCT	2315	230

From *Database Systems: Design, Implementation, and Management*, 5th edition, by ROB/CORONEL (p. 60). 2002. Reprinted with permission of Delmar Learning, a division of Thomson Learning: www.thomsonrights.com. Fax 800 730–2215.

Keys

The concept of keys is fundamental to the relational model. A key is defined as an attribute that determines other attributes or defines some type of functional dependence between attributes and the entities they describe. There are four basic types of keys: superkeys, primary keys, foreign keys, and secondary keys.

A superkey is an attribute or combination of attributes that uniquely identifies each entity. An example for the entity students would be the unique student identification number. The primary key is the attribute that uniquely identifies any given entity or row; each table must have a primary key. An example of a primary key for a row of data on a business transaction might be the unique number identifying the transaction. A foreign key is an attribute whose values match the primary key values in the related table. This key is vital is establishing relationship between entities. An example of the use of the foreign key is a situation in which the unique identification for a student appears as the primary key in the student entity table, but also appears as an attribute (but not the primary key) in another related table entitled tuition fees. The identification number attribute in the tuition fees entity table is the foreign key, and it provides a link and creates a relationship between the two tables. From a relational database point of view, an ideal table is one in which each foreign key matches the related table's primary key name. A secondary key is defined as a key used primarily for data retrieval purposes. It provides other access points or additional descriptors of the entity. In a student table, the last name of the student would be a good example of a secondary key. The unique student number would be a poor choice for the secondary key, because it is an attribute that is hard to remember.

Normalization

Once the attributes are defined, designers initiate a process known as normalization (Rob and Coronel, 2002; Whitten and Bentley, 1998). Normalization is a process whereby data redundancies are minimized, and by extension, data anomalies that result from these redundancies are much reduced or eliminated. There are stages or forms of normalization, labeled 1NF, 2NF, 3NF, 4NF.

In Level 1NF the requirements are that all key attributes are defined, no repeating groups in the table exist, and all attributes are dependent on the primary key. Level 2NF adds the requirement that no attribute is dependent on only a portion of the primary key. Level 3NF specifies that no attribute is dependent upon another attribute that is not part of the primary key—a condition known as transitive dependency. For most business databases, 3NF is as far as the institution needs to go in the normalization process. In some, very specialized instances, systems may also be subjected to a denormalization process in which a larger amount of redundant data is purposely retained in the system. This process is used most often when there is a need to retain historical data in the operational systems or in specialized systems like data warehouses.

THE DATABASE MANAGEMENT SYSTEM (DBMS)

As mentioned at the beginning of the chapter, a database management system (DBMS) is a critical feature of the relational database model. A DBMS is a set of programs that is used to create, access, control, and manage the database. Rob and Coronel (2002) identify nine functions performed by the DBMS. Yevich and Lawson (2001) provide a detailed description of how one type of database management system functions.

The functions of a DBMS most important to recordkeeping include:

System Metadata and Data Dictionary Management

System metadata is stored in the System Catalog or Data Dictionary. These catalogs or directories provide detailed documentation about all tables and sometimes all objects within the database. The data dictionary typically will include some or all the following data categories:

1) data elements defined in all the tables—names, data types, display format, internal storage format, and validation rules;
2) tables defined in all databases—name, date of creation, access authorizations, and number of columns;
3) indexes defined for each database—names, attributes used, location, specific index characteristics, and creation date;
4) end users and administrators;
5) programs that access the database, including screen formats, report formats, application programs, and SQL queries;
6) access authorizations for all users;
7) relationships among data elements—which elements are involved, mandatory or optional, connectivity and cardinality requirements.

Figure 3.9

Example of a Data Dictionary

Table Name	Attribute Name	Contents	Type	Format	Range	Required	PK or FK	PK Referenced Table
Customer	CUS_CODE	Customer account code	CHAR (5)	99999	10000-99999	Y	PK	
	CUS_LNAME	Customer last name	VCHAR (20)	Xxxxxxxxx		Y		
	CUS_FNAME	Customer first name	VCHAR (20)	Xxxxxxxxx		Y		
	CUS_Initial	Customer middle initial	CHAR (1)	X				
	CUS_RENEW_DATE	Customer insurance renewal date	DATE	DD_MM_YYYY				
	AGENT_CODE	Insurance agent code	CHAR (3)	999	100-999		FK	AGENT
Agent	AGENT_CODE	Insurance agent code	CHAR (3)	999		Y	PK	
	AGENT_AREACODE	Agent's area code	CHAR (3)	999		Y		
	AGENT_PHONE	Agent's telephone number	CHAR (8)	999 – 9999		Y		
	AGENT_LNAME	Agent's last name	VARCHAR(20)					
	AGENT_YTD_SALES	Agent's year-to-date sales	NUMBER (9,2)	9,999,999.99	0.00-9,999,999.99	Y		

From *Database Systems: Design, Implementation, and Management*, 5th edition, by ROB/CORONEL (p. 77). 2002. Reprinted with permission of Delmar Learning, a division of Thomson Learning: www.thomsonrights.com. Fax 800 730–2215.

3) concurrent backups that take place while the user is working on the database

4) transaction log backups that copy the transaction log operations that have occurred since a previous backup of the database

Backups can also be assigned to occur at different time intervals. Another decision regarding backups is determining how many backup versions will be preserved and how many will be retained on-line. At some point, most system designers and administrators decide that the oldest backup will either be deleted or will be taken off-line and stored on some separate medium.

Data Integrity Management

The DBMS promotes and enforces integrity rules in a variety of ways. The data relationships stored in the data dictionary and lookup tables are used to enforce data integrity. SQL commands assist in maintaining integrity. For example, when the command UPDATE CASCADE is used, all foreign key references to a primary key are updated when the primary key is changed. The command DELETE CASCADE deletes the targeted data in all rows in every table that the data appears. Databases also store procedures to do multiple updates, and batch routines to update master table fields in a single operation. Other mechanisms for enforcing integrity are Triggers, which are a procedural SQL code that is automatically invoked and executed by the DBMS upon the occurrence of a data manipulation event. Triggers can be used to update table values and audit logs, enforce business rules, and create replica tables for backups.

In addition, the DBMS strictly controls and manages database transactions. A computer transaction is defined as "a logical unit of work that must be entirely completed or aborted" (Rob and Coronel, 2002: 460). For example, registering for a course requires updates to several tables to complete the business transaction. Updating only one of the tables would not be acceptable to the system. In managing the transaction the DBMS will not allow the transaction to end until the goal is reached of a consistent database state where all data integrity requirements are satisfied. To ensure this consistency every computer transaction must begin with the database in a known consistent state and must end in a consistent state with all SQL operations completed. As part of this transaction management process, the DBMS also maintains a transaction log, which was discussed above.

PRESERVING HISTORICAL DATA

As already noted, the primary design goals for operational databases are maintaining data integrity and processing speed. Most texts on database design devote very little if any time on describing techniques for preserving historical data. A good example is the Rob and Coronel text, which consists of over 800 pages but only devotes two pages to the discussion of preserving historical data. However, there are times when designers must sacrifice primary goals to fulfill certain critical information needs. Preserving historical data on transactions is one of those needs. For example, universities routinely preserve indefinitely a great deal of data and information on students, including most importantly grade information and courses taken. To accommodate the need to deliver a transcript on demand, the database of student data must ensure that certain data elements that comprise the transcript are preserved and remained unchanged over time.

Over the decades database designers have developed several techniques for preserving this historical data.

Redundant Data Approach

The strategy of planned redundancies involves intentionally duplicating a data value under a different attribute name in another table. For example, for financial transactions, the users and designers might agree that a history of the cost of the products they are selling must absolutely be retained for five years. To ensure that this occurs the database designer could use the following strategy. The entities defined for this process might be the customer, which would contain attributes on the buyer (name, phone number, etc.); the invoice, which would contain attributes on the bill (dates, number, etc.); and the product, which would contain attributes on the merchandise (name, price, code number, etc.). The price of the item in the product table would be the current price, and of course this would change frequently over time. So how does one maintain a record of what a particular customer paid at a point in time? One approach is to duplicate the value for the price that the customer paid for the item in another table entitled customer transaction under a different attribute name, for example historical price instead of simply price. By designing this data redundancy into the database, two major design features are achieved: the current price for the product is available in the database, and the historical record of the price of the product paid by an individual customer at some specific point in time is also preserved.

Archiving Historical Tables

This is a process of archiving or preserving data at a certain point in time. The classic example is the storage of data on a 13-month cycle where the oldest month is dropped or moved to an off-line environment as a new month is begun. This strategy can be implemented in various ways. Some applications require access to historical data within a time period (organizing element is date and then some unique ID). Other systems require access to records of a certain type within a date range (organizing element is unique ID and then by date). Most often these historical tables are transferred off-line and stored on tapes and other media.

Effective Dated Tables

Effective dates is a strategy for indicating when the data in a database row goes into effect or becomes part of the system and when activities can be performed on the data. The effective date is determined through the comparison of the system date to the effective date associated with the transaction being processed. Effective dating allows one to store historical data, see changes over time, and enter future data.

The PeopleSoft system categorizes effective-dated rows into three basic types:

Future: These are data rows that have effective dates greater than the system date. There can be more than one of these rows in an effective dated table. An example of future dating is establishing a new account on March 15, 2006 with an effective date of April 1, 2006. Because the account is future dated, no journals or transactions from that module can be posted to the newly created account unless the transaction has an effective date equal to or greater than April 1, 2006.

Current: These are data rows with the most recent effective date that is closest but not greater than the system date of the computer. An effective dated table can contain only one current row.

History: These are data rows that have effective dates less than the effective date of the current data row. For example, the current effective date for a row of data is March 10, 2006. Historical data would be any rows of data that are dated earlier than the 10th of March. Using an earlier effective date on that data is the equivalent of prohibiting any further updating or processing of this data, and at the same time allowing this information to be retained for historical purposes. There can be more than one row of historical data in an effective dated table.

In PeopleSoft, the types of actions that can be performed on rows of data are dependent on the effective date assigned to that row. When users attempt to retrieve, modify, or insert rows in an effective dated table, the update and correction actions apply specific rules based on the effective date. Figure 3.10 shows the template for effective dates in PeopleSoft. Figure 3.11 shows an example of effective dating.

In data rows assigned the history effective date, no updates or changes are allowed except for the Correction action, which is an action that is normally restricted to a select group of users.

In People Soft, effective dates are accompanied by Effective Date Status codes designated as either active or inactive. These codes enable the maintenance of historical changes within a table by recording the time period that the data is active along with the periods the data is inactive. The inactive status prevents use or changes of the data during the active period, while still allowing use of the data for historical reporting.

Figure 3.10
PeopleSoft Effective Dated Records

Type of Action	View Records	Change Records	Insert New Rows
Update/Display	Permissible in Rows Designated as Current or Future	Permissible Only in Rows Designated as Future	Permissible in Rows Where Effective Date is Greater Than or Equal to Current Row
Update/Display All	Permissible in Rows Designated as History, Current and Future	Permissible Only in Rows Designated as Future	Permissible in Rows Where Effective Date is Greater Than or Equal to Current Row
Correction	Permissible in Rows Designated as History, Current and Future	Permissible in All Existing Rows	No Effective Date Restrictions for This Type of Action

Source: Richard Gillespie and Joann Gillespie, *PeopleSoft Developer's Handbook* (New York: McGraw-Hill, 1999), 19.

Figure 3.11
Example of Effective Dating

Row No.	Department	Effective Date
1	Physics	Sep-01-2008
2	Physics	Nov-01-2008
3	Physics	Dec-01-2008

Row numbers that are...

Calendar Date	History	Current	Future
Sep-08-2008	—	1	2,3
Nov-04-2008	1	2	3
Jan-02-2009	1, 2	3	—

Source: University of Houston, Office of Finance, effective dating example. Available at: www.uh.edu/finance/Glossary/Eff_Dating_Link.doc

Challenges and Problems in Preserving Historical Data

While all these strategies for preserving historical data have been implemented and do work, there are challenges and problems associated with each of them.

1) Redesign problems: Preserving historical data should be addressed at the design stage. If planning does not take place at this stage, problems will occur. As one expert on DB2 has written: "A comprehensive design at the very beginning must address structuring the data, archiving the data, archiving associated or related data, archiving the data structures, tracking the archived data by period and storage medium, and restoring the data for a short period. If these issues are not addressed at the very beginning of the design, difficult and sometimes insurmountable problems will occur later" (Yevich and Lawson, 2001: 242).

2) Growth of historical data over time: Typically, at the design state, the volume of historical data that will be accumulated over time is not properly assessed. At some point the sheer volume of historical data will mandate that some changes occur in design of the database, and as indicated above, redesign can be difficult and expensive.

3) Access to data: It is often forgotten by system designers that the need for efficient access does not go away just because data is archived or taken off-line. Once data and information is moved to a near-line or off-line system, management and access strategies must be created to ensure that this information remains useful to those who have need of it.

4) Complexity of relationships: Modeling all the relationships to ensure the integrity of current but also of historical data is a difficult and challenging process. It is especially difficult to ensure that the relationships between and among historical data are maintained over time. For example, experts on DB2 design have written that effective dates are "at best very difficult to define properly for all access . . . there are two dominant access needs: the need to change the data while retaining the old data and the ability to reconstruct what the data looked like at any point in time. The issue becomes more complex where a parent table is bounded by effective dates and changes must be made to a child table that is also bounded by effective dates" (Yevich and Lawson, 2001: 240–241). An institution implementing the effective dates strategy also uncovered problems in maintaining relationships between effective dated data rows in different tables. "For example, two tables 'A' and 'B' have related data. To get the correct data from table 'B' that relates to the row you are processing from table 'A' you must find the row in table 'B' that has an effective date less than or equal to the effective date of the row you are processing in table 'A'. This results in a complicated conditional join that effects SQL access" (Cornell University, 2001, "PeopleSoft Effective Dating").

Most of these potential problems with preserving historical data in relational databases link back to the same issues—preserving historical data in a relational database must be very carefully planned, and if at all possible, the strategies must be incorporated into the database at the initial design stage. Even when this planning does occur, it is still very difficult to model and maintain all the relationships between historical data over the life cycle.

SUMMARY OF THE PRIMARY CHARACTERISTICS OF THE RELATIONAL DATABASE MODEL

Database Design Features
Database designers must reconcile three often contradictory require-ments: design elegance and performance, processing speed, and information requirements.
Most of the design emphasis is on achieving processing speed and data integrity.
Data storage is optimized to support the creation and updating of a high volume of transactions.
The guiding principles are to create data that is current, accurate, and consistent; minimize the amount of data stored in the system; improve overall efficiency of the system; remove obsolete data, and provide an organizational resource to current data.

Database Models
Business processes are represented by individual data items docu-menting the things involved in the process (entities and attributes) and relationships between and among them.
Relationships are classified into one of three categories: as "one-to-one" (1:1), one-to-many" (1:M), and "many-to-many" (M:N or M:M).
Relationships can be also be defined in a variety of other ways, in-cluding Cardinality (number of occurrences), Strength (dependent or independent), Participation (mandatory or optional), and Degree (unary, binary, ternary).

Database Structure
A relational database is perceived by the user to be a collection of tables in which data are stored.
Tables represent an entity or an entity set; in essence, a relational database stores a collection of related entities or tables.
Tables are logical and not physical constructs.
The concept of Keys is fundamental to the relational model. Keys are attributes that determine other attributes or define some type of dependence or relationship between attributes and the entities they describe.
Each table must contain a Primary Key that uniquely identifies an entity.
Although tables are independent, they can be linked by shared or common attributes called a Foreign Key.
Normalization is a process whereby data redundancies are minimized.

Database Management System (DBMS)
A DBMS is software that manages the structure of a database and access to the data.
DBMS performs a variety of critical functions, including the creation and storage of metadata on the system and on transactions, security management, transaction management, data integrity management, and access management.

Historical Data in Relational Databases
Historical data is preserved in databases by means of a variety of techniques, including preserving redundant data, archiving historical tables, and effective dating.
All strategies for preserving historical data present certain challenges, including the problems of redesigning systems to accommodate the growth of historical data, dealing with the complex relationships between data and tables, and access to historical data that is in an off-line system.

TRANSACTION PROCESSING SYSTEMS AS RECORDKEEPING SYSTEMS

Are transaction processing systems good recordkeeping systems? A favorite answer of many designers regarding most performance questions is "It depends. Most of the interesting questions do not have a simple answer. . . . While 'it depends' is completely correct, it is also completely useless unless we go on to explain more about the dependencies and issues" (Yevich and Lawson, 2001: xxv). To determine the answer to this question, let us review how well TPS and relational databases meet the functional requirements for a recordkeeping system that were identified in chapter 2.

IMPORTANT QUESTIONS TO CONSIDER

1. Are records present in the TPS relational database?

Yes, business records are present in the database. The database was created or modeled on reality or on the business environment. Database transactions reflect real-world transactions like registering for a course or buying a product.

This being said it must be reemphasized that records are not represented in the relational database as objects but rather as separate pieces of data found in the attributes of entities which are related one to another through a variety of techniques. Another way of saying this is that the database is not built around records of business processes. It is constructed using a different model, the E-R model that views the world in terms of subjects or entities and their characteristics and not directly in terms of business processes and records. Consequently, the records or the products of events are not identified by tables or even rows within tables, but rather by means of the union of data, usually from different tables, representing subjects or things involved in the business transaction. The attributes only become records when the various data elements are pulled together and united by the software to create the record. This process becomes more complicated when the data comprising the records of the business processes has to be assembled from various tables in the database.

Clearly, records exist in the database. The harder questions relate to whether the records are authentic, i.e., are they reliable (are they complete), and do they have integrity (are mission-critical records changed or unintentionally deleted over time)?

2. Are records protected from unauthorized and undocumented alteration or deletion within the TPS?

Within the TPS, database methodology employs a variety of methods for ensuring that records are accurate and protected, primarily through the ability of the DBMS to manage data integrity, security, and transactions. In addition, the transaction logs and audit controls track changes and assist in reconstructing data and records. Finally, as was seen in the discussion on preserving historical data, database designers have developed various strategies for managing and preserving historical data over time.

Nonetheless, there are a number of challenges with preserving records in a database structure. Some of these problems are inherent in the relational database model and methodology and some relate to the potential inadequacy of strategies for managing the records over the life cycle.

1) Modeling historical data—Maintaining some relationship between related data stored in a variety of tables is a challenge. This problem is magnified when these relationships must be maintained over long periods of time.

2) Database rules for maintaining the integrity of data can actually

work against the preservation of records—The primary objectives of operational databases are to create data that is current, accurate, and consistent and to improve the overall efficiency and speed of the system. To achieve these objectives there are rules and procedures like normalization to minimize data redundancies and anomalies. In addition, SQL commands and operations can initiate massive changes in tables throughout the database. While all these procedures and commands promote data integrity, they can work against the preservation of historical records, particularly if the planning for historical data is not perfectly modeled and all proper relationships defined.

3) Lack of archival input on identifying records with historical or long-term value—Archivists, records managers, auditors, and legal counsel are seldom involved in the database design process. Consequently there is the potential to improperly identify records with long-term legal or historical value, or to not include enough detailed metadata describing a business process.

4) Lack of a preservation strategy—Most databases systems do not have a set of procedures for preserving data and records over time. There are back-up systems, but rarely are there procedures for converting or migrating this data to new system hardware, software, and storage media. We will look at this problem in more detail under question number five.

3. Does the TPS systematically preserve reliable or fully documented records?

Again, the relational database employs various methodologies and strategies for documenting processes. Primary among these are the data dictionary, transaction logs, and audit trails. In addition, the E-R model provides a systematic methodology for identifying attributes and a variety of ways to model and describe the relationships between entities.

However, as with record integrity, the reliability of records in a database is potentially threatened by problems that are inherent in the relational database model or in the strategies for managing the records over time.

1) Completeness of metadata—The data dictionary and the transaction logs within an information system are very useful, but my experience reviewing these systems would suggest that these sources do not provide all the recordkeeping metadata that archivists/records

managers would recommend. System designers think first and foremost about types of metadata required to document the structure of the system, describe data models and content, and manage the integrity of the transactions. What is often missing is sufficient metadata on the context of creation and transmission over time. Another way of expressing this problem is that systems typically do not include sufficient audit trail documentation for all processes that create, update, delete, transfer, import and export, access, and use data and records over the life cycle. Information systems also typically lack enough metadata on the business functions and processes that the data and records describe.

2) Modeling complex data types and relationships—One of the disadvantages of using E-R modeling is that it can be difficult to model complex data types and complicated business processes. Ralph Kimball, the noted authority on data warehouses, writes that in his opinion entity-relationship modeling is incomplete in that the "entities and relationships on any given diagram represent only what the designer decided to emphasize, or was aware of. There is no test of an E/R model to determine if the designer has specified all possible one-to-one, many-to-one, or many-to-many relationships." Kimball also suggests that E-R models are "ideal, not real" portrayals of the enterprise, and that these "models are rarely models of real data." Kimball concludes by stating that "while E/R modeling is a useful technique for beginning the process of understanding and enforcing business rules, it falls far short of providing any kind of completeness or guarantee" (Kimball, 2000; also Kimball, 1995 and Kimball, 1997).

In large part these criticisms of E-R modeling can be traced to the lack of semantic content in the models. Semantics or the definition of meaning or relationships can be very effective in portraying dynamic data behavior and in providing a more natural and realistic representation of real world objects. Data representation as undertaken in the E-R model constitutes a rather static view of the environment that is being modeled. Thus for example, E-R models cannot easily define relationships between attributes in entities, represent entities that have multiple relationships with other entities, or model certain data constraints. In terms of recordkeeping, one cannot help but be concerned about the ability of E-R modeling to represent all the relationships between data in a very complex business process, that might involve ten or more activities and produce many records before the process is completed.

The need to better represent more complex data types and relationships was instrumental in the development of object-oriented databases. This model adds semantic content to the attributes that are defined. The result is a much richer and more accurate representation of real world processes. For this reason, a new type of relational database has emerged—the extended relational data model (ERDM)—that integrates many of the best features of the object oriented model into the relational database model. The latest versions of Oracle 8 and DB2, for example, contain object oriented components within a relational database structure.

3) Tendency to not spend enough time on modeling business processes—Modeling business processes is the first step in E-R modeling. However, it has been my experience that system designers do not spend enough time on understanding the business processes. Often the analysis will end at the function or sub-function level, and business transactions and activities are not fully explored or modeled. Since the meaning and context of records can only be understood at the business transaction and activity level, there exists a real potential for databases to lack the metadata defining the context of creation and the relationships between records.

4) Linkages between metadata and the data and records—One of the requirements of a recordkeeping system is that the metadata be logically linked to the records they document, so that users can review the metadata when they retrieve records. These logical links do not always exist. I have discovered metadata in separate tables not logically linked to the data they described; in some cases, this metadata was a paper document existing totally outside the automated system. Another concern is ensuring that the back-up schedule maintains the linkages necessary to recreate the business records. In other words, are the tables containing the metadata backed up on the same schedule as the records they describe?

4. Does the TPS support a classification scheme for defining relationships between and among records?

As demonstrated earlier in the basic review of the database model, a complex network of descriptors and other devices are used to define relationships between and among entity sets. As a result, the ability clearly exists to reconstruct the relationship between database tables and data elements.

PeopleSoft, for example, does provide a means of associating data panels with particular activities within a business process (Gillespie and

Gillespie, 1999). These processes are available within the Application Designer of the PeopleTools. However, some databases do not offer these kinds of tools, and consequently it can be more difficult to link records to business processes. For many archivists and records managers the lack of a direct relationship between data and business processes is a real deficiency, since strategies for managing electronic records are often based largely on initially linking records to the processes that created them. Once the record is associated with the business process, the archivist can use that information to: 1) provide a means of determining that all the right records are captured; 2) create linkages between records related to specific functions and activities; 3) provide metadata on the context of creation; 4) determine appropriate retention periods for classes of records; 5) assist in establishing user permissions for access to classes of records; and 6) define responsibility for managing classes of records over time.

5. Does the TPS provide for the long-term preservation of records?

In most institutions the typical strategy for protecting data is to generate backups of system data. While the back-up strategy is a necessary and useful activity, it must be regarded more as a disaster preparedness plan than as a preservation strategy. Unlike a true preservation strategy, the back-up solution does not deal with the root causes of the deterioration and obsolescence of digital records: hardware obsolescence, storage medium deterioration, and the biggest problem of all, software dependence.

To preserve records over time, the system must ensure that records, components of records, audit trails, metadata, links to metadata or to files, and classification schemes can be converted or migrated to new system hardware, software, and storage media without loss of vital information. Unfortunately, TPS and most other information systems do not include strategies and procedures for systematically migrating or converting records over time. Backups in many cases are created, moved off-line, and essentially forgotten until needed, at which point the data may already be corrupted or may be un-useable because it is in a format or application that is no longer available.

From a recordkeeping perspective, it is also critical that the system document the back-up and preservation processes. This documentation would include metadata on who had responsibility for performing the process, when it was done, what was done, the impact of the preservation process, and the definition of how the data was stored. My experience is that some of this critical metadata is not available in the typical TPS.

6. Does the TPS provide for the systematic retention and disposition of records?

As we saw in the section on historical data, various methods are used to preserve data in the relational database, but some of these strategies are difficult to implement or have other problems associated with them. If we look specifically at strategies for systematically destroying data and records in databases, experience would indicate that a common practice among database managers and, for that matter, the managers of most information systems, is to avoid making appraisal decisions about the destruction of data. The primary disposition strategy in many systems consists of copying most of the data, and moving this data to near-line and eventually off-line storage status.

From an archivist's perspective another issue and potential problem related to the retention and disposal of data and records in a database is the lack of adequate documentation on the disposal process. Archivists and records managers would like to include in the metadata associated with the records the definition of the disposal authorization or the warrant, the disposal date, and the identification when the record was destroyed and by whom. This level of documentation is not available in most databases.

7. Does the TPS provide for the long-term security of records?

Most transaction process systems have very robust security functionality. Nonetheless, the archivist and records manager cannot take for granted that security requirements for records are being met. Particular attention must be paid to smaller systems further down in the business hierarchy. My experience auditing various systems at universities would indicate that the biggest security deficiencies are in systems at the school, department, and individual administrative unit level and not within the larger, central systems. The most serious problems relating to the security of records exist for the data and records that have been transferred to near-line or off-line storage. This data sometimes simply "falls off the map," in the sense that the resources devoted to the management of this data are not sufficient to do the job.

In defining other potential security problems, it is useful to review some relevant items within the functional requirements statement and the metadata specifications. Questions to consider include:

- Does the system control access to the records according to well-defined criteria?
- Are records linked to citations and references to laws, policies, and best practices that impose a requirement to control access to and use of a record?
- Are records linked to statements defining the terms under which the record may be accessed and used?
- Does the system allow only authorized personnel to create, capture, update, or purge records, metadata associated with records, files of records, classes in classification schemes, and retention schedules?
- Is the audit trail data unalterable?
- Does the system ensure that any function to delete records on an ad hoc basis (outside of the disposal process) is restricted to only the highest level of administrator?
- Does the system identify who accessed and used the record, and when this action occurred?

8. Does the TPS provide for the long-term access to records?

Short-term access, or access for active, on-line records, is well managed in most transaction processing systems. However, as with security, the management of access deteriorates rapidly once data is moved to near-line or off-line storage. Records in the off-line environment should be available for easy access and retrieval in a timely manner in the normal course of all business processes or for reference or secondary uses. My experience with users seeking to retrieve off-line data is that this type of retrieval is not always possible. I have been told by several users that their requests for off-line data were met with the response that the data existed but that it would take two or three weeks to retrieve it.

Other questions to consider regarding access include:

- Can all components of a record, including contents, relevant metadata, notes, attachments, etc., be accessed, retrieved, and rendered as a discrete unit or group and in a single retrieval process?
- Can the system search all metadata elements?
- Can the system search at different levels, i.e., within electronic files, across files, and at any level within the classification scheme hierarchy?

Are transaction processing systems good recordkeeping systems?
TPS can meet recordkeeping requirements. They do create business records and can recreate these records as needed. They do employ a variety of strategies for protecting data over time from unauthorized alteration and deletion. The relational database does use various tools such as the data dictionary and transaction logs to document processes and records. They do employ strategies such as systematic backups to ensure the recovery of data and records. They use a variety of strategies for preserving data and records with long-term value. Finally, they provide an accessible and secure environment for on-line, primarily active or current data.

This being said, it is my opinion that, overall, TPS and the relational database environment have more flaws than virtues as a recordkeeping system. The biggest flaws relate to the overall objectives of the database and to the design process. As has been stated repeatedly, operational database systems are primarily concerned with providing an organizational resource to current data that will support on-going business needs; they are not designed primarily for long-term recordkeeping. Moreover, databases create records based on a strategy of assembling individual data elements into record objects again and again as needed. This requires that all the data that comprise the record must be carefully managed and preserved over time. If this is not done that particular record as originally created can never be reassembled.

It is much easier to imagine designing a recordkeeping strategy in which the record object, including all metadata, is assembled and captured just once, and all the management strategies are then focused on managing that object. This capture-once strategy offers the distinct advantage of not having to manage the separate data elements and all the relationships between and among data over long periods of time. The strategy of reassembling records repeatedly, particularly for records with long-term retention, demands precise planning at the design stage and, in my opinion, is a strategy that may be asking too much from a system designer.

Other critical problems with relational databases as recordkeeping systems include:

- Data models that have trouble modeling complex relationships
- Strategies for preserving historical data that are difficult to implement and manage

- A design process that routinely omits the input of archivists and records managers
- The distinct absence of a preservation strategy for routinely migrating data
- The absence of critical metadata on processes for managing the data over time
- A tendency for system designers to not spend enough time on modeling business processes
- A tendency to devote most of the management resources on the on-line, active record and to neglect the management of off-line, historical records.

To sum up, TPS constructed on the relational database model have some major flaws as recordkeeping systems. These deficiencies can summarized as problems associated with 1) preserving data and metadata and the relationships between and among data over the life cycle so that authentic and reliable records can be recreated as needed; and 2) creating a management regime for accessing, protecting, preserving, and disposing of historical data over time.

MAKING TRANSACTION PROCESSING SYSTEMS BETTER RECORDKEEPING SYSTEMS

There are four basic strategies for transforming TPS into better, more effective recordkeeping systems:

OPTION 1: ADD FUNCTIONALITY TO EXISTING OR NEW TPS

It is far easier to incorporate recordkeeping requirements into a database at the design stage than it is to modify an existing, legacy system. In an existing system, some of the modifications listed below may be far too complicated or expensive to actually implement.

The goals in this first option are to review the functional requirements and metadata specifications and incorporate as many of these requirements as possible into the database structure. There likely will be limitations on how many requirements can be applied, and consequently prioritization will be required. The value of the requirement will be measured against the need, costs to implement, and available resources. One of the primary responsibilities of the archivist and records manager is to determine where he/she can compromise and which of the requirements is so essential that compromise will in essence undermine the very concept of a recordkeeping system.

Listed below are the requirements that I believe are most critical or will make the biggest difference in transforming the database into a more effective recordkeeping system.

Add archivists/records managers to the system design and data management teams. Since most design teams do not include archivists and records managers, the records management and life cycle management perspective is under-represented in the planning process. Adding archivists and records managers to the system design and data management teams would be beneficial for several reasons. The major contributions would include: a) providing more information in the appraisal discussions on the long-term, secondary value of records; b) emphasizing business process modeling and the need to create models down to the transaction and activity level; and c) stressing the need to design systems that will manage data and records over the entire life cycle.

Incorporate into the database more metadata that describes the data in relation to business processes. In my opinion, associating system data and metadata with business transactions is the one modification that will have the most significant impact in transforming an information system into a recordkeeping system. Many other decisions and activities are ultimately dependent on knowing this relationship. Understanding the relationship between the record and the processes that created it provides a strategy for: a) determining that we are capturing all the right records; b) providing metadata on the context of creation; and c) building a classification structure that will effectively manage these records over time. In other words, once the products (records) are linked to the events (business events) that produced them, we can build our strategies for the capture, retention and disposal, preservation, access, and use of records.

Add more metadata of other types. Earlier, we noted that the database contains a great deal of system metadata. What is often lacking is detailed metadata on the context of creation and transmission over time, and metadata on how the system is managing activities such as retention and disposal and preservation. More specifically metadata that typically needs to be added or enhanced in most information systems include: a) Audit trail metadata for all processes that create, update or modify, delete, transfer, import and export, access and use data and records over the life cycle; and b) Management metadata on retention and disposal, access and use, and preservation. This category of management metadata would include documentation identifying citations and references to laws, policies, and best practices that impose a requirement; terms under which the record may be accessed and used; who (person, system, organization) is responsible for performing or authorizing the activities; what specific preservation activity was initiated (e.g., backed-up, imaged, medium refreshed, microfilmed, migrated); the effect of preservation activities on the form, content, accessibility, and use of the record; and activity types and dates for the next scheduled preservation activity.

Create an automated system for applying retention and disposition decisions. The objectives in regard to this goal are to systematically apply some type of authorized and approved retention schedules to records in the database, to assign retention periods to data producing records, and then to have the system implement the retention decision. The challenge for the archivist and records manager is to develop a strategy for equating and linking disposal decisions to the data stored in the various tables in the database.

One strategy is to use business process models to identify where records are created and retention schedules to indicate how long the record series must be retained, and then to use this information to evaluate which data elements that constitute these records must be preserved and for how long. This is the most thorough and accurate way to preserve records in databases, because it will likely uncover all the records created by the environment being modeled. However, it is certainly the most time consuming (modeling is a laborious process) and difficult process, in that one is trying to use tools and methodologies based on evaluation of records as objects within a database system that is organized around data. This strategy will be most effective in the initial design of database systems, and it will be least effective in creating better appraisal systems for existing, legacy systems.

A second strategy is to use process models and retention schedules to appraise and evaluate the outputs of the system. This methodology is easier to apply because objects and not data elements are the focus of the analysis, and it will be less time consuming because it does not involve the precise modeling of all business processes. However, this strategy has several weaknesses as an appraisal methodology. Reviewing and appraising only outputs will likely not reveal all the relationships between and among data, nor will it identify all the critical metadata. Moreover, there exists the distinct possibility that an analysis focused on outputs will fail to reveal all records created by processes. In addition, after one completes this analysis of outputs, there is still the challenge of integrating the appraisal decisions about outputs into the database structure, i.e., you must convert the decisions about outputs into the database structure built around data elements in tables. This strategy likely will be used most effectively and realistically in creating better appraisal systems in existing, legacy systems, but it will not be the strategy of choice in designing new systems.

A third strategy is to use the tools developed by designers, such as data and metadata models, to review how decisions were made and which data elements are being preserved to produce records. This strategy provides the most direct route to gaining information about appraisal decisions. However, these data-oriented tools are not familiar to archivists and records managers and will be more difficult to interpret. Ultimately, archivists and records managers must become more familiar with and use the tools created by system designers. However, I think these tools will always be used in conjunction with more traditional tools, such as retention schedules for records series and models of business processes.

Create a preservation strategy. As discussed above, many database systems do not include a true preservation strategy for data and records. Archivists and records managers must make the creation of a strategy for preservation and not just data recovery a major priority in system design and modification. Addressing this problem demands administrative planning as well as technology solutions. Undoubtedly, there will be quite a number of technological decisions to be made about how to implement specific preservation strategies. However, these decisions must be accompanied by the creation of a management regime for implementing the technological solutions. Definition of the management strategy would include identifying people who will be responsible for implementation, defining the financial resources to meet commitments, establishing a schedule for the conversion or migration of resources, and carefully documenting all activities.

Develop better management systems for off-line records. One of the biggest contributions an archivist and records manager can make is to enhance and strengthen the management of off-line systems comprised of inactive and historical data and records. As indicated earlier, IT personnel typically do not devote the necessary resources to manage off-line records properly. The archivist and records manager can help rectify this situation by drawing attention to the problem, providing arguments for devoting more resources to the management of these records, and by identifying strategies for providing better access to and enhancing the security of the data.

If all these activities are implemented, the transaction processing system will surely be a better recordkeeping system. This being said, ultimately it will be difficult to transform TPS into viable recordkeeping systems. There are two fundamental problems archivists face in implementing this transformation—undertaking the analysis and implementing the results.

Let us first look at the analysis issue. The archivist's and records manager's methodology is based on reviewing and managing records as objects. For example, archivists and records managers appraise records and record series, i.e., objects and groups or classes of objects. The product of this appraisal is a retention and disposal schedule that identifies the record series and links the series to a time period that it must be retained. However, in the database environment data and not objects are the focus. Consequently, when the archivist and records manager attempts to review relational databases, they are at a distinct disadvantage because their methodologies and tools are not directly compatible with the models and structures created by database designers. This compatibility issue directly impacts their ability to not only appraise records but also to identify records and metadata in the database, establish relationships between records, and review how the system is managing records over the life cycle. In short, archivists' and records managers' methodologies for managing records do not transfer very well to a database environment where data is king. Obviously, this difficulty in analyzing databases will impact implementation.

Another challenge in implementing changes in databases relates directly to the differences in the overall design and functionality of relational databases and recordkeeping systems. Quite simply, the primary objectives of the relational database and the modeling process and structures designed to realize these goals are not good matches for a recordkeeping system.

Because of these fundamental differences between records management and database methodologies and tools, and between the primary objectives and design of database and recordkeeping systems, I think a better strategy for managing records produced in a database is to extract and transfer data and tables from the database system and into a new environment that has its own recordkeeping requirements and is managed by a different set of information professionals with their own unique skills, i.e., records managers and archivists. The other three options for transforming transaction processing systems into better recordkeeping systems all use this strategy.

OPTION 2: USE BACK-UP FILES AS THE HISTORICAL REPOSITORY

The advantages to this option include:

- This is an option that fits well into the database management strategy and will likely be supported by IT personnel. In fact, this is the strategy most often endorsed by IT personnel I have consulted.
- This strategy will likely capture most of the important data. Decisions on what data to back up and how frequently backups are made is based in large part on how vital the data is to the institution.
- One does not need to worry about maintaining historical data in an ever changing, active operational system.
- By getting the data out of the operational environment, one has a better chance of establishing a new and different set of requirements geared more towards recordkeeping and preserving and managing inactive, historical data and records.
- Appraisal decisions are less difficult and made at an aggregate level. Decisions on what to back up are typically made at the table level or even for sets of tables; consequently appraisal of data and all the difficulties of conducting this analysis in a database are less of an issue.
- Storage is cheap so the high volume of data produced by this option is not a major cost factor.

The disadvantages of employing this strategy:

- Some updated records will not be captured in the backups. Not all tables are copied on the same schedule; the frequency will depend on an assessment of the value of the data and of the resources available for this activity. Without question, backups completed once or even two or three times a week will be missing records that were updated and changed more than once during that time.

- In this option, one would still face the challenge of preserving records over the life cycle that are contained within a database model and structure that is based on the management of data elements and not records as objects. Although the data comprising records is no longer part of the operational system, the records are still represented as discrete data elements, and this makes the archivist's job more difficult.
- Accessing and manipulating data in this massive database could be a major problem. Though access software is improving and will continue to improve, it will still be a challenge to retrieve records in the vast repository that will be created by this strategy. In essence this option shifts responsibilities and resources from conducting appraisals to developing access strategies and tools. In particular this option will require that considerable resources be devoted to the creation of metadata to retrieve records within this vast repository.
- Significant resources must be allocated to properly manage this massive resource over time. This option requires the conversion of the back-up system originally designed to simply reconstruct the operational database into a system now designed to manage a key intellectual resource. As the primary resource for inactive and historical data, many of the gaps and shortcomings in the management of backups must be rectified. More specifically more resources must be allocated to creating better access systems, designing and implementing preservation strategies, and managing the security of the back-up system.

OPTION 3: ARCHIVING SELECTED TABLES TO A HISTORICAL REPOSITORY COMPRISED OF DATA WITH LONG-TERM VALUE

Advantages of employing this option:

- Like backups, this is a strategy that is already deployed by institutions. Data warehouses, consisting of select data tables that have been transferred out of the operational system, have been in existence for decades. Because IT personnel are already familiar with the concept and have established management strategies for a similar type of system, there is the potential for IT to understand and support the concept of a recordkeeping system based on this strategy.

- Because data warehouses already exist there is the potential to gain support for devoting some of the storage space and functionality in the data warehouse environment to recordkeeping. There are similarities in mission and objectives between the two environments, and this could result in a partnership between the recordkeeping and data warehouse communities.
- In this option one does not need to worry about maintaining historical data in an ever changing, active operational system.
- This option is based on a selection of data and tables. Consequently, it will result in a repository that is smaller than the repository based on backups; as a result it will be less costly to manage, and it will be easier to develop strategies for access and retrieval.

The primary disadvantages of employing this option:

- As with the back-up option, one must deal with the complex world of data in related tables to reconstruct records.
- Using this option one still must overcome most of the challenges of converting a relational database into a better recordkeeping system. This option addresses the problem of managing records in a volatile, operational environment; however, all the other problems associated with converting databases into recordkeeping systems still exist in the historical repository.
- It is a new system (even if it is analogous to the data warehouse environment) that will need additional resources devoted to its management.
- Unlike the back-up option, there is the additional challenge of selecting the right data and tables to reconstruct the historical records one is seeking to preserve. In this option, much more attention and planning will be required to ensure that the right tables and data are transferred to the historical repository.

OPTION 4: DEVELOP AN AUTOMATED MECHANISM FOR CAPTURING RECORDS (CONTENT PLUS METADATA) AS OBJECTS

This option attempts to capture records as objects rather than as discrete data elements. There are a number of different ways to achieve this. One way is to preserve forms or outputs of the database. This strategy has the advantage of being easier to implement and less time consuming than some other alternatives. However, it is very likely that the analysis and capture of outputs will not result in a complete set of records, nor will this analysis likely identify all the critical metadata or reveal all the relationships between and among records. In my opinion, the analysis of outputs can only be effective for small database systems.

For larger systems, other strategies are required. In most instances, the strategy that makes the most sense to me is to capture record content plus metadata as they are assembled in the context of an automated business process workflow system. Once captured, these records as objects containing both content and metadata would be transferred to a recordkeeping system, where the objects would be managed according to the requirements established for recordkeeping.

At one point, Indiana University began to model this type of strategy as part of a NHPRC funded electronic records management project. The planning never got beyond the point of high level conceptual models and certainly never to the point of implementation. Nonetheless reviewing the conceptual design of the IU strategy can provide some sense of how this strategy might work. Figure 3.12 shows the conceptual design of the portal, applications, and infrastructure. (For a description of the strategy, see Flynn [2001].)

The IU recordkeeping strategy for capturing operational data as record objects began as part of the larger IT project to implement the PeopleSoft enterprise-wide operational database system and to reengineer other legacy applications to Web-enable them. As part of this strategic plan, IU's technology department also began to review strategies for creating an enterprise-wide portal environment made up of components, such as a workflow engine and a global inbox for administrative messages, that could be shared among applications, The workflow engine was instrumental in the recordkeeping strategy we were developing. Workflow has been defined as "the automation of a business process, in whole or part, during which documents, information or tasks are passed from one participant [human or machine] to another for action, according to a set of procedural rules" (Flynn, 2001: 4). The primary goals of the IU workflow engine were to route electronic transactions to individuals or systems for completion, approval, or notification, and to provide an audit trail of all routing and actions taken on electronic transactions.

In addition to the workflow application, plans were made to create a variety of other modules, including one for recordkeeping.

Recordkeeping was viewed as both a separate application that would eventually be integrated into the system like other enterprise applications and as a set of requirements that the portal, workflow engine, and other components needed to incorporate. As part of the development of the concept, a member of the IU archives project team worked with IT staff on developing the requirements for documentation creation and workflow. Figure 3.13 shows the EDEN workflow engine and how it relates to electronic recordkeeping.

The best way to explain how the workflow engine would work and would interact with the recordkeeping module is to use an example. Let us say that IU's Financial Management Services (FMS) is processing a request for travel reimbursement. The process begins when someone submits an electronic travel reimbursement form to the travel management department. Document creation applications send an XML version of the electronic document to the workflow engine. The workflow engine then submits the XML document to the routing modules. The route modules return a list of action requests, scan the XML for specific route controls, and match the document information to the action request rules. The next step is activating the action request which results in the request being sent to a person's inbox by the workflow engine. The person then reviews the action list in the portal, along with the routing log and other header information. The action list refers the user to the original application to see any business information in the document. The application then consults the workflow engine to determine what elements of the document to show the user, if any. After reviewing the document, the user takes some action (approves, asks for more information, etc.). After the user completes his/her activities, the updated XML contents of the document and a description of the action taken by the user are again routed through the workflow engine. Once the engine has determined that all routing is complete, it then notifies the application post-processor.

What IU added to the conceptual design was a recordkeeping component. To begin the process, archivists, records managers, auditors, and legal counsel would determine which records created in the business process would be captured. It may be the products of all activities, or it could be only the final output. For example, for the travel reimbursement process, there may well be a variety of versions as the result of adding more information to an earlier form or of correcting errors. At some point a decision must be made on whether we needed to capture and maintain all versions of the travel reimbursement form or just the final product. Once this appraisal is completed the decisions are programmed into the workflow engine. To capture the document when it becomes a record or evidence of a transaction, routing rules would direct the document to the recordkeeping node. The attached inbox would have a conduit that passes the document into a recordkeeping system or repository to be managed. Each document in the recordkeeping system would include the metadata attached at its creation in addition to all metadata gathered whenever it is routed through the engine. Since the record has been captured as part of its associated process, we can be assured that the metadata also contains all of the appropriate contextual information that may be missing if captured outside the workflow process. This process would also assign to the record a unique number and a date when the record moved into the recordkeeping environment.

The last several years have witnessed the emergence of technologies that should promote the strategy of capturing data as objects. One of these developments is the emergence of business process manage-

Figure 3.12
Conceptual Design of Portal, Applications, and Infrastructure

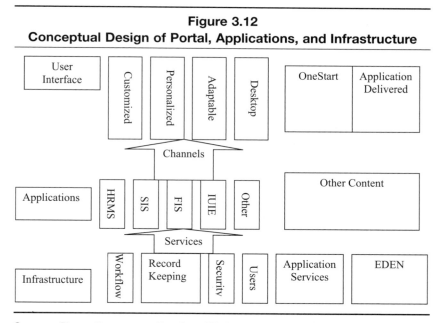

Source: Flynn, Rosemary. *OneStart/EDEN—A Description of IU's, Transaction Processing/Recordkeeping Environment.* http://www.indiana.edu/~libarch/ER/flynn-saa2001.pdf.

Figure 3.13
EDEN Workflow Engine and Electronic Recordkeeping

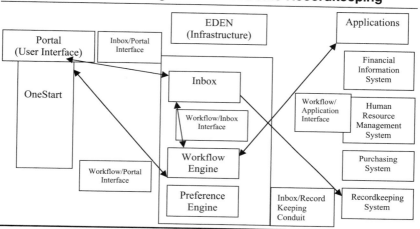

Source: Flynn, Rosemary. *OneStart/EDEN—A Description of IU's Transaction Processing/Recordkeeping Environment.* http://www.indiana.edu/~libarch/ER/flynn-saa2001.pdf.

ment systems or BPMS or e-process applications. These tools provide the means to create more robust, more comprehensive automated workflows that integrate with all business processes. In essence these tools create automated workflows that are more than just routing mechanisms designed to include only those documents that require review and approval. BPMS integrates with all processes including ad hoc activities, and as a result provides automated workflows or process models that can more comprehensively support the identification and capture of records as they are created and used. Another development that supports the strategy of capturing records as objects is the emergence of enterprise-wide portals. These portals provide an enterprise-wide gateway to systems that can be used to implement automated business process applications and to capture data as records as these objects are assembled and used. Consequently the portal can be viewed as a mechanism for extracting the data as an object or record out of the transaction processing system.

We not only have more sophisticated mechanisms for getting the information out of the TPS; there now exist very robust systems in which to deposit the objects. The emergence of enterprise content management systems, which we will discuss in the next chapter, and of more integrated data warehouses, which we will discuss in chapter 5, provide the kind of managed repositories that are required to support the strategy of managing data in TPS as objects in a document repository. Finally, the emphasis on the integration of systems within the enterprise encourages vendors of TPS and ERP systems to develop strategies for integrating their products with other systems. For example, the Gartner Group describes a new type of ERP, the "ERP II," that not only manages data in the ERP environment but can also move that data in various formats into other information systems where it can be used for other purposes (Line56, 2001).

A good real-life application of the strategy of capturing data as objects is SAP's ArchiveLink application. This product implements the automatic archiving of data as documents as these objects are created within the SAP WebFlow process. In addition, ArchiveLink will automatically capture documents produced by SAP Smartforms, such as print, fax, or e-mail documents, and will do ad hoc archiving of incoming documents. As testimony to the potential value of this application and the power of the concept of integration, several companies dealing with document and records management have created the tools to integrate documents in the SAP document repository into their own document and records management environments. For example, TRIM, the Australian records management application, includes software to automatically accept SAP documents and to manage them as part of the TRIM Context Information management database. In this way documents created in SAP can be managed in accordance with the robust document and records management functionality found in TRIM but not within the SAP system. Perceptive Software, developer of the ImageNow document management software, has also created a module, which will allow SAP users to incorporate ImageNow's document management functionality into the SAP ArchiveLink (for more information on the SAP Archive Link product, see the SAP Web site.

The advantages to the option of developing an automated mechanism for capturing records as objects include:

- This strategy is more likely to capture authentic and reliable records, because it is reconstructing the record once and then capturing the entire object. Since records do not have to be reassembled as needed, there is not the additional burden of ensuring that all the individual data elements that constitute the records are preserved over time.

- Because the strategy is designed to capture records as objects it will be far easier for archivists and records managers to apply traditional methodologies and tools in the analysis process.
- In this option one does not need to worry about maintaining historical data in an ever changing, active operational system.
- By getting the data out of the operational environment, one has a better chance of establishing a new and different set of requirements geared more towards recordkeeping and preserving and managing inactive, historical data and records.
- This strategy is more likely to capture complete records, because it is binding related metadata to record content at the point of creation. Again, one does not have to worry about maintaining complex relationships between data and metadata stored in different tables.
- By capturing records in the context of a business process and workflow, the strategy provides a more efficient mechanism for appraising records and for establishing strategies for managing the access and preservation of records.
- This strategy will result in a smaller historical database than the back-up option because records will be retained and disposed of according to a systematic appraisal process. Ultimately this will result in fewer resources required to manage the repository.
- This strategy promotes enterprise-wide integration of information by combining structured database records with semi-structured and unstructured objects within one single system or repository.
- The trend toward the development of more robust business process management tools and enterprise-wide portals makes this strategy easier to design and implement.
- As indicated above, this strategy is starting to be implemented, albeit on a small scale, which will allow archivists/records managers to provide real-life data on costs and benefits.

Disadvantages to this option:

- This strategy is not consistent with the design scheme of relational databases, and represents a different strategy for IT that will require them to use new tools and methodologies. Some IT personnel may be reluctant to make these changes.

- Capturing records as objects and moving them to a recordkeeping system adds another level of complexity and cost to the information systems managed by the institution.
- There are likely to be some significant and complex technological solutions that need to be addressed to make this strategy work. There are very few implementations of this strategy, and consequently there are many unanswered questions, particularly relating to costs and benefits.
- IT may not be convinced that the present system requires this level of redesign. Most IT personnel I have talked to feel the database model does a decent job of capturing and preserving records. They recognize that some tweaks may be needed, but few individuals that I consulted felt the radical redesigning of the system advocated by this strategy was justified.
- Although the repository for these records will be smaller than that produced by the back-up option, it will still be a very large repository that will require considerable resources to build and manage.
- It may be difficult to capture all pertinent records as objects at the point of creation. BPM systems are still not widely used. A more typical workflow engine is more accurately described as a routing mechanism for reviewing and getting approval for certain types of records. Since not all records are routed for review and approval, this workflow engine would not capture all records generated by the business. Another way of saying this is that many workflow engines only work with structured business processes. They will not deal with the more loosely structured, unstructured and ad hoc processes that form a major part of any organization's business processes.

REFERENCES

Bellaver, Richard, and John M. Lusa, eds. 2002. *Knowledge Management Strategy and Technology*. Boston: Artech House.
Bielawski, Larry, and Jim Boyle. 1997. *Electronic Document Management Systems: A User Centered Approach for Creating, Distributing and Managing Online Publications*. Upper Saddle River, NJ: Prentice Hall.

Boddy, David, Albert Boonstra, and Graham Kennedy. 2004. *Managing Information Systems: An Organizational Perspctive.* Harlow, UK: Prentice Hall.

Chaffey, Dave, and Steve Wood. 2005. *Business Information Management. Improving Performance Using Information Systems.* Harlow, UK: Prentice Hall.

Cornell University. 2001. Human Resource/Payroll Data Warehousing Web Site FAQ (May 18). Available: www.cit.cornell.edu/services/datadelivery/datamarts/hrpdw/help.html

Davenport, Thomas. 2000. *Mission Critical: Realizing the Promise of Enterprise Systems.* Boston: Harvard Business School Press.

Davenport, Thomas. 2002. *Information Ecology: Mastering the Information and Knowledge Environment.* New York: Oxford University Press.

Dollar, Charles M. 1999. *Authentic Electronic Records: Strategies for Long-Term Access* Chicago: Cohasset Associates.

Flynn, Rosemary. 2001. "OneStart/EDEN—A Description of IU's Transaction Processing/Recordkeeping Environment." Available: www.indiana.edu/~libarch/ER/flynn-saa2001.pdf

Gillespie, Richard, and Joann Gillespie. 1999. *PeopleSoft Developer's Handbook.* New York: McGraw-Hill.

Kimball, Ralph. 1995. "Is ER Modeling Hazardous to DSS?" *DBMS Online* (October). Available: www.dbmsmag.com/9510d05.html

Kimball, Ralph. 1997. "Dimensional Modeling Manifesto." *DBMS Online* (August). Available: www.dbmsmag.com/9708d15.html

Kimball, Ralph. 2000. "There Are No Guarantees: Entity-relation modeling is far from being a universal solution for data warehouse business rules." Intelligent Enterprise Web site. Available: www.intelligententerprise.com/000801/webhouse.jhtml

Laudon, Kenneth C., and Jane P. Laudon. 1999. *Essentials of Management Systems.* 4th ed. Englewood Cliffs, NJ: Prentice Hall.

Line56. 2001. "CEO: What Is ERP II? Is it Better than ERP I?" The General Center for Internet Services Inc. Available: www.gcis.ca/english/cdne–077-aug–16-2001.html

Marshall, Chris. 2000. *Enterprise Modeling with UML: Designing Successful Software Through Business Analysis.* Reading, MA: Addison-Wesley.

McGee, James, and Laurence Prusak. 1993. *Managing Information Strategically.* New York: John Wiley and Sons.

Montgomery, Stephen. 1994. *Object-Oriented Information Engineering: Analysis, Design, and Implementation.* Boston: AP Professional.

Pearlson, Keri E., and Carol S. Saunders. 2005. *Managing and Using Information Systems.* New York: John Wiley and Sons.

Rob, Peter, and Carlos Coronel. 2002. *Database Systems: Design, Implementation and Management.* Boston: Course Technology.

SAP Web Site. Available: www.sap.com/usa/index.epx

Schmidt, Bob. 1999. *Data Modeling for Information Professionals*. Upper Saddle River, NJ: Prentice Hall.

Stair, Ralph. 2003. *Principles of Information Systems: A Managerial Approach*. Boston: Course Technology.

Sutton, Michael J. D. 1996. *Document Management for the Enterprise: Principles, Techniques, and Applications*. New York: John Wiley and Sons.

Taylor, David A. 1990. *Object-Oriented Technology: A Manager's Guide*. Reading, MA: Addison-Wesley.

Tenner, Arthur, and Irving DeToro. 1997. *Process Redesign: The Implementation Guide for Managers*. Reading, MA: Addison-Wesley.

Tom, Paul L. 1987. *Managing Information as a Corporate Resource*. Glenview, IL: Scott Foresman.

Turban, Efraim. 1993. *Decision Support and Expert Systems: Management Support Systems*. New York: Macmillan.

Whitten, Jeffrey L., and Lonnie D. Bentley. 1998. *Systems Analysis and Design Methods*. Boston: Irwin McGraw-Hill.

Williams, Brian, Stacey Sawyer, and Sarah Hutchinson. 1999. *Using Information Technology. A Practical Introduction to Computers and Communications*. Boston: Irwin McGraw-Hill.

Yevich, Richard, and Susan Lawson. 2001. *DB2: High Performance Design and Tuning*. Upper Saddle River, NJ: Prentice Hall.

4

Enterprise Document Management and Content Management Systems

During most of automation's history, the emphasis has been on managing data and not documents or objects. However, in the last ten to fifteen years this focus has changed, in large part because so much corporate knowledge is now stored as documents. Current estimates are that only 20 percent of business information is stored as structured data in databases, and that 80 percent or more exists as unstructured or semi-structured data in the form of digital objects (Sutton, 1996). This recognition of the importance of documents or objects rather than data has resulted in the rapid development of systems to manage documents. These applications began appearing in the 1980s and have evolved dramatically in the last decade. In fact, document management systems have likely been subject to more growth and change over time than any other type of application. These applications have evolved from fairly simple systems that managed mostly text documents and possessed some basic records management functionality to the new massive systems referred to as Enterprise Content Management (ECM) applications, designed to manage all types of content over the entire life cycle in a very integrated environment. Figure 4.1 demonstrates the differences between data and documents.

DOCUMENT MANAGEMENT SYSTEMS IN THE EARLY TO MID 1990S

Were document management systems of this period good recordkeeping systems? To begin the process of answering this question, let us first review the functionality of a typical document management system as it existed about ten years ago. Document management systems of this time period were client server applications, in which the client contained the critical functionality that typically would work independently of other applications as a stand-alone application. However, most systems had the capability to integrate with other popular applications, particularly Microsoft products, web browsers, and imaging systems. The server's primary functions were to communicate with the client database and file system, to manage queries and to update the database. Figure 4.1 shows a logical model of how an electronic database management system (EDMS) of this period worked. Within this client server architecture, there existed a number of sub-applications that managed the system. One commentator describes the architecture and functionality of these systems in terms of seven different manager applications (Sutton 1996, 13–15).

DOCUMENTBASE MANAGER

This is the file structure or repository where the actual document objects are stored and managed. Systems at this time could handle a variety of objects, including text, graphics, voice, image files, videos, and multimedia documents. Documents could be organized around functions such as human resource or financial activities or around subjects, and could be placed into file folders or containers that stored documents on the same subject or business process. Some of the primary functionality of these repositories included:

Check-in: The check-in process involved the transfer of the document into the repository and the identification of metadata describing the object. Typical metadata elements gathered at this point would include author, title, subject, date, and type of document. The number of metadata items that could be assigned to objects varied from application to application; some provided only a limited number of document attributes, while others allowed users to augment standard lists with customized attribute lists.

Figure 4.1
Logical Model of the EDMS Architecture

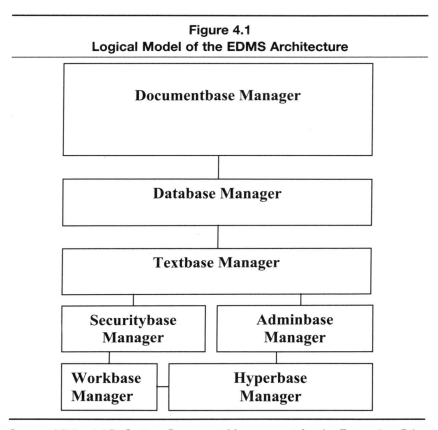

Source: Michael J.D. Sutton, *Document Management for the Enterprise: Principles, Techniques, and Applications* (New York: John Wiley and Sons, 1996), 14. Reproduced with permission of John Wiley and Sons, Inc.

Check-out: During the check-out process users could create a read-only copy of the document or a fully functional copy that could be edited. While the document was checked out, the original in the repository was locked and was not available to other users.

Version Control: Each time a document was updated several activities occurred: a new copy of the file was placed alongside the previous version in the file system, a new version number was created, and a corresponding entry on the new document was made in the database. In most systems, the creation of a new version occurred during the check-in or check-out process. In some systems, versioning was linked to workflow/routing modules, which assisted in controlling and managing the editing of documents associated with a business process.

Archiving: Document management systems of this time period provided the means to move non-essential documents to near-line or off-line media.

DATABASE MANAGER

The metadata or object attributes were stored in a database, which in the vast majority of cases was a relational database. The database manager created indexes, supported retrieval via SQL, and maintained an audit trail of actions performed on documents and files.

TEXTBASE MANAGER

The textbase manager preserved or deleted pointers to the location and position of text contained in the document objects. These processes were implemented whenever documents were added, deleted, modified, searched, or indexed.

ADMINBASE MANAGER

This sub-application maintained administrative controls over the processes of backup, recover, rebuild, install, un-install, startup, restart, restore, verify integrity, and shut down.

SECURITYBASE MANAGER

The securitybase manager administered the security controls throughout the application. The security system was typically built around a classification structure that equated a user's or groups' role or position in the organization with a security level which allowed that class of user to perform specific activities within the application. For example, a group of users could be granted permissions only to view and copy documents but not to edit or delete. Of particular importance were the controls built around the processes of check-in, check-out, and versioning. Permissions could be granted at the repository, file, or document level. The security system also controlled the generation, cataloging, and reporting of security logs.

HYPERBASE MANAGER

This sub-application administered and maintained the links between the parts of compound or hypermedia documents.

WORKBASE MANAGER

This sub-application administered the workflow processes, and maintained the workflow map, participant roles, and relationships. This workflow software was primarily designed for routing documents that needed review and approval.

EARLY TO MID 1990S DOCUMENT MANAGEMENT SYSTEMS AS RECORDKEEPING SYSTEMS

Let us compare the functionality of these systems to our set of recordkeeping requirements.

SYSTEM CAPTURES RECORDS FROM A VARIETY OF APPLICATIONS

These systems did have the ability to capture different types of objects, such as text, photographic images, video and audio, and compound, complex documents. They were integrated with other popular applications, such as Lotus and prominent Web browsers. Consequently, there was the potential to move records from these environments into the document management system. Finally, the document management systems of this period included workflow/routing engines, which could be used to capture some record content and metadata as part of a business process. Nonetheless, these systems had some severe limitations as record capture systems. Most importantly, the ability to integrate with other information systems was limited; by today's standards these systems were still more of a stand-alone application. The workflow engine had limited functionality, and it was primarily a tool for routing documents that required review and approval.

SYSTEM SUPPORTS A CLASSIFICATION SCHEME

Most systems of this period included some type of classification scheme for organizing objects into folders. However, classification schemes and files plans were not prominent features of the systems of this period. There was still a tendency within these applications to manage documents as individual objects and not to include a robust record classification scheme that would bring together objects or records on the same or related business processes.

SYSTEM ASSIGNS METADATA

These systems could capture and manage metadata at the check-in process, and through use of pointers they could relate or associate this metadata to the objects they described. They could also create relationships between records on similar functions or subjects and organize them into folders. However, on the whole they did not capture the range of metadata required for recordkeeping, particularly metadata that defined the context of creation and the relationships between documents. On average, the standard metadata lists included with systems of this period were incomplete, and the ability to customize the lists was limited.

SYSTEM SUPPORTS AUDIT CONTROL

Document management systems of this period did maintain transaction logs and audit controls that could track changes to the status of records and could assist in reconstructing data and records. Nonetheless, these systems generally did not include the detailed audit trails required in recordkeeping systems and, on the whole, lacked the very rigorous controls required to protect the authenticity of records.

SYSTEM MANAGES RETENTION AND DISPOSAL

Some of the systems of this period possessed a limited ability to manage the disposition of objects, but on the whole this functionality was underdeveloped. This inability to manage systematically the retention and disposal of records was certainly one of the greatest liabilities as a recordkeeping system of document management applications of this period.

SYSTEM MANAGES SECURITY AND CONTROL

These systems had the potential to protect records by means of its various security controls, such as access control lists, security logs, and the strict controls built around the check-in, check-out, and versioning processes. However, these systems generally lacked the much tighter controls on access and permissions required to maintain authentic and reliable records.

SYSTEM MANAGES PRESERVATION

These systems did have an ability to "archive" documents by moving them off-line, and to migrate documents to other systems. They also included the functionality for backup and recovery, restoring and rebuilding the system, and verifying integrity. What was missing from these systems, however, was a defined and well managed preservation strategy that included automated mechanisms for preserving objects over time by systematically converting or migrating records as needed. In part this deficiency was a result of designing systems that still did not as yet place a great emphasis on adhering to national and international standards and on developing strategies for interoperability.

OVERALL ASSESSMENT

Electronic document management systems of this period clearly possessed some of the functionality of a recordkeeping system. However, on the whole these document management systems were still rather poor recordkeeping applications. These deficiencies began with the design and overall purposes of the systems. Their primary purpose was not to create a secure repository for authentic and reliable records, but rather to provide current documents for everyday use. Consequently, these systems lacked the types of strict controls and functionality required of a recordkeeping system designed to manage authentic records over the entire life cycle. Specific deficiencies included:

- Inadequate security controls to ensure records would not be inappropriately changed or deleted
- Insufficient record disposition controls to automatically manage retention and destruction of records
- Lack of detailed audit trails documenting activities on the status of the record
- Incomplete metadata describing the context of creation and use
- Systems not adequately built upon standards and interoperability which would enhance record capture from a variety of applications and facilitate the process of record preservation.

CHANGES IN ENTERPRISE DOCUMENT MANAGEMENT SYSTEMS IN THE LAST DECADE

In the last few years document management applications have changed dramatically as more functionality has been added. These changes can be summarized in terms of two major developments: the emergence of records management (RM) applications and the creation of enterprise content management (ECM) systems.

Let us first examine why these changes are occurring. While one can point to a number of factors, without question the primary driver is compliance with new legislation aimed at reducing financial impropriety and on increasing the transparency of processes and accountability within businesses. In a 2004 survey by AIIM, organizations ranked the need to comply with new laws and regulations as the second most important factor motivating them to buy ECM applications (AIIM 2004, 5). Laws such as Sarbanes Oxley, HIPAA, Basel II, the Gramm-Leach-Bliley Act, and a host of others typically contain requirements for better internal controls and for protecting the privacy of citizens. (We will review these laws in more detail in chapter 7.) In addition, they often include severe penalties for non-compliance. At the heart of much of this legislation is a requirement to better manage records that will provide evidence of activities and of the institution's compliance with the provisions of the acts.

The other main thrusts behind the development of ECM and RM are cost reductions and the belief that by better leveraging content, new opportunities and business advantages will be generated and efficiencies will be realized. The AIIM survey in 2004 found that the most important factor motivating businesses to purchase ECM applications was improving efficiency (AIIM 2004, 5). Corporate directors have discovered that any strategies designed to more effectively manage content and make it more accessible to users will result in millions of dollars of saving.

THE ADDITION OF RECORDS MANAGEMENT FUNCTIONALITY TO DOCUMENT MANAGEMENT APPLICATIONS

Early records management applications were offered by smaller, niche vendors, like Tower, TrueArc, Provenance, and Tarian. These were stand-alone systems that attempted to combine the functionality of traditional document management systems with records management functionality. More specifically, this new records management software augmented document management applications by adding the capability of implementing a record file plan, i.e., the ability to declare and classify records and to manage them by means of an automated retention and disposal schedule. In addition, these record management applications provided additional metadata to define relationships between objects, more rigorous controls to ensure the authenticity of records, and the ability to manage new types of records such as e-mail.

Eventually, some of the larger players in the world of document management, such as FileNet and IBM, recognized the value of adding more record management functionality to their products. Initially, they achieved this by teaming up with the smaller record management software companies. For example, FileNet partnered with Provenance to offer a product that loosely integrated FileNET IDM Content Services 5.1.1 and ForeMost Enterprise 2.0.

These initial implementations from IBM and FileNet were loosely integrated applications. They essentially consisted of two products with a gateway to move documents between the two environments. As a result they were not very efficient applications, especially since many functions were shared or performed jointly by the two products. For example, a Department of Defense review charted how FileNet and ForeMost performed various functions. The results are shown in figure 4.2.

As the demand for record management functionality grew, these loosely integrated products no longer met businesses' needs. For example, 48 percent of institutions consulted in a 2004 survey claimed that integrated records management functionality within an ECM environment was a top priority (AIIM, 2005: 6). Even large companies like Microsoft have gotten this message as witnessed by the inclusion of records management functionality, such as the ability to assign retention schedules to documents, within their Sharepoint application.

This demand for more efficient and integrated records management functionality resulted in several developments. Larger companies sought to integrate records management more tightly into their ECM suites. Some achieved this by buying out the smaller records management vendors. Other companies, like Tower and Hummingbird, enhanced their existing record management software, and integrated it into their suite of ECM applications. Most of these products could be employed as stand-alone systems that combined records management and document management functionality. Ultimately, how-

Figure 4.2
DoD Comparison of FileNet and ForeMost

	DoD 5015.2-STD	FileNET	ForeMost	Comments
Para	Requirement			
2.1.1	Managing Records	✔	✔	Separate operations
2.1.2	Accommodating Year 2000	✔	✔	Separate operations
2.1.3	Implementing Standard Data	✔	✔	Separate operations
2.2.1	Implementing File Plans		✔	
2.2.2	Identifying and Filing Records	✔	✔	Joint operations
2.2.3	Filing E-mail Messages	✔	✔	Separate operations
2.2.4	Storing Records	✔	✔	Separate operations
2.2.5	Scheduling Records		✔	
2.2.6	Screening Records		✔	
2.2.7	Retrieving Records	✔	✔	Separate operations
2.2.8	Transferring Records	✔	✔	Joint operations
2.2.9	Destroying Records	✔	✔	Joint operations
2.2.10	Access Control	✔	✔	Separate operations
2.2.11	System Audits	✔	✔	Separate operations
2.2.12	System Management	✔	✔	Separate operations

Source: Assistant Secretary for Command, Control, Communications, and Intelligence. *Design Criteria Standard for Electronic Records Management Software Applications.* DoD 5015.2-STD. June 19, 2002. Available: http://jitc.fhu.disa.mil/recmgt/p50152s2.pdf.

ever, the goal of all of these vendors was to make records management an integrated and robust sub-application with the suite of products offered within their Enterprise Content Management (ECM) application.

ENTERPRISE CONTENT MANAGEMENT

The term enterprise content management began to be commonly used around 2000 to describe an application that combined the functionality of enterprise document management systems with the services of content management applications. The ECM concept differs from other applications in that it attempts to be a very integrated product that addresses business needs at the enterprise level. ECM integrates traditionally independent content technologies including document management, enterprise collaboration, knowledge management, e-mail management, archiving solutions, records management, and Web management into a secure, unified platform.

In 2002, early implementers like Hummingbird and FileNet described their new applications as a move from electronic document management systems to enterprise document management systems. Functionality was listed as: Web based; integrated library services; integrated search and retrieval; more robust workflow and life cycle management tools; ability to collaborate around documents; enhanced ability to incorporate legacy systems into the application; greater ability to integrate with more popular applications such as Microsoft Office, Outlook, Lotus Notes, and PeopleSoft; greater multi-level security; and enhanced ability to quickly capture and store information in a variety of formats, including scans, e-mail, Web documents, and custom applications. A good example of ECM software from 2001–02 is FileNet's Panagon system.

Present day ECM systems have improved upon this list of services by adding new functionality and expanding upon and improving other management tools. Today, ECM systems are generally considered to be an amalgamation of the following distinct but interrelated and integrated applications. A good description of modern-day ECM functionality can be found at the Hummingbird Web site.

Document Management for library services such as check-in and check-out, version control, and user and document level security.

Web Content Management for collecting, assembling, and staging content for the purpose of publishing to Web sites or intranets.

Records Management for long-term archiving and the automation of retention and compliance policies.

Business Process Management (BPM) or Workflow for routing content and support of business processes. BPM software is more than a routing engine; it actually integrates with all business processes. As one expert has written: "Instead of attempting to map business organizations to technology, it utilizes technology to mirror the processes that essentially define the business" (Thompson 2004, 3). A primary driver of this new workflow technology is E-Commerce, where the goal is to create a Web-based workflow to support collaborative commerce. These e-process applications are also being used with portal technology, where they can serve as the integration point for interacting with various applications, including ERPs like PeopleSoft and SAP.

Content Integration for providing data integration capabilities between data sources and for migrating and consolidating repositories without programming.

Collaboration for sharing, organizing and controlling document based collaborative processes.

Document Capture and Document Image Management for capturing and managing paper documents and electronic objects.

E-mail Management for capturing and managing business-related e-mail communications

Another way of portraying the functionality of modern ECM systems is shown in Figure 4.3.

Figure 4.3
Enterprise Content Management Functionality

Requirement	Description
Management of Electronic Objects	• Ability to capture, control, and deliver content objects in a wide variety of formats, including traditional object types like office documents, but also new object types such as email • Requires a repository that provides traditional library services, such as check-in and checkout and version control
Web Content Management	• Ability to capture and manage the dynamic presentations of content via the Web
Life Cycle Management	• Ability to manage content objects from creation through active use, destruction, and deposit in an archives • Requires library services as well as records management functionality
Process Management	• Ability to automate and manage business processes and workflows
Integration	• Ability to integrate with other information systems and desktop environments

A survey in 2005 revealed that ECM vendors reported strong growth during the year. 77.1 percent reported that revenues increased or increased significantly in 2005, and 46 percent reported net profits in excess of 10 percent. Ninety-one percent believed that 2006 would be an even more profitable year. Vendors responding to the survey reported selling ECM applications most often to:

Banking, finance, insurance = 77.4 percent
Healthcare = 66.5 percent
Government = 64 percent

Functionality most often requested from the vendors included:

RM/archiving=77.7 percent
DM = 76.9 percent
Information Capture = 67.2 percent
(AIM 2005, 6).

Forrrester Research, Inc. estimates the "market for enterprise content management (ECM) license software will exceed $3.9 billion in 2008, outpacing the software market with a forecasted 19 percent compound annual growth rate" (McNabb et al., 2005, Executive Summary).

MODERN DOCUMENT MANAGEMENT/RECORDS MANAGEMENT APPLICATIONS AS RECORDKEEPING SYSTEMS

Are the modern age DM/RM applications good recordkeeping systems? To answer this question, let us return to the set of recordkeeping requirements and review how some of the leading products measure up. Applications that are reviewed here include products from Tower, IBM, Hummingbird, Filenet, EMC, and Open Text. It should be noted that this analysis only reviews functionality present in the application; it does not measure its ability to implement the functionality (DM/RM systems).

SYSTEM CAPTURES RECORDS FROM A VARIETY OF APPLICATIONS

Capturing the Record

These products support the capture and import of many types of records, including e-mail, Web pages, all MS Office applications, and more specialized applications such as CAD drawings and Visio diagrams. Interoperability with other systems will increase as DM/RM applications become more fully integrated with other modules in the ECM environment, such as e-mail management, Web management, business process management, and image management. In regard to capture mechanisms, they typically include several methods for filing records. Users can file records directly into the DM/RM repository from the main client; they can file records from the Web using a Web browser such as Explorer; they can file records into the repository from within Microsoft products; and they can use personal or shared selection lists to file records. All these applications have the capacity to capture and store e-mail from Outlook into the DM/RM repository. They can store the e-mail messages and an attachment as a single record or can file the e-mail and attachment as separate documents.

Registering the Record

At the time of filing, all these application assign a unique record identifier and a date/time stamp to each record. Users cannot modify either field. Once documents are registered as records, unauthorized changes or deletions cannot be made.

Adding Classification and Other Metadata

These systems capture classification and other metadata at the point when the record content is captured. Typically the metadata captured at registration includes: document name, free-text description, classification, and perhaps some user defined fields to further describe or classify the record. For e-mail, most of these applications automatically capture the message transmission and receipt data to populate the author/originator, addressee(s), publication date, and subject record profile fields.

Summary

Compared to earlier versions, present day DM/RM software is able to integrate with and capture records from a much broader set of applications. This functionality will be enhanced as the DM/RM module becomes more integrated with other sub-applications within the ECM environment. Moreover, these new applications do a far superior job of registering and protecting records at the point of capture, and of providing some initial metadata and classification data when the record enters the recordkeeping system.

SYSTEM SUPPORTS A CLASSIFICATION SCHEME

All of these applications include a file classification or file plan module that allows organizations to build a classification scheme that reflects their own, unique processes. They include standard, out of the box workflows, which through the use of a set of workflow tools can be modified and configured to match specific business processes. These modules also allow the user to classify or describe their records according to record types. Typically classification profiles within these applications include the following information: "Reason(s) for Classification," "Initial Classification," "Current Classification," and "Declassify On" fields. Compared to earlier versions, the workflow modules in present day DM/RM software are more robust and flexible. Unlike workflows of the past they can be more than simple routing mechanisms; they can be configured and used to truly integrate with business processes. These modern day workflow modules can become tools for capturing records on all business processes, including ad hoc processes. This ability to capture records within business processes will become more effective as DM/RM systems become more integrated with the Business Process Management sub-application within the ECM environment.

SYSTEM ASSIGNS METADATA

Compared to earlier versions, these present day applications include the ability to add far more metadata documenting record content, the context and use, and the management of the record over time. In addition to standard lists of metadata, these applications offer greater capability than earlier systems to create customized lists of metadata. In essence these modern day DM/RM are far more capable of meeting the metadata specifications required for recordkeeping systems.

SYSTEM SUPPORTS AUDIT CONTROL

All these applications capture audit logs documenting activities performed on the records. Users determine which events to audit. Typically they include some or all of the activities associated with capturing, adding, deleting, copying, updating, moving, and viewing records; with editing metadata; with login and logout; and with changes to security classifications, disposition schedules, file plans, and workflow. In addition, a history audit trail will capture replaced metadata values and the name of the user who entered that value. Users can view, copy, save, and print the audit log based on their access permissions. In comparison to earlier DM/RM systems, the newer applications have a greater capacity to track a much broader set of activities performed on records. The result is an audit trail that provides far greater information on how the record was managed over time. This translates into more reliable records that have greater integrity over time.

SYSTEM MANAGES RETENTION AND DISPOSAL

Modern-day DM/RM systems have the ability to create and maintain disposition schedules and file plans. These schedules can either be created within the application or imported from another source. Disposition instructions are created separately within the system and then assigned to the disposition schedule or file plan. The applications automatically track and implement the disposition schedules. Subcomponents listed under a higher level of classification, for example a folder within a record series, inherit the same disposition instruction unless another instruction is specified for that lower level component. Records targeted for destruction are aggregated and submitted for approval by authorized personnel. File plan and disposition and retention data are typically stored in a relational database within the application. This level of retention and disposal functionality was not found in earlier DM/RM applications. The addition of this functionality signals real progress towards the development of robust and truly effective records management applications.

SYSTEM MANAGES SECURITY AND CONTROL

These applications use several methods to control user access to records held in the repository. The most basic method is to control access to data by defining the level of access based on the roles, activities, or position in the hierarchy of end users. These applications typically assign users or groups of users a classification (security) level of Top Secret, Secret, Confidential, or Unclassified. Security levels are hierarchical, therefore, those users assigned a "Secret" security level will only see documents marked Secret and below. Another method of managing security in these applications is to provide support for multiple levels of access to activities related to implementing the file plan and disposition schedule and to performing activities on the records. For example, only certain "privileged" users would be able to delete records or files associated with a file plan, to alter retention periods, or to edit and delete audit logs. This security can be managed all the way down to the field level. All in all, the security to protect and manage records over time is far superior in these new systems. There are simply many more controls in the modern day record management applications that govern who can perform certain activities on records. The result is the potential for preserving more authentic records.

SYSTEM MANAGES PRESERVATION

Like older DM/RM systems these newer applications also include the functionality for backup and recovery, for restoring and rebuilding the system, and for verifying integrity of data. However, the modern day DM/RM applications are much more committed to interoperability and to integrating standards into their products. This strategy of integrating with other products has positive implications for preservation of electronic information. The primary benefit is that a greater potential exists for being able to more efficiently and effectively migrate information out of older, outdated systems and to keep the information alive over time. The ability to efficiently migrate records will increase as DM/RM systems become more integrated with the Content Integration module within the ECM environment.

SYSTEM MANAGES NON-ELECTRONIC RECORDS

These newer applications are capable of classifying and managing non-electronic, physical records and of managing electronic and non-electronic records in an integrated manner. This type of functionality was not well developed in earlier DM/RM applications.

OVERALL ASSESSMENT

The functionality of these new document management/records management applications is better in almost every respect than that found in systems a decade ago.

Their superiority can be summarized in terms of three basic qualities:

1) Tighter system controls and more complete audit trails governing and documenting the creation, receipt, transmission, maintenance, and disposition of records throughout their life cycle.

The result of the tighter controls and more detailed audit trails is the potential for preserving more authentic records.

2) Creation of additional metadata to document the context of creation and use. A major factor here is the inclusion of better workflow modules, both within the DM/RM systems and the BPM sub-application, that can potentially capture objects and metadata as part of any business process. The result of these additions in functionality is the potential for more reliable records.

3) Creation of strategies for managing records over the entire life cycle. Of particular importance here is the addition of functionality for the automated retention and disposal of records.

Over the past decade, document management/content management systems have witnessed the addition of more recordkeeping functionality than any other type of application. For the foreseeable future this is the arena where discussions between IT and archivists and records managers will be occurring on how best to manage records over the entire life cycle. In the future, we will likely see improvements in the recordkeeping capabilities of these applications. More specifically, we should see improvements in the following areas:

- More efficiently capture records from a larger set of systems and use portal technology to achieve this
- Integrate the record capture process more effectively into the workflow modules and make more transparent the assignment of classification data to records
- Automate more fully the capture and assignment of metadata to records
- Improve and automate more fully the process of destroying records that no longer have long-term value
- Improve the efficiency and effectiveness of the conversion/migration process.
- Integrate the DM/RM systems more fully into the sub-applications of the ECM environment.

REFERENCES

AIIM. 2004. "Why Enterprise Content Management? Why Now?" Available: www.aiim.org/viewpdfa.asp?ID=28967.

AIIM. 2005. "State of the Document Management Service Provider Industry." Available: www.aiim.org/article-industrywatch.asp?ID=
32703

DM/RM systems: For descriptions of the functionality of Tower, IBM,
Hummingbird, FileNet, EMC, and Open Text products see Web pages
at:

www.hummingbird.com/products/index.html
www.towersoft.com/global/Product/EDM/EDM
www.306.ibm.com/software/info/contentmanagement/
www.filenet.com/English/Products/FileNet_P8_Platform/
http://software.emc.com/products/content_management/content_
    management.htm
www.opentext.com

Hummingbird Ltd Web Site. Available: http://connectivity.hummingbird.
com/products/index.html

McNabb, Kyle, Connie Moore, Robert Markham, and Colin Teubner.
2005. "ECM Growth Outpaces the Overall Software Market."
Forrester Research, Inc. Available: www.forrester.com/Research/
Document/Excerpt/0,7211,36935,00.html

Sutton, Michael J. D. 1996. *Document Management for the Enterprise: Principles, Techniques, and Applications.* New York: John Wiley and Sons.

Thompson, Michael. 2004. *Process, People, and Content: Working in a Syn-
ergistic Environment.* Butler Direct Limited. Available: www.aiim.org/
article-dosrep.asp?ID=28051

5

Decision Support Systems and Data Warehouses

DECISION SUPPORT SYSTEMS

The ultimate purpose of any information system is to make the information available to end users for analysis and for assisting in decision making. Over the decades numerous business systems have been developed for this purpose. The first of these systems, developed in the mid 1960s, were referred to as Management Information Systems (MIS). MIS have been defined as "an integrated man/machine system for providing information to support the operations, management and decision-making functions in an organization" (Power, 2002: 3). General characteristics of these information systems included:

- Problem Solving Abilities: These systems did not have much analytical power; they were designed to address fairly structured questions that were well defined in advance; they were unable to analyze ad hoc, unforeseen information needs.
- Inputs and Outputs: These systems used simple routines such as summaries and comparisons to address fairly routine information needs; inputs to the system were typically transaction and accounting data, such as bills, orders, and paychecks; outputs

were typically summarized reports and budget summaries; systems captured information in batch routines run in the middle of the night.

- Interaction with Users: These systems were unable to work in an interactive mode with users; they required technicians to work with users to define searches and extract information (Whitten and Bentley, 2005; Williams, Sawyer and Hutchinson, 2006; Laudon and Laudon, 2004; Holsapple and Whinston, 1996).

In the late 1960s, a new type of information system became practical. These systems were model-oriented Decision Support Systems (DSS) or management decision systems. These systems were more sophisticated and useful than the management information systems. DSS have been defined as: "Computer systems at the management level of an organization that combine data and sophisticated analytical models to support semi-structured and unstructured decision making" (Laudon and Laudon, 2004: 374). Another source defines DSS as "an interactive, flexible, and adaptable computer-based information system (CBIS), specially developed for supporting the solution of a non-structured management problem for improved decision making. It uses data, provides easy user interface, and can incorporate the decision maker's own insights" (Turban, 1995: 77). From these definitions we can identify the primary characteristics of DSS as:

- Adaptability: Responsive to unplanned as well as planned information requests and reporting needs.
- Interactive: Users can work directly with these systems.
- Flexible: Users can change the search strategy or redefine the search parameters "on the fly."
- Customizable: The user can choose between numerous options and configurations and customize outputs.
- User Friendly: Systems employ user friendly software and graphical interfaces so that users with limited knowledge of technology can use them; as a result users are no longer as dependent on technical staff to define searches and extract results.
- Sophisticated Tools: DSS use sophisticated analysis and reporting models and other tools that assist decision makers to solve complex problems (Power, 2002; Laudon and Laudon, 2004; Marakas, 1999).

TYPES OF DSS

DSS systems can be very different and there are a wide variety of types of applications. At the conceptual level, one expert identifies five types of DSS: model-driven DSS, knowledge-driven DSS, data-driven DSS, document-driven DSS, and communication-driven DSS (Holsapple and Whinston, 1996; Power, 2002).

Model-driven decision support systems are the most common type of DSS. Model-driven DSS use mathematical and statistical methods to obtain solutions to user defined problems. Simple statistical and analytical tools, like spreadsheets, provide the most elementary level of functionality. Typically, however, these systems use more complex financial, simulation, optimization or multi-criteria models to provide decision support. Models include accounting and financial models, such as break-even analysis, budget financial models, and ratio analysis, and decision analysis models, such as forecasting, network and optimization, and simulation models. Very large databases are not usually required for model-driven DSS, but data for a specific analysis may need to be extracted from a large database. Outputs from the models may be expressed in mathematical expressions, in natural language statements or as a computer program. An example of a natural language query is the question by an executive: Should the company invest money in expanding a present product line? To answer this question a model-driven DSS would analyze trends and patterns over time based on national purchasing trends and provide a recommendation based on the findings.

A **knowledge-driven DSS** differs from a conventional model-driven DSS in the way that the information is presented and processed. Instead of statistical and analytical models, the knowledge-driven DSS uses problem solving expertise stored as facts, rules, and procedures. In essence, a knowledge-based DSS uses representations of human knowledge to obtain a solution to a problem. The knowledge-driven DSS is comprised of two basic components: the knowledge base and the inference engine. The knowledge base contains the facts, rules, and procedures. The inference engine is the software that actually performs deductions and inferences based on the rules and facts and determines the possible responses to the query. The most common type of knowledge-driven DSS is known as an expert system, which will be examined in more detail later in this chapter.

A **data-driven DSS**, or data-oriented DSS, emphasizes access to and manipulation of large databases of structured, internal company data. At the core of many data-driven DSS are data warehouse systems, which will be reviewed in detail later in this chapter. Examples of specific types of data-driven DSS include Executive Information Systems (EIS) or computerized systems designed to provide current and appropriate information to support executive decision making, and databases using On-Line Analytical Processing (OLAP), which is software for manipulating data from multiple databases and applications and for creating multi-dimensional views and representations of the data. Both of the systems will be examined in more detail later in this chapter.

A **document-driven DSS** manages, retrieves and manipulates unstructured information in a variety of electronic formats, including audio and video. Examples of document-driven DSS are document/content management systems, as discussed in chapter 4.

A **communications-driven DSS** is a type of DSS that emphasizes communications, collaboration, and shared decision making. Communications-driven DSS software has at least one of the following characteristics:

- enables communication between groups of people
- facilitates the sharing of information
- supports collaboration and coordination between people
- supports group decision tasks

A simple bulletin board is the most elementary level of functionality, and groupware or software intended to support and augment group activity is an example of a more complex type of communications-driven DSS. Examples of group support tools are: audio conferencing, Web conferencing, document sharing, electronic mail, computer supported face-to-face meeting software, and interactive video. Communications-driven DSS are often categorized according to the time/location matrix using the distinction between same time (synchronous) and different times (asynchronous), and between same place (face-to-face) and different places (distributed).

EXECUTIVE INFORMATION SYSTEMS (EIS)

EIS are an example of a data-driven DSS and are one of the earliest types of decision support systems. The term executive information systems was coined at Massachusetts Institute of Technology (MIT) in the late 1970s and early 1980s, and the systems became popular in the mid 1980s and the early 1990s as a tool for enhancing the strategic planning and decision making of executives. An Executive Information System (EIS) has been defined as "a computer-based system intended to facilitate and support the information and decision making needs of senior executives by providing easy access to both internal and external information relevant to meeting the strategic goals of the organization" (Marakas, 1999: 185–186). Basic characteristics of the EIS include:

- Designed primarily for senior executives; however, newer EIS are aimed at a broader audience including middle managers
- Designed to require little or no training to use
- Has an interface that is intuitive, flexible, and easily managed by the non-technical user
- Can present information in graphical, tabular, and textual formats
- Provides a wide variety of reports
- Provides on-line tools to perform the following types of analysis: trend analysis and detection, drill-down analysis, problem monitoring, competitive analysis, and key performance indicator monitoring
- Provides access to information from a broad range of internal and external sources (Power, 2002; Marakas, 2003; Holsapple and Whinston, 1996).

Initially, executive information systems were developed as mainframe computer-based programs. The first programs were proprietary and very expensive. With the advent of local area networks (LANs), several EIS products for networked workstations became available. These systems had the advantage of requiring less support and less expensive computer hardware. In the last decade Executive Information Systems have become closely tied to the data warehouse. This convergence is so pronounced that some commentators argue that the traditional EIS as it was known in its earliest manifestations "has all but disappeared" (Inmon, 2002: 248). Today, EIS integrate information stored on mainframes, personal computer systems, and minicomputers, and are available to many users in the enterprise at the personal computer level or workstation level. Future trends in EIS will be to develop systems that are more integrated with other information systems, are connected to the Web, use sophisticated analytical tools such as data mining applications, and integrate multi-media resources such as voice and images.

ARTIFICIAL INTELLIGENCE: EXPERT SYSTEMS

An expert system is a knowledge-driven DSS that captures the expertise of a human in a limited domain of knowledge and experience and uses that expertise to recommend actions. Expert systems use techniques developed in the field of artificial intelligence (AI). AI is a branch of computer science defined as "the effort to develop computer based systems that can behave like humans with the ability to learn languages, accomplish physical tasks . . . and emulate human expertise and decision making" (Laudon and Laudon, 2004: 406). This class of programs were first developed by researchers during the 1960s and 1970s and applied commercially throughout the 1980s. By the mid–1980s, a more powerful set of AI applications emerged, such as fuzzy logic, heuristic reasoning and neural networks, data visualization, multidimensional analysis, and intelligent agents.

The expert system includes two major components: 1) the knowledge base of rules and data and 2) a logic inference engine that creates new rules and data based on accumulated knowledge. The inference engine performs three basic steps: it matches rules with given facts; selects the rule that best fits the situations, and executes the rule. An inference rule is a formal way of specifying a recommendation, directive, or strategy, expressed in an **IF** premise **THEN** conclusion structure.

There are two ways an inference engine can manipulate rules. The first is forward chaining, where an inference engine starts from known facts, examines the **IF** statement in the inference rules to find any matches and then proceeds to find additional rules that apply to the user's responses. Forward chaining starts with a known body of data and proceeds to find logic in the rules so as to analyze the data. The second method is known as backward chaining. This technique involves starting the inference engine with a hypothesized solution by looking at the right-hand **THEN** statement, and working backwards to find the starting conditions that are necessary to arrive at that solution and to match a user's responses. In this technique, the logic moves downward or backward from the solution to an analysis of the data in order to determine if a possible goal is appropriate for a user (Marakas, 1999; Holsapple and Whinston, 1996; Power, 2002; Laudon and Laudon, 2004).

ARTIFICIAL INTELLIGENCE: DATA MINING

Data mining refers to a class of analytical applications that search for hidden patterns and relationships in data. With the application of data mining techniques important and previously unknown business patterns can be discovered, relationships between obscure and otherwise unnoticed variables can be examined, and long-term trends can be measured. There are two main kinds of models in data mining: predictive and descriptive. Predictive models are the most common types, and are used to uncover patterns or values that are based on known patterns of behavior. Descriptive models describe patterns in existing data, and are generally used to create meaningful subgroups such as demographic clusters.

In the 1960s and 1970s, data mining was referred to as statistical analysis, and companies employed business analysts who used statistical packages like SAS and SPSS to perform trend and cluster analyses on data. Today there are many more sophisticated tools for data mining. The five most common categories of data mining tools include:

- Case-based reasoning: This category of tools finds records in a database that are similar to specified records. Case-based tools are used with a five-step problem-solving process: 1) Presentation: a description of the current problem is input to the system; 2) Retrieval: the system retrieves the closest-matching cases stored in a database of cases; 3) Adaptation: the system uses the current problem and closest-matching cases to generate a solution to the current problem; 4) Validation: the solution is validated through feedback from the user of the environment; and 5) Update: if appropriate, the validated solution is added to the case base for use in future problem solving
- Data visualization: Data visualization tools are data mining tools that translate complex formulas, mathematical relationships or data warehouse information into graphs or other easily understood models.

- Fuzzy query and analysis: This category of data mining tools is based on a branch of mathematics called fuzzy logic. Fuzzy logic consists of a variety of concepts and techniques for representing and inferring knowledge that is imprecise, uncertain, or unreliable. Fuzzy logic can create rules that use approximate values of this incomplete or ambiguous data.
- Genetic algorithms: Genetic algorithm software is based on biological mechanisms of natural selection and adaptation. One expert defines this technique as viewing "learning as a competition among a population of evolving candidate problem solutions. A 'fitness' function evaluates each solution to decide whether it will contribute to the next generation of solutions. Then, through operations analogous to gene transfer in sexual reproduction, the algorithm creates a new population of candidate solutions." Like other data mining techniques, this quantitative model is used to find patterns among very large sets of data.
- Neural networks: Neural networks consist of hardware or software that attempts to emulate the processing patterns of the biological brain. Neural networks seek to learn patterns from data directly by repeatedly examining the data to identify relationships and then building a model. They build these models by a trial and error process which involves three iterative steps: predict, compare, and adjust. Neural networks are commonly used in a DSS to classify data and to make predictions. According to a study in 1997, neural networks were at that time the most common type of data mining technique (Laudon and Laudon, 2004; Marakas, 2003; Holsapple and Whinston, 1996).

ON-LINE ANALYTICAL PROCESSING (OLAP) SYSTEMS

In 1993, E.F. Codd, the so-called "father of the relational database," introduced the term on-line analytical processing (OLAP) to refer to the technology that allows users of multidimensional databases to generate on-line descriptive or comparative summaries of data and other analytic queries. A data analyst may use Multidimensional OLAP (MOLAP) to view data in a multidimensional format, as shown in figure 5.1, rather than in the two-dimensional row and column format as in a relational database. The intersecting cells of the three dimensions contain the actual data that the user requested. For example, the concept of how many units of a product were sold could be viewed in the dimensions of a product model, geography, time, or some additional dimension. In this case, sales or items sold are known as the measure attribute of the data cube and the other dimensions are the feature attributes.

Another type of OLAP, relational OLAPs (ROLAP), are run as a SQL query against a large relational database and return a result set to the desktop. There are also Hybrid OLAP (HOLAP) which combine functionality from both multidimensional and relational OLAP applications (Marakas, 2003; Power, 2002).

BUSINESS INTELLIGENCE (BI)

BI is the umbrella term coined in the mid–1990s to define the functionality of the present-day and near-future type of DSS environment. In the most general sense, Business Intelligence (BI) are data-driven DSS that include a broad category of applications and technologies for gathering, storing, analyzing, and providing access to data to help enterprise users make better business decisions. However, BI has also become known as the use of high-level, cutting-edge software for business applications. BI applications have evolved into integrated appli-

---

Figure 5.1
Three-dimensional Data Cube

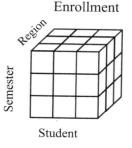

Enrollment   Dimensions: Student, Region, Semester

Source: "Concepts of Dimensional Modeling." *IBM Informix Database Design and Implementation Guide.* Available: http://publib.boulder.ibm.com/infocenter/idshelp/v10/index.jsp?topic=/com.ibm.ddi.dec/ddi232.htm

cations that combine a wide variety of decision support tools, including data mining, OLAP, statistical and forecasting models, query and reporting tools, visualization features, and data warehouse functions. In a sense BI applications presently represent the most sophisticated set of tools now available for decision support. (For a definition of BI from the perspective of vendors see Oracle, "Unified Business Intelligence Meets the Needs of 21st Century Business"; for a definition of BI from the perspective of an information management consultant, see Claudia Imhoff [2005].)

An example of a typical modern day BI application is the product offered by one of the most popular vendors, SAS. According to SAS literature, the primary goal of the SAS Enterprise BI Server is to create an integrated, comprehensive, end-to-end platform. To this end the product offers a single interface for managing and configuring an organization's entire intelligence environment; easy-to-use Web and desktop reporting interfaces; advanced analytics that include predictive analytics, such as scenario planning, optimization, and data mining; online analytical processing (OLAP) storage that is optimized to pre-summarize and store large amounts of data at different levels of detail; Web-based, wizard-driven query capabilities; an open, integrated metadata foundation; and Extract/Transformation/Loading (ETL) capabilities (SAS BI Web site).

In a very real sense, the modern BI applications represent the "best of breed" planning about the need for integrated access to a wide variety of tools for managing information and for using that knowledge to make better decisions.

OPERATIONAL DATA

In the 1960s, the common wisdom was that a single, large database could be used for all types of processing. Experience demonstrated that this strategy was not going to work. Consider the executive trying to answer this question: In the last six months, has our company made a profit, and is our revenue stream comparable to other businesses who sell the same product? The manager contacts his IT department and is told that they can provide this information, but it will likely take a good deal of time to tweak this information out of the operational system. In his frustration, the executive goes into the operational system to try to obtain the information himself. After many false starts and zero results, the manager gives up and resigns himself to waiting for IT to deliver the information. Increasingly managers and executives discovered that they could not easily obtain the information they needed for decision making from operational systems. This is not surprising since, as we saw in chapter 3, the design and primary goals of transaction processing systems and information systems differ significantly. The technology, processing characteristics, the data requirements, and the users are all fundamentally different. A summary of the many differences is listed in figure 5.2. (For more information on why operational systems did not meet the needs of managers see Kelly [1994] and Poe, Klauer and Brobst [1998].)

One response to this problem was to redesign the operational systems to meet these information needs. However, for most organizations this proved to be an unsatisfactory solution, for several reasons.

Reduced productivity—processing requests from executives resulted in reducing the productivity and response time of the operational systems.

Resources required—the time and resources to undertake a massive restructuring of operational systems proved to be immense.

Disruption of business—the disruption to conducting everyday business while the systems were reengineered was not acceptable (Inmon, 2002).

Eventually most organizations made the decision to separate the operational functions from the informational and analytical functions by creating separate and distinctly different systems for the managers and executives seeking summary and historical information. The three most common strategies were the operational data store (ODS), sometimes called on-line data processing systems (ODP); data marts, and data warehouses.

OPERATIONAL DATA STORE

The form that these separate systems first assumed was the Operational Data Store, or ODS. According to Bill Inmon, an ODS is "a hybrid structure that has some aspects of a data warehouse and other aspects of an operational system." The ODS "contains integrated data and can support DSS processing. But the ODS can also support high-performance transaction processing" (Inmon, 2002: 301; Inmon,

Figure 5.2
Differences between Operational Data and Derived DSS Data

Primitive Data/Operational Data	Derived Data/DSS Data
Application-oriented	Subject-oriented
Detailed	Summarized, otherwise defined
Accurate, as of the moment of access	Represents values over time, snapshots
Serves the clerical community	Serves the managerial community
Can be updated	Is not updated
Runs repetitively	Runs heuristically
Requirements for processing understood a priori	Requirements for processing not understood a priori
Compatible with the SDLC	Completely different life cycle
Performance sensitive	Performance relaxed
Accessed a unit at a time	Accessed a set at a time
Transaction-driven	Analysis-driven
Control of update a major concern in terms of ownership	Control of update no issue
High availability	Relaxed availability
Managed in its entirety	Managed by subsets
Nonredundancy	Redundancy is a fact of life
Static structure; variable contents	Flexible structure
Small amount of data used in a process	Large amount of data used in a process
Supports day-to-day operations	Supports managerial needs
High probability of access	Low, modest probability of access

Source: Inmon, William, *Building the Data Warehouse*, 3rd edition, 2002, p. 15. Reproduced with permission from John Wiley and Sons, Inc.

1998b). In the ODS data is organized around different subjects or business functions, such as products, orders, and customers. The data, which comes from multiple operational systems, is integrated to some degree to resolve redundancies and inconsistencies and enforce business rules. The data in the ODS is current or as close to "real time" as possible. Finally the data in the ODS is volatile, i.e., the data in the ODS is updated just as it is in the operational system. For example, if a customer's phone number changes, the old number in the ODS would be overwritten. Other characteristics are that an ODS typically contains thirty to sixty days of information, and includes mostly aggregated or summarized data and relatively small amounts of transaction level data.

Businesses that make most effective use of ODS are those that do a lot of online transaction processing, such as banks and airlines. However, in most enterprises, the ODS has either been abandoned or transformed. Recently a strategy has emerged to redefine the ODS as either a staging area for other repositories, such as the data warehouse, or to actually integrate the ODS into the data warehouse. Ralph Kimball has argued for this second strategy. Kimball asks, "So why is my ODS a separate system? Why not just make the ODS the leading, breaking wave of the data warehouse itself?" To this end, Kimball would redefine the ODS as a "subject-oriented, integrated, frequently augmented store of detailed data in the enterprise data warehouse" (Kimball, 1997b). A characteristic of this strategy is to view the ODS as part or the "front edge" of an existing data warehouse, and not as a separate system.

The second significant change in Kimball's redefinition is to augment data in the ODS, i.e., to retain previous data values and not overwrite them with current values. In other words, the critical transformation in Kimball's strategy is to make the ODS a historical repository of data.

Whatever the future of ODS, these systems represent a strategy, often the initial step, in developing an information system separate from the operational system. ODS in most organizations typically are separate systems (not part of a larger data warehouse) that contain data that was subjected to limited amounts of transformation into summarized information. In addition, these ODS still share characteristics with the operational systems in that data is current and constantly changing. Because of these characteristics ODS only meet some of short-term, less sophisticated information needs of decision makers.

DATA MARTS

Another type of repository for information derived from operational systems is the data mart. A data mart, like the ODS and the data warehouse, is a database, or collection of databases, designed to help managers make strategic decisions about their business. The data mart shares many characteristics with the data warehouse. In both systems, data from the operational systems goes through an integration process, and most of the data is significantly transformed by being aggregated or summarized. However, as we shall see in the section on data warehouse, data marts and data warehouses are very different in their design and purpose. Among the most important differences are:

- Data marts are created for specific business units that have particular data analysis needs.
- Organizations can have multiple data marts built around functions, such as sales, marketing, etc., each one relevant to one or more business units for which it was designed.
- Data marts are smaller than a data warehouse. A data mart can run in size from megabytes to gigabytes; a data warehouse may run from gigabytes to terabytes. In modern applications, many data marts are built from a larger data warehouse.
- Data marts typically contain less historical data than a data warehouse.
- Data marts typically have many more indexes than a data warehouse.
- Data marts contain much more summary data than a data warehouse. Data marts are built for rapid, ad hoc analysis of data, usually at the aggregate level.
- Data marts, unlike ODS and some data warehouses, contain very little, if any, detailed data.

A data mart may have a different data structure than the data warehouse. The data mart is almost always organized as a one dimensional model in a star schema made up of a fact table and multiple dimension tables (we will examine this structure in more detail in the section on data warehouses). Data warehouses are constructed around two data models, the relational model and the dimensional model (Marakas, 1999; Inmon, 1998a; Inmon, 2002).

Initially, data marts were developed as independent structures that existed separately or independently from each other. Eventually, however, institutions discovered that the independent data mart architecture did not offer the best solution. As William Inmon writes, the flaws in these independent information systems were "massive redundancy of detailed and historical data from one data mart to another, inconsistent and irreconcilable results from one data mart to the next, an unmanageable interface between the data marts and the legacy application environment, etc." (Inmon, 1998a).

Eventually, data architects arrived at the strategy built around dependent rather than independent data marts. In a dependent data mart architecture, a centralized data warehouse delivers data and information to the data marts. William Inmon writes that "this architecture is sometimes called the 'hub and spoke' architecture, where the data marts are the spokes and the data warehouse is the hub" (Inmon, n.d.). Because the data going to the marts is coming from a single source, the data warehouse, where the data has undergone a process of integration, the problems associated with data inconsistency and duplication are alleviated. This hub and spoke architecture where data marts are fed data from a data warehouse is the most popular strategy within institutions today.

It should be noted, however, that some institutions may not have developed data marts or ODS. In other words there is not necessarily a sequential development process from ODS to data mart to data warehouse that must be followed. Some institutions never developed an ODS and have gone right into data marts; some developed an ODS, never created data marts, and eventually moved into a data warehouse; finally, some institutions never developed either an ODS or data mart, but moved immediately into a data warehouse. Archivists/records managers will need to examine their own environment to determine the evolution of these systems within the business.

DATA WAREHOUSES

As dissatisfaction with the usefulness of ODS and data marts grew, more ambitious strategies for building repositories of data to support analysis and planning began to emerge. Certainly the most ambitious of these information strategies was the data warehouse. Data warehouses became a distinct type of computer database during the late 1980s and early 1990s.

DEFINITION AND CHARACTERISTICS

William Inmon, the recognized father of the data warehousing concept, defines a data warehouse as a subject-orientated, integrated, time variant, non-volatile collection of data in support of management's decision-making process (Inmon, 2002; Inmon, n.d).

Subject-oriented: Data in the warehouse is often organized around subjects, such as customers, products, employees, or vendors. However, some systems are organized around functions and processes, such as finances, marketing, or human resources.

Integrated and transformed: Most data in the warehouse is not merely moved into the warehouse unchanged; it undergoes some form of integration and transformation. We will look at these processes in more detail later. For now, remember that most of the data in the data warehouse is not the same data that once resided in the operational environment. The data may be changed by altering the format or the structure of the data, or by summarizing, aggregating, filtering, cleansing, and condensing the data to some degree. These transformations are important to note because these changes in the data have tremendous impact on the ability of the data warehouses to serve as recordkeeping systems.

Time variant: Data in the warehouse is time stamped and associated with defined periods of time. This means that all data in the warehouse is accurate as of some moment in time. This differs, as we will remember from our earlier discussion, from operational systems where data is intended to be as current as possible and accurate at the moment of access.

Non-volatile: Data in the warehouse is not only time stamped; it does not change over time. In other words, snapshots of data in the warehouse are fixed in time; they are static and not dynamic and cannot be overwritten or updated. Data in the warehouse is in read-only format. This characteristic is fundamentally different from the operational systems where constant updating of data occurs. Consequently, data warehouses can accurately be described as a series of historical snapshots of real life events or of the data as it existed at that particular moment. The effect created by these snapshots is a warehouse of data that provides a historical sequence of activities and events. This historical data can go as far back as ten years, but most often is in the 5–10 year range.

Other important characteristics of the data warehouse include:

- Data warehouses are physically separated from operational systems, even though the operational systems feed the warehouse with source data.

- Data warehouses' applications are designed primarily to support executives, senior managers, and business analysts in making complex business decisions. They provide historical information, support analysis, produce various types of reports, and can combine data from various sources to meet user queries.
- Data warehouses are designed so that users with limited knowledge of computer systems can access and retrieve information from the systems without assistance from IT staff.
- Data warehouses are not defined by the type of stored data. Most warehouses are composed of primarily transactional data—95 to 99 percent—extracted from operational systems. However warehouses can and do contain objects, such as textual documents, photographic material, audio and video. In some industries, such as healthcare, the warehouses may be comprised primarily of textual documents.
- Data warehouses are not defined by the form or structure of stored data. Data can be stored in a relational database, multidimensional databases, flat files, hierarchical databases, object databases, etc.
- Some data from the operational system is never transferred to the data warehouse. Extraction of data for the warehouse is a selective process in which the data most likely to be useful for decision making is identified.
- The data warehouse contains both detailed, atomic data at the transactional level and summarized and aggregated data. Decision makers require the ability to "drill down" to the most atomic or elemental data as well as the ability to view summaries of many transactions over time.
- Data warehouses are most often very large repositories. Because of the need to retain a great deal of historical information over relatively long periods of time, warehouses in large companies or institutions typically contain terabytes of data.
- A data warehouse contains external as well as internal data. Types of external data include economic forecasts, political information, data on competitors, data on technological developments, trends regarding inflation and taxation, and consumer demographic data.
- A data warehouse contains both normalized and denormalized data. However, compared to operational systems, the warehouse includes much more denormalized data, created primarily to provide historical perspective.

- A data warehouse contains a great deal of metadata on the structure, contents, and context of information in the system.
- A data warehouse includes a much more robust and sophisticated indexing structure than is found in operational systems.

Now that we have developed a basic profile, let us look more closely at the architecture and functionality of the data warehouse (for more information on the general characteristics of data warehouses, see Marakas [2003]).

BASIC ARCHITECTURE

A data warehouse is comprised of eight basic and distinct systems or layers (Marakas, 2003).

Data Sources Systems or Operational Data Stores

These are the systems that feed data to the warehouse. These sources include any electronic repository of information that contains data or digital objects that might be of interest to managers, such as mainframe databases, client-server databases, PC databases, spreadsheets, the various types of document management systems, and external systems. Data from these systems is moved to the warehouse on a regular cycle or as the transactions occur in the case of real-time data warehouses.

Data Warehouse Staging Layer

This is the area or layer of the warehouse that receives the incoming data from the internal and external systems and then integrates, standardizes, and transforms the data before it is loaded into the warehouse repository. This transformation of data can be performed either by manually created code or more commonly by a specific type of software called an Extract/Transform/Load (ETL) tool.

Data Warehouse Repository or the Physical Data Warehouse Layer

This is where the actual data resides. The data warehouse is usually a relational database, but it does not have to be. Because of their size, most data warehouses exist in a client/server environment, where the data warehouse resides on a mainframe which operates as a giant server (this is the most typical configuration) or the data warehouse actually resides in the client server environment.

Metadata Layer

As indicated earlier, metadata of all types is an extremely important feature of the data warehouse. This metadata is used to inform IT personnel about the status or management of the warehouse and users of the system about the information within the warehouse.

Data Access Layer

This layer allows the Information Access Layer to talk to the Operational Layer. It is an interface between the various tools for extracting and analyzing data and the databases in the warehouse. The common data language for this interaction is Standard Query Language (SQL).

Information Access Layer

This layer includes the software and hardware used by the end user to extract and analyze data, and to display and print reports, charts, graphs, and spreadsheets. In the past, this was achieved primarily by means of SQL commands. In the last decade, applications for accessing data warehouses have gone well beyond SQL and now include all or most of the analytical tools described in the section on decision support systems.

For example, the Microsoft's SQL Server product includes OLAP, data mining, and sophisticated reporting tools. IBM's DB2 Data Warehouse Edition includes an SQL warehousing tool, data mining, and OLAP. Finally, Oracle's Data Warehousing application offers data mining, OLAP, and sophisticated tools to enable Excel users to mine the database and analyze the results. William Inmon contends that data mining in particular is an effective analysis tool in the data warehouse environment for three basic reasons: data in the warehouse is integrated, cleansed and scrubbed; the warehouse contains historical data; and the warehouse contains both summary data and detailed data. Inmon contends that the data miner requires all of these in order to retrieve and analyze the patterns and relationships that are of interest to the corporation (Inmon, 2002). This use of more sophisticated tools for analyzing data in the warehouse is very closely related to the development of real-time data warehouses. If warehouses are to become active systems that are linked to real time decision making and collaboration, the tools for analysis and reporting must become more sophisticated. At the same time, these complex tools must be created so that non-technical staff can use them effectively, and this requirement has proven to be a bit more difficult to accomplish.

Operations or Process Management Layer

The operations layer schedules the various tasks that must be undertaken to build and maintain the data warehouse and metadata directory. This layer manages the processes of loading, manipulating and extracting data from the data warehouse, user management, security, capacity management, and related functions.

Application Messaging Layer

This layer, also known as middleware, transports data and information throughout the computer network. We will now look more closely at two of these layers: the data warehouse staging layer and the metadata layer.

DATA STAGING LAYER: LOADING THE DATA AND INFORMATION

Identifying Requirements

Before the loading process can occur, there must be some extensive discussion about what data will be collected. As indicated earlier, the data warehouse does not replicate the operational or source systems. It is a selective process that extracts data based on some defined criteria. One such process is called Business Question Assessment (for more information on business question assessments, see Dan Montgomery, 2000).

This process includes a number of different activities. One of these activities is to define the business requirements and information needs of the enterprise. The information is gleaned from analyzing fundamental business processes and transactions, by reviewing critical documentation produced by the business, and by live interviews with managers at various levels. As a result of these interviews and focus sessions, designers of the warehouse uncover the information needs of users and identify how managers measure, manage, and monitor the business. Once this input is received, a decision is made on which subject areas will be populated and in what order. Once the requirements have been gathered, they are prioritized based on their business value, impact, and overall importance to the enterprise. This analysis typically moves forward one subject area at a time. During the process, information needs of users continue to be identified and fine tuned. As user needs are being defined, IT representatives begin evaluating the feasibility of implementing the project and the availability of resources to deliver the various products.

Snapshots of Data

The data warehouse has been characterized as a series of snapshots of data captured in time. Most of these snapshots are the product of an event—the completion of a business transaction, the result of data being accumulated over a period of time, or the result of a certain project or activity, such as an audit. The snapshot itself includes the primary key data or data that serves to identify the record or the business process; a unit of time when the snapshot occurred or when the data was captured; data that describes the event; and any optional secondary data that further describes the business process. Inmon (2000b, 2002) identifies four types of snapshots:

Four Types of Data Snapshots

Wholesale Database Snapshots: This type of snapshot replicates tables within the database on a certain timetable. In practice, this would rarely mean replicating the source systems in their entirety. Typically, total replication of the TPS occurs only when the volume of data is small and the data is very stable, and when there is an overwhelming need for detailed historical data. In most cases the transaction processing system environment contains some data that is relevant only to the operational functions and is considered of no particular importance for analysis and reporting. Based on the requirements and assessment of needs, tables and certain fields are typically filtered out or eliminated before the transfer of data to the warehouse. Wholesale database snapshots are the simplest and easiest strategy to implement because very little design or complex programming is required. It also has the advantage of extracting a great deal of detailed transactional data, which can increase the flexibility and potential usefulness of the warehouse. An example of a wholesale database snapshot is shown in figure 5.3.

Ralph Kimball argues very emphatically for the inclusion of a great deal of transaction grain data collected at the lowest level of a business process. To accommodate this data Kimball proposes a data model that includes both a detailed transaction and a snapshot table. He argues that only in this way can one perform many powerful analyses that cannot be done on any form of summarized data. "Transactions and snapshots," Kimball (1998a) writes, "are the yin and yang of an operational data warehouse. Transactions give us the fullest possible view of detailed behavior, and snapshots allow you to measure the status of the enterprise quickly. . . . Used together, transactions and snapshots provide a full, immediate view of the business, and when they are part of the overall data warehouse, they blend gracefully into the larger views across time and across the other main dimensions." William Inmon (2002: 155) agrees that transactional level data is important in a warehouse and in general recommends that "the level of granularity of the data warehouse must be sufficiently low to feed the lowest level of data needed anywhere in the corporate information factory. This is why it is said that the data in the warehouse is at the lowest common denominator." However, Inmon also argues that the level of granularity of the system must be assessed in terms of other factors, particularly on the amount of data to be found in the source system and how often that data changes. He writes, "As a rule, the faster the rate of change, the fewer and more cumulative snapshots are taken. Conversely, the slower the rate of change, the more wholesale snapshots are taken" (Inmon, 2000b: 12). Consequently Inmon argues that wholesale copying of database tables is a strategy that cannot routinely be applied with large source systems that are frequently updated.

Selected Records Snapshot: A second type of snapshot identified by Inmon is the "selected records snapshot," or what Ralph Kimball calls the "periodic-snapshot grain" (Kimball, 1998a). This snapshot is created as a result of an event or a regular repeating measurement that the enterprise routinely captures. Figure 5.4 depicts a selective database snapshot. These snapshots are selected based on the criteria established in the requirements stage. In this strategy, rather than copy tables wholesale, only selected fields and data often from several tables are copied. For example, a decision based on use and needs might be to only extract data on financial transactions that were greater than $500 or to routinely capture only a monthly balance of all bank accounts. Inmon states that this is the most common strategy for capturing data in source systems. Advantages are that this strategy is based on information requirements stated by managers, and as a more selective strategy than the wholesale database approach, it will result in a less voluminous repository that will consume fewer resources to access and manage. Inmon (2000b) reminds us, however, that this strat-

Figure 5.3
Wholesale Database Snapshot

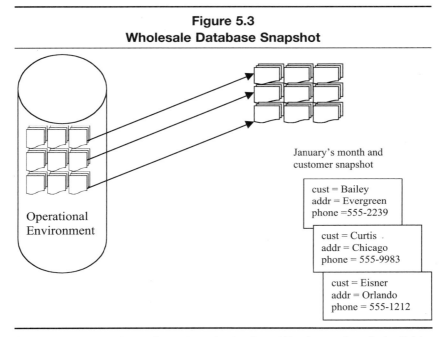

January's month and
customer snapshot

cust = Bailey
addr = Evergreen
phone =555-2239

cust = Curtis
addr = Chicago
phone = 555-9983

cust = Eisner
addr = Orlando
phone = 555-1212

Operational
Environment

Source: Inmon, William. "Snapshots in the Data Warehouse," p. 4. Available: www.inmoncif.com/registration/whitepapers/ttsnap–1.pdf. Reproduced with permission of William Inmon.

egy has the disadvantage of requiring more complex programming so as to extract this select data from the tables.

Exceptional/Special Snapshot: A third type of snapshot is the "exceptional/special" snapshot. With this type of snapshot, an even more select group of fields and data is extracted from the source system. In this type of snapshot, many transactions over time are represented by one snapshot which portrays the total effect of all these transactions. For example, a snapshot could be created whenever an account became overdrawn, or snapshots might be extracted showing only the balances of over $100,000. The advantage of this strategy is that it uses less storage space and resources. The disadvantages are the data from these snapshots occur infrequently and do not form anything like a continuous record of transactions over time.

Cumulative Snapshot: The final type of snapshot Inmon identifies is the "cumulative" snapshot or, as Kimball calls it, the "accumu-

Figure 5.4
Selective Database Snapshot

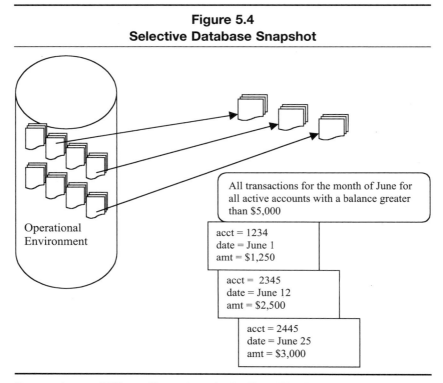

Source: Inmon, William. "Snapshots in the Data Warehouse," p. 6. Available: www.inmoncif.com/registration/whitepapers/ttsnap–1.pdf. Reproduced with permission of William Inmon.

lating snapshot grain" (Kimball 1998a). This type of snapshot is shown in figure 5.5. In this snapshot related records are extracted, summarized, and then aggregated and calculated. An example of this type of snapshot would be to display profits calculated for a given month created from daily transactions existing within the source system. Advantages to this approach are that it provides managers with summary information, which does not have to be repeatedly aggregated, and the data requires less storage space and consumes fewer resources. The disadvantage is that the detailed data which might be needed for other information needs is not available in the warehouse environment.

It should be noted that these types of snapshots are not mutually exclusive. Some or all of these four strategies can and will be used at different times to populate the data warehouse.

Figure 5.5
Cumulative Database Snapshot

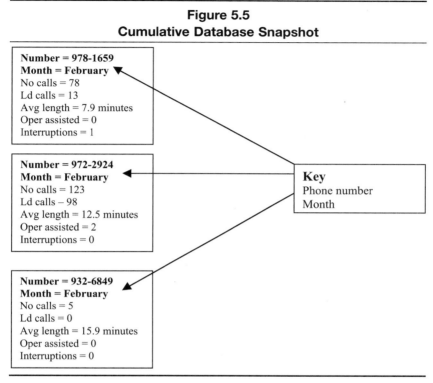

Source: Inmon, William. "Snapshots in the Data Warehouse," p. 9. Available: www.inmoncif.com/registration/whitepapers/ttsnap–1.pdf. Reproduced with permission of William Inmon.

DATA STAGING LAYER: DATA INTEGRATION

Data Integration

Integration is a complex process that requires a great deal of planning and resources. It is estimated that up to 75 percent of development dollars for building the data warehouse are consumed by the planning and implementation of the integration process (Inmon, n.d.). In general terms data integration represents the process of combining data from different sources into a common model and presenting the user with a unified view of the data. Figure 5.6 depicts the data integration process. Data going into the warehouse typically comes from various operational and information systems within the organization. These systems often are inconsistent in the way they structure, encode and format data, and assign and name attributes. For example, each operational system might have a different way of defining a customer or how they represent a particular characteristic or attribute of an entity or subject. Some systems may represent a female student with the code "F", and another system with a "1". The process of integration will ensure that within the warehouse a consistent representation of female is applied to all values that define that attribute.

Operations involved in the integration process can be placed into two major categories: data consolidation and data conversion.

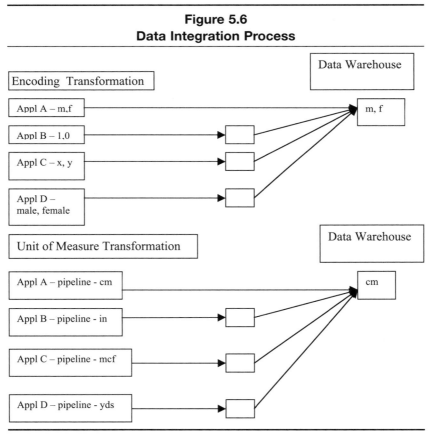

Figure 5.6
Data Integration Process

Source: Inmon, William, *Building the Data Warehouse*, 3rd edition, 2002, p. 84. Reproduced with permission from John Wiley and Sons, Inc.

Data Consolidation

Data consolidation focuses on the structure of the data and seeks to consolidate the data from the source systems into a single integrated target structure. In the design of data warehouses two models are prominently featured: the relational or entity-relationship (E-R) model, as discussed previously, and the dimensional data model, which is advocated by Ralph Kimball. The relational model for building the data warehouse uses traditional and conventional entity-relationship modeling techniques of the type described in chapter 3. However, it should be noted that one of the primary differences between traditional E-R modeling employed in building operational systems and that used in data warehouses is that for the warehouse more tables will be denormalized to add redundant data so as to display historical information (Inmon, 2002, and 2000a).

The other approach for building the data model for the data warehouse is dimensional modeling or the star schema structure. This strategy is advocated most prominently by Ralph Kimball. In chapter 3, we examined some of the shortcomings of E-R models in depicting the business or the reality it is designed to represent. Kimball adds another problem he perceives in E-R modeling, namely the difficulty for users in understanding, navigating, and effectively using E-R models. In Kimball's words, "E/R models lead to absurdly complex schemas that defeat the primary objectives of information delivery. Every designer is aware of how complex an enterprise level E/R model can become . . . These huge schemas thwart the basic data warehouse objectives of understandability and high performance" (Kimball, 2000c, and Kimball, 1995, and Kimball, 1997a).

Dimensional Models-Fact Tables

Dimensional modeling is also called a star schema because the diagram of this schema resembles a star, with points radiating from a central table. The center of the star consists of a large fact table and the points of the star are the dimension tables. This logical design technique "divides the world of data into two major types: measurements and descriptions of the context surrounding these measurements" (Kimball, 2002a). The measurements or facts are numeric or text data that document a single transaction or event or aggregate that data to measure the business process over time; they are quantitative or factual data about the subject that answer the question how much or how many. In a typical business, the measures or facts might be prices, product sales, inventory, and revenue. In a university they might be courses, enrollment, and grades.

These facts are stored in fact tables, an example of which is shown in figure 5.7. A dimensional database that documents multiple business process would contain many fact tables. Fact tables are often defined by their grain or granularity, which is a measurement of the level of detail captured about the business processes. For example, the fact or measurement could contain data documenting that John Doe received an "A" in a course in archival management in the fall semester of 2006, or it could measure all grades of A for classes throughout the whole university for the fall semester. In other words, fact tables will typically contain values representing both transaction level facts and aggregations of data into sums or measurements over a period of time. Ralph Kimball argues for the creation of two types of fact tables: a transaction level fact table and a second, separate snapshot table.

Dimensional Models-Dimension Tables

The descriptions or dimensions, which are typically textual data, provide information that describe or classify the transaction in various ways. Dimensions can be thought of as the qualifiers that make the measurements in the fact table more meaningful, because they answer the what, when, and where aspects of a question. These dimensions consist of an element that defines the subject and one or more attributes of that element. For example, in defining the subject or fact called customer, the dimension element might be a customer account, and the attributes for the account would be an account number and

Figure 5.7
Fact Table

Product Code	Account Code	Day Code	Units Sold	Revenue	Profits
1	5	32104	1	82.12	27.12
3	17	33111	2	171.12	66.00
1	13	32567	1	81.12	27.12

Source: *IBM Infomix Database Design and Implementation Guide.* "Building a Dimensional Data Model." Available: http://publib.boulder.ibm.com/infocenter/idshelp/v10/index.jsp?topic=/com.ibm.ddi.doc/ddi232.htm

account name. Defining the time frame is an important part of any dimensional model. The dimension of time period usually contains data defined by year, quarter, month, and day of the year. Dimensions also are comprised of hierarchies of related elements. An example of this hierarchical structure would be the state of Indiana defined within the region known as the Midwest. This hierarchical structure allows users to "roll up" data and information at a higher level (all accounts in the Midwest) or "drill down" to a lower level (all accounts within Indiana) as needed. All of these descriptions are stored in dimension tables, which contain the element and the attribute, if appropriate, for each level in the hierarchy. A dimension is defined along the top of the table and the attributes are the data items in the columns below the elements, as shown in figure 5.8.

The Strengths of Dimensional Models

Proponents of the dimensional model argue that it makes it easier for staff with limited information technology experience to understand and use the data warehouse. As Ralph Kimball writes, "the dimensional model is a predictable, standard framework. Report writers, query tools, and user interfaces can all make strong assumptions about the dimensional model to make the user interfaces more understandable and to make processing more efficient" (Kimball, 1997a, "Strengths of DM").

William Inmon argues that Kimball's "series of star schemas and multi-dimensional tables are brittle . . . [They] cannot change gracefully over time." He writes further that "this basic lack of flexibility is at the heart of the weakness of the star schema model as the basis of the data

Figure 5.8
Dimension Table

Acct Code	Account Name	Territory	Salesman	Region	Region Manager
1	Joe's Diner	10	P. Bantin	Great Lakes	C. Walters
2	Jake's Cafe	15	R. Lee	Mid-Atlantic	K. Walker
3	Village Deli	25	D. Kellams	Southwest	N. Mares
4	Uptown Cafe	50	B. Cook	Northeast	E. Bartheld

Source: *IBM Infomix Database Design and Implementation Guide.* "Building a Dimensional Data Model." Available: http://publib.boulder.ibm.com/infocenter/idshelp/v10/index.jsp?topic=/com.ibm.ddi.doc/ddi232.htm

warehouse" (Inmon's quotes on problems with dimensional tables can be found at Katherine Drewek, 2005). Inmon believes that the star schema structure will work fine within the smaller, more specialized data marts, but that for the larger, enterprise-wide data warehouses, the relational database design employing database management software is the best solution. Inmon concludes that this "should be no surprise since the DBMS technology the data warehouse runs on works the best with a relational database design" (Drewek, 2005).

Converting and Cleansing Data

The other primary operations undertaken during data integration can be categorized under the term data conversion. Part of the conversion focuses on mapping the source attributes and values to the data warehouse models. The other part of the conversion process deals with data cleansing or data scrubbing or a process of decomposing, reassembling, and redefining the data. Ralph Kimball identifies four essential steps in the data cleansing process (Kimball, 1996a, 1996b).

The first step is what he calls "elementizing" or parsing the data, a process which isolates data and applies structure to each data element. The second step is to standardize the elements, and the third step is to verify the consistency of the standardized elements and to uncover any mistakes in the content data. The last step is comparing or matching the standard values to other instances of that data element to ensure consistency.

The process of converting and cleaning data integrates dissimilar data, reconciles data definitions, standardizes names and values, establishes common access paths, codes data consistently, and reformats data. As a result, the data sets that are being merged into the data warehouse are more consistently and accurately defined. This work is typically undertaken using data conversion tools or software designed to automate the process of extracting data from heterogeneous sources, mapping the source data to target data, and generating the code to convert or manipulate the data.

DATA STAGING LAYER: DATA TRANSFORMATION

The other primary operation that occurs in the data staging layer is data transformation. The following activities typically occur in the transformation process.

- **Data is summarized and aggregated.**

  In previous sections of this chapter, we have discussed the issue of granularity of data or the level at which the data will be available in the data warehouse. In the data staging layer, these transformations of data tables are implemented. For example, numerous individual rows of data within a table can be summarized to create a profile or an aggregate computer record in which many different, detailed occurrences of operational data are combined into a single view or composite. A simple example is daily bank account balances aggregated into one record that provides the balance at the end of the month. Other types of data transformations that occur are taking the average of data elements or capturing only the most recent or oldest values of a series of transactions. There are a host of other types of aggregations and summaries that can be created depending on needs and requirements. Because of the creation of all these summaries and aggregations, numerous detailed transactions within the operational systems never make it into the data warehouse.

- **Database structures within the operational systems are altered by denormalizing or by adding data redundancy**
- **Tables that have data in common are merged**
- **Data is taken out of an existing table and placed in an additional table**
- **Data is partitioned**

  Given the high volume of data in the warehouse, partitioning of data is absolutely necessary. Partitioning refers to the breakup of tables of data with similar structures into separate physical units that can be handled independently and more efficiently by the system. A typical example is the partitioning of data within subject areas in the warehouse by date, organization units, function, or geographic region.

- **Data relationships are summarized in the warehouse**

  William Inmon writes that the "data relationships found in classical data modeling are for the operational environment. Those relationships assume that there is one and only one business rule underlying the relationship. . . . However, for a data warehouse there usually will be MANY business rules between tables of data . . . Thus the classical representation of relationships between tables as found in classical data modeling is inadequate for the data warehouse" (Inmon, 2000a: 8). To represent relationships between data and information in the warehouse, designers typically create an "artifact" or a snapshot in time that defines the part of the relationship that is most important to define and recreate in the warehouse. The creation of relationship artifacts is shown in figure 5.9. Typically this artifact only captures some of the key relationship data and, of course, only as it exists at one point in time. Consequently, a good deal of the logical relationship data created for the operational system is never captured in the data warehouse.

- **Data is deleted.** Some data in the staging layer is deleted because upon further review it was determined that this data would not likely be useful to decision makers.

Much of the data that enters the data warehouse is radically transformed. It is subjected to various degrees of aggregation and summarization, filtering, cleaning, subtracting from, adding to, combining

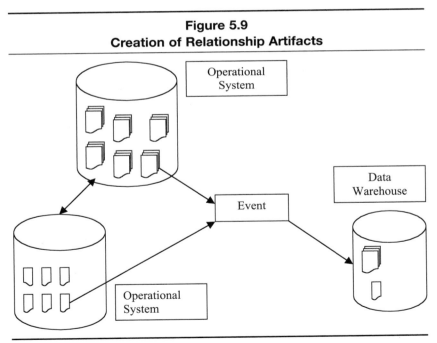

Figure 5.9
Creation of Relationship Artifacts

Source: Inmon, William. "Metadata in the Data Warehouse," 2000, p. 9. Available: www.inmoncif.com/library/whiteprs/earlywp/ttmeta.pdf. Reproduced with permission of William Inmon.

and breaking apart. Only a relatively small proportion of data in the typical data warehouse exists exactly as it appeared in the operational system (for more detailed descriptions of the summarizing process, see Inmon [2000a]).

METADATA LAYER

Metadata was not part of the first generation of data warehouses, in large part because the immediate need was to get these systems off the ground as soon as possible. As corporations matured in their understanding of the warehouse environment, metadata became a more important component. There are a number of reasons for the growing importance of metadata in the warehouse environment. Certainly one of the major needs was for more metadata to define the context of creation and use. Bill Inmon makes this point when he writes: "Because of data warehousing and its emphasis on information management over time, we are now embarking on the exciting new world of the understanding and management of context of information. We are but in our infancy as a professional in coming to grips with the context of information" (Inmon, 1995). Like archivists and records managers, users and designers of data warehouses have come to understand that in order to interpret and understand information over time, metadata on content and context is essential. In operational systems where many data elements are typically retained for a few weeks to 90 days, contextual metadata is not always critical. However, within the data warehouse where data is typically retained for 5–10 years, this metadata is essential.

Another reason for the emergence of metadata in data warehouses was the need to document the transformations to data that occur in the data staging layer. This metadata would address where the data originated and what happened to it before it entered the warehouse. A third need was for more management-oriented metadata on preservation, access, security, usage strategies, and implementation so IT could manage the information more effectively and efficiently over time. In short, data warehouse users and designers arrived at the conclusion that for systems that manage historical information it is essential to have metadata on the structure and management of the data and on the context of its creation and use.

Experts have typically identified the following categories of metadata which should be present in the data warehouse (for a detailed discussion of the types of metadata that should be included in the data warehouse, see Ralph Kimball [1998b]).

Business Metadata

This metadata is about adding information about the context of creation and use and about making meaning more explicit and defined. It includes the following categories of metadata:

- Definitions/descriptions of data
- Business descriptions of each source including metadata about the business processes
- Definitions of relationships between data and tables—at a minimum this would include descriptions of relationship artifacts, but ideally it would provide a more extensive definition of relationships, including tables participating in the data relationship, effective dates of the relationship, constraints in effect, cardinality, and description of the relationship.

Management and Audit Metadata

The literature on data warehouses identifies the following categories of management metadata:

- Owner/Stewardship Metadata: Who owns and administers the data?
- Access Metadata: Access rights and privileges, and legal requirements.
- Security Metadata: Settings for extract files, software, and metadata; security settings for data transmission (passwords, certificates, and so on); network security user privilege profiles, authentication certificates, and usage statistics; file usage in the data staging area including duration, volatility, and ownership; usage and access maps for data elements, tables, views, and reports.
- Query and Access Patterns Metadata: Data on tables being run; tables being accessed; fields being used; data on how long queries take to execute, and how the data is being used.
- Archives and Recovery Metadata: Data staging area archive logs, recovery procedures, and archive security settings.
- Aging/Purging Metadata: Descriptions of when this was done and the impact.

Metadata Documenting the Extract/Transformation/Loading (ETL) Process

- Mapping (from operational system to warehouse) Metadata: Identification of source field, attribute to attribute mapping, attribute conversions, encoding/reference table conversions, naming changes, algorithmic changes, and key changes
- Results of specific extract jobs including exact times, content, completeness, and the number of records inserted
- Data enhancement and mapping transformations metadata
- Data transform run-time logs, success summaries, and time stamps
- Data cleaning specifications
- Aggregate definitions and modification logs
- Summarization algorithms used in summarizing and calculating data

Technical System Metadata

This category includes:
- Basic description of table structure, keys of those tables, and the attributes and how they change over time
- Volumetrics metadata: Number of rows in the table, growth of the table, statistical profile of the table, and byte specifications for the table
- Reference tables/Encoded data
- Data model used to create the warehouse
- Relationship to other metadata stores such as the Data Dictionary
- DBMS system tables
- Partition settings
- Indexes
- View definitions
- Stored procedures and SQL administrative scripts

The advent of the modern data warehouses has given rise to the marriage of context and content of information. Users and designers of data warehouses have come to recognize that more than technical system metadata is required to make the information in the warehouse useful for analysis. They have realized that to be useful this historical information must be supported by contextual metadata documenting the processes of creation and use of the data and its transformation as it entered the warehouse from the operational system. Moreover, designers of warehouses have come to recognize the power of metadata in documenting the processes involved in managing the warehouse over time. Consequently, metadata management has emerged as an integral part of the data warehouse development process. It is no longer an afterthought as in the past. As the warehouse is designed and populated, the metadata is automatically collected. Slowly but surely the metadata requirements for data warehouses are beginning to resemble the set of metadata requirements established by archivists and records managers for recordkeeping systems.

DATA WAREHOUSES: FUTURE DEVELOPMENTS

Experts on warehouses who are closely monitoring the market and the trends have identified several likely areas where product development will occur. (For discussions on the future of data warehouses, see William Inmon's articles on the Corporate Information Factory [CIF]; Neil Raden and Ralph Kimball [2003]; Ralph Kimball [2000b]; and Ralph Kimball [2000a].)

Near Real-time Data Warehouses

The most anticipated development is the widespread development and use of near real-time data warehouses, which are also referred to as active data warehouses. Data warehouses have "evolved beyond a decision support enabler to the enterprise platform for making near-real-time business-critical decisions" (Brown, 2005: 2). They are being transformed from rather passive, off-line reporting structures that were disconnected from day-to-day business process into more active systems that are linked to real-time decision making and collaboration and are able to interact with operational systems. Data warehousing applications and online transaction applications are converging and becoming integrated systems.

One way this is being done is by updating the warehouse more frequently than once a day. Ultimately this could mean that every time data is added, deleted, or updated in the operational system the same change would occur simultaneously or in near-real-time in the data warehouse. This integration is also being achieved by increasing the access response times in the warehouse so that users can get answers to questions in seconds rather than minutes or hours. It also means extending access to the data warehouse to a larger number of concurrent users or processes at a level or degree of availability that matches those of the operational system. The result of all these transformations is a data warehouse application that can be used to drive real-time tactical and event-based decisions.

Wider Variety of More Sophisticated Tools

The trend of integrating more sophisticated analytical tools into the data warehouse will continue. Recent research by International Data Corp. found that the data warehousing tools market grew at a double-digit clip and generated enormous annual revenues. Across all segments, the data warehousing tools market grew by 11.3 percent and generated $9.6 billion in worldwide sales in 2005 (Vesset, 2005). The challenges for the future will be to make these tools not only more sophisticated in what they can achieve but also more user friendly for non-technical staff. This is particularly important in light of the trend toward real-time data warehouses that will be used by more and more staff for routine decision making. The inability of some of the analytical tools to be used by non-technical staff is one of the reasons Ralph Kimball believes that data mining will ultimately not be effective in the real-time data warehouse environment. Kimball argues that using data mining tools involves training and knowledge that only data mining experts possess. In his mind the typical end user will not be effective in using data mining tools in the warehouse for decision support, which in the end will undermine the strategy for creating warehouses that can be used to drive real-time business decisions (Kimball, 2002b).

Federated or Distributed Environments

As with other applications, integration of the data warehouse with other systems is a major priority. Some experts discuss this strategy in terms of a transition to a federated or a distributed information environment (Inmon, 2002). The architecture of a distributed data warehouse is shown in figure 5.10.

In a distributed or federated structure all internal business processes, external data sources, and the databases of suppliers and customers are all part of the enterprise data warehouse. One of the primary advantages to this strategy is that data from all systems undergoes transformation and cleansing before it enters the warehouse. The result is a uniformity and consistency of data no matter where it originated and an approximation of the goal of a "single version of the truth."

Figure 5.10
Architecture of a Distributed Data Warehouse

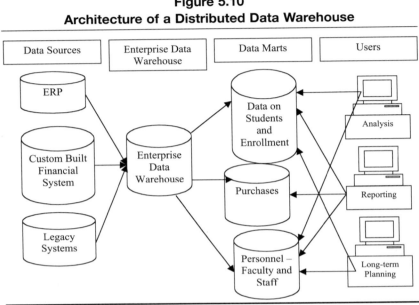

Source: Inmon, William. 2002. *Building the Data Warehouse.* 3rd edition. New York: John Wiley and Sons.

Tighter Integration with the World Wide Web

The Web is an ideal source for external data that would be useful in the data warehouse. The challenges are to ensure that this data and information is transformed, cleansed, converted, and integrated into the warehouse, and to develop strategies for determining the accuracy and quality of the information. There is also the issue of moving integrated data from the warehouse back into the enterprise's Web site. The data warehouse can also be an ideal source of information for the institution's Web based e-business environment. However, this strategy will only work if the information delivered to the Web site is accurate, complete, and arrives on time. Response times in particular have proven to be a major challenge for data warehouse designers seeking to incorporate information from the warehouse into the corporation's e-business Web site.

Incorporation of Unstructured Records into the Warehouse

It is by no means guaranteed that unstructured information will become a major component of the data warehouse. Content management systems are flourishing, and these systems are designed to manage this unstructured information. However, some new data warehouse systems are being designed to capture e-mail and other textual documents into the warehouse repository. Perhaps the primary challenge in implementing this strategy is determining how best to integrate this unstructured data into the structured environment based on fields and tables that exist within the warehouse. (For a vision of the next generation data warehouse, see William Inmon [2006].

DECISION SUPPORT SYSTEMS BASED ON THE DATA WAREHOUSE AS RECORDKEEPING SYSTEMS

A number of archivists and records managers have recounted this experience. They have gone to an IT manager to talk about recordkeeping systems. After a short description of the functionality of these systems, the IT manager responds: we have a data warehouse. Doesn't the warehouse meet your requirements for a recordkeeping system? To determine the answer to this question, let us review how well data warehouses meet the functional requirements for a recordkeeping system that were identified in chapter 2.

IMPORTANT QUESTIONS TO CONSIDER

Are records present in the data warehouse?

Yes, there are records in the data warehouse. A great deal of detailed, transactional data is transferred directly from the operational system to the warehouse. As related earlier, the warehouse is composed of snapshots of data captured in time, and these snapshots can represent the data created after the completion of a business event. In relational models, this data would be available in the tables that were created for the operational system. In dimensional models, this data would be available primarily in the fact tables. This being said, there are some major problems with the records in the warehouse.

- **Transformed:** As discussed earlier, most of the data in the warehouse has been changed in some fashion; this includes format and structure changes, summarizing, aggregating, filtering, cleaning and condensing, partitioning, and denormalizing of data. Many transactional records recorded in the operational system do not contain the same data or characteristics within the data warehouse. In many instances, these data warehouse records do not document the original transaction. They are no longer records or evidence of transactions or activities.
- **Selective:** Some data from the operational system is never transferred to the warehouse. The data warehouse is not meant to duplicate the operational system. As related earlier, the most typical strategy for extracting data is to capture from the operational system only those snapshots of data or tables that are considered useful for decision making. A strategy based on wholesale replication of data in the operational system is far less common, because as Inmon (2002) reminds designers such a strategy would increase dramatically the volume of data; it would impact significantly on the number of resources required to manage the system; and it would make the warehouse more difficult to use for high-level analysis and decision making. Wholesale replication of data in the warehouse would make it a different type of system; it would become more like a recordkeeping system than like an environment for decision support.
- **Frequency of capture:** Most systems do not capture data from the operational systems in real-time or as the event occurs. Most data warehouses capture the data on a daily or even a weekly schedule. Inmon (2002: 115–118) recommends that in most cases the capture schedule be managed according to "the wrinkle of time" concept, which states that "at least 24 hours should pass from the time the change is known to the operational environment until the change is reflected into the data warehouse." The reasons he gives for this are that if the warehouse attempts to capture changes in real-time or within several minutes or hours of changes, it will add tremendous cost and complexity to the system. For a recordkeeping system, delays of 24 hours or more in capturing snapshots is a definite problem. In that time period several changes might occur to that data or table which would never be captured.

- **Data Relationships Are Summarized:** As indicated earlier, relationships between tables, data, and records within the operational system are often simplified and summarized in the data warehouse, and consequently only a portion of the relationships between records may be represented.
- **Based on Relational Model**: Most data warehouse are constructed around the relational data, model, and as a result warehouses incorporate all the problems with managing records as data that were outlined in chapter 3.

Are records protected from unauthorized and undocumented alteration or deletion within the data warehouse?

Within well-managed data warehouses, the answer to this question is yes. One of the primary characteristics of a data warehouse is that data within the system is read-only. Snapshots of data within the warehouse are fixed in time and cannot be overwritten or updated. This is a dramatic difference from operational systems which are designed to provide the most current and accurate data, and where constant updates occur. Data integrity is one of the greatest shortcomings of operational systems as recordkeeping systems, but is perhaps the greatest strength of data warehouses in terms of their recordkeeping functionality.

The major problem in this area is the amount of time data is retained in the warehouse. The data is appraised on the basis of how long it is needed for decision making and planning, not in regard to the evidential and informational needs of users outside the enterprise. Consequently, few records in the warehouse have long-term or indefinite value; the life span of data in the warehouse is typically less than a decade (Inmon, 2002). The decisions on appraisal of data in the warehouse go back to the original design purposes of the system. It is a system created to support decision making and not to preserve historical records for other types of use.

Do data warehouses systematically preserve reliable records or complete, fully documented records?

As we have seen, one of the potential strengths of a data warehouse is the inclusion of a great deal of metadata for describing data and its management over time. Ideally, data warehouses should do a very good job documenting the creation, use, and management of data in the system.

However, there are problems to be aware of. One of these is the completeness of the metadata describing the context of creation. As I reviewed the literature on metadata in warehouses, I was struck by how little attention was still being given to the identification of business context metadata. Designers of data warehouses are only beginning to understand the value of contextual metadata. At this time, much more attention is devoted to describing structural and management metadata. Consequently, there is still a need for an archivist and records manager to help define business process related metadata.

This problem is compounded by the relative inability of the relational data model to identify the metadata in complex processes, and for data modelers to not spend enough time analyzing business processes, particularly at the transactional level. The result is a metadata model that is again incomplete in its description of the context of creation and use over time.

Does the data warehouse support a classification scheme for defining relationships between and among records?

One of the primary characteristics of the data warehouse is that data in the warehouse is organized and classified. Users require the creation of these classification schemes so that they can combine data in various ways to conduct their analyses. As result, data warehouses do provide the means to create or reconstruct relationships between data and records. This is definitely the strength of the data warehouse as recordkeeping system. Most often this scheme is based on subjects, such as customers or products. However, some data warehouses do organize the data around functions and business processes.

As with operational systems it would be much more useful to the archivist/records manager if the classification schemes were linked directly to business processes rather than subjects. For many archivists and records managers the lack of a direct relationship between data and business processes is a real deficiency, since strategies for managing electronic records are often based largely on initially linking records to the processes that created them.

Do data warehouses provide for the long-term preservation of records?

The data warehouse is viewed as a historical repository for data and information. Consequently, designers and managers of these systems are aware that they must keep the data alive over time. Most strategies, however, still focus on backing up systems according to a defined schedule and do not articulate a well-defined strategy for preserving records over time. The warehouse literature on "archiving" and preservation typically focuses on strategies for transferring older, less useful data, or the more detailed and voluminous transaction level data to off-line storage. For example, Inmon (2002) discusses a strategy for keeping two years' worth of data in the active, online warehouse and moving any data older than two years into alternate, less expensive storage. However, one does find the occasional mention of the need to migrate or convert data so that it will remain useable as hardware and software change. For example, Ralph Kimball discusses the warehouse and the preservation of data in regards to recent legislation such as Sarbanes-Oxley. In light of more rigorous requirements for preserving authentic and reliable records, Kimball advises warehouse designers to develop better recordkeeping strategies for managing archival copies of warehouse data (Kimball and Ross, 2004). So, certainly there is emerging a stronger recognition than in operational systems that the data in the warehouse must be managed and that measures must be taken to keep the historical data accessible over time.

This being said, this discussion has not reached the level of attention that would be required of a recordkeeping system. In large part this is a consequence of the data in the warehouse not being viewed as having indefinite or long-term value. As expressed earlier, data in the warehouse typically is viewed as having a life span of 5–10 years. In this time frame, one conversion of data would likely be required, and in some cases, the data would be readable even if nothing were done to it. Because of this time frame there is a certain lack of urgency or concern on preservation issues in the data warehouse literature.

Do data warehouses provide for the systematic retention and disposition of records?

As indicated above, data warehouse do capture records on a regular schedule, usually within 24–48 hour time frames. Data is deleted from the data warehouse as it is no longer useful to users. What is not clear is whether this data is deleted on a regular schedule, and how these decisions are made. I uncovered no real discussion in the literature on the need to create record schedules, or even discussions about defining what criteria will be used to make retention decisions related to specific types of records or business processes. Clearly the definition of a methodology for making document retention and disposal decisions is an area where the archivist and records manager can make a real contribution in the management of data warehouses. Critical issues to bring to the table would be the capture of some data on a more frequent timetable for recordkeeping or historical purposes, and the appraisal of data from a broader perspective that takes into account the needs of other users and researchers with broader evidential and informational needs. Of course, these arguments begin to run counter to the defined purpose of the data warehouse as a repository to support executives and mangers in making business decisions.

Do data warehouses provide for the long-term security of records?

Most data warehouses appear to have very robust security functionality. Users typically have read-only privileges, and the primary user community is well defined as executives and managers. However, a recent trend in data warehouse design has been to broaden or expand the community of users. As this user group grows, it will be imperative that the following issues be carefully addressed: a) Does the system control access to the records according to well-defined criteria? b) Are records linked to citations and references to laws, policies, and best practices that impose a requirement to control access to and use of a record? c) Are records linked to statements defining the terms under which the record may be accessed and used? d) Does the system identify who accessed and used the record, and when this action occurred?

Do data warehouses provide for the long-term access to records?

Access to data and tools for manipulating data in the warehouse are the greatest strengths of the systems. The tools for retrieving and analyzing data from the warehouse are plentiful and are becoming more and more sophisticated. Again, the primary challenge relating to access will be to ensure that managers with limited technical knowledge can use these sophisticated tools.

Summary

Data warehouses fulfill many of the requirements of a recordkeeping system. Most importantly, data and records in the repository are inviolate and secure and are relatively well documented by various types of metadata. However, data warehouses have one fatal flaw in regard to recordkeeping: they do not routinely and systematically capture authentic records. In large part this deficiency derives, as it always does, from the design objectives of the data warehouse. The primary design feature of the data warehouse is to select data that supports decision making and to integrate and transform the data so that it can be used for analysis. To achieve these objectives, data warehouse designers selectively capture data and records from the operational systems based on the potential and known value of the information for decision makers, and they transform the data in various ways in an attempt to create more integrated, consistent, and useable information. These activities run counter to the primary goal of a recordkeeping system which is to capture and manage authentic records of business processes. This difference is so basic and so fundamental that one can only conclude that data warehouses are not viable recordkeeping systems.

MAKING DATA WAREHOUSES BETTER RECORDKEEPING SYSTEMS

As with TPS we can undertake a number of activities that will make data warehouses more viable recordkeeping systems. We can attempt to add archivists and records managers to the system design and data management teams; we can incorporate into the database more metadata that describes the data in relation to business processes; we can create an automated system for applying retention and disposition decisions; and we can develop a preservation strategy for the warehouse. All of these changes will make a positive difference in the management and preservation of data as records.

Ultimately, however, these changes will have little effect unless the primary difference between the two systems—the ability to capture and manage authentic records of all primary business processes—is addressed. There are three ways to achieve this: 1) add more detailed transactional data to the warehouse; 2) capture this data in real-time as changes occur in the operational system; and 3) ensure that this detailed data is not transformed or changed as it moves from the operational system to the warehouse.

As discussed earlier in this chapter, there is a trend to adding more detailed transactional data to the data warehouse. Ralph Kimball in particular argues for the inclusion of more detailed transactional data to allow users to drill down to the transactional level if necessary. This argument is supported by the fact that storage space is becoming cheaper and more accessible and that decision support tools for analyzing data are becoming more sophisticated and better able to analyze massive amounts of data. As documented earlier, there is also a trend to create real-time data warehouses that capture operational data as changes occur. Data warehouses are getting away from being passive, offline, after-the-fact reporting structures that are disconnected from business processes, and are becoming linked to real-time decision making and collaboration. Both of these changes definitely make the data warehouse a more effective recordkeeping system; as a result of these transformations the warehouse would capture more detailed transactional records and more updates and revisions as they occur.

However, the third requirement of ensuring that data is not changed or transformed as it enters the warehouse will be much more difficult to achieve in my estimation because it runs counter to the essential design qualities of the data warehouse. The key to the value of the data warehouse as a tool for decision makers is its ability to provide consistent, integrated data. To achieve this means most data must undergo various types of transformations. Now certainly there are some transformations that may not impact on authenticity issues, such as some reformatting. However most transformations of data entering the warehouse, such as changing values or aggregating, summarizing, or merging data, will result in the creation of a new record that does not accurately reflect the original transaction as it was recorded in the operational system. One way around this problem is to convince designers that the data warehouses can serve two functions: as an integrated resource to decision support information and as a recordkeeping system preserving authentic records. To achieve these goals the warehouse will have to contain two types of data: detailed transaction-level data that has not been transformed or changed in any way to serve the recordkeeping function, and selected detailed and summary data that has been transformed and integrated to serve the decision support function. It appears to me that there is some chance of achieving this goal using Kimball's dimensional model that includes two types of fact tables: a transaction-level fact table and a second, separate snapshot table. However, one can argue that a warehouse based on Kimball's design would be immense in size and would require very significant resources to manage over time.

Ultimately, it is unlikely that transforming the data warehouse by adding recordkeeping functionality will work. Theoretically, it is possible, but there are many factors working against it. In particular the strategy subverts and undermines the primary goals of the warehouse. Although the recordkeeping and warehouse systems share much in common and in some ways are converging even more, they are different at the most fundamental level. Recordkeeping systems capture and manage authentic records; data warehouses capture and manage integrated information that is useful for decision support.

A better solution than transforming the data warehouse into a recordkeeping system is to implement strategies for making the content management systems a better recordkeeping environment, for several reasons:

- Recordkeeping requirements have already been incorporated into many content management systems.
- Content management systems are presently the most integrated environments within most businesses, and most enterprises are investing a great deal of money into making these systems the focal point of its information management strategy.
- Content management systems handle all types of information, structured and unstructured; data warehouse are still very focused on managing structured data.
- The majority of records created in the enterprise are unstructured records, and many would argue that most archival records are unstructured as well. Consequently focusing recordkeeping strategies on content management systems will result in more "bang for the buck."

Although the archivist and records manager may not be able to transform data warehouses into recordkeeping systems, this does not mean the professions should ignore these systems and the staff that manage them. One of the best strategies the archivist and records manager can employ is to develop strong partnerships with personnel who manage the warehouse. Because warehouses share so many design features with recordkeeping systems, data warehouse personnel can be ideal partners for the archivist and records manager. Both professional groups share a concern for historical data, metadata that defines information, useful access tools, solutions to capture data from operational systems, and ultimately for managing the repository over time. Data warehouse personnel can be advocates for recordkeeping systems, and archivists and records managers are well advised to seek out and aggressively develop working partnerships with them.

REFERENCES

Brown, Douglas. 2005. "Teradata Active System Management: High-Level Architectural Overview." Available: www.teradata.com/t/pdf.aspx?a=83673&b=145622

Drewek, Katherine. 2005. "Data Warehouse: Similarities and Differences of Inmon and Kimball." Available: www.b-eye-network.com/blogs/drewek/archives/2005/03/data_warehouse_3.php

Holsapple, Clyde, and Andrew Whinston. 1996. *Decision Support Systems: A Knowledge-Based Approach*. Minneapolis/St. Paul, MN: West Publishing.

IBM Informix Database Design and Implementation Guide, Version 10.0/8.5, 2004. Available: http://publib.boulder.ibm.com/infocenter/idshelp/v10/index.jsp?topic=/com.ibm.ddi.doc/ddi232.htm

Imhoff, Claudia. 2005. "A New Paradigm for Enterprise Business Intelligence." Available: www.b-eye-network.com/view/1705

Inmon, William. 1995. "Data Warehouse and Contextual Data: Pioneering a New Dimension." Available: www.inmoncif.com/view/30

Inmon, William. no date. "The DSS Environment: Data Warehouse, Data Mart, and Data Mining." Available: www.inmoncif.com/view/23

Inmon, William. 1998a. "Data Mart Does Not Equal Data Warehouse." *DM Review* (May). Available: www.dmreview.com/article_sub.cfm?articleId=608

Inmon, William. 1998b. "The Operational Data Store: Designing the Operational Data Store" *DM Review* (July). Available: www.dmreview.com/article_sub.cfm?articleId=469

Inmon, William. 2000a. "Creating the Data Warehouse Data Model from the Corporate Data Model." Available: www.inmoncif.com/registration/whitepapers/ttdwdmod-1.pdf

Inmon, William. 2000b. "Snapshots in the Data Warehouse." Available: www.inmoncif.com/registration/whitepapers/ttsnap-1.pdf

Inmon, William. 2002. *Building the Data Warehouse*. 3rd ed. New York: John Wiley and Sons.

Inmon, William. 2006. "DW 2.0 – The Architecture for the Next Generation of Data Warehouse." Available: http://inmoncif.com/home/

Inmon, William. "Corporate Information Factory (CIF)." Available: www.dmforum.org/portal/downloads.asp?keywords=bill+inmon&do_search=1

Kelly, Sean. 1994. *Data Warehousing. The Route to Mass Customisation*. Chicester, UK: John Wiley and Sons.

Kimball, Ralph. 1995. "Is E-R Modeling Hazardous to Your Health?" Data Warehouse Architect. *DBMS* (October). Available: www.dbmsmag.com/9510d05.html

Kimball, Ralph. 1996a. "Mastering Data Extraction." Data Warehouse Architect. *DBMS* (June). Available: www.dbmsmag.com/9606d05.html

Kimball, Ralph. 1996b. "Dealing with Dirty Data." Data Warehouse Architect. *DBMS* (September). Available: www.dbmsmag.com/9609d14.html

Kimball, Ralph. 1997a. "A Dimensional Modeling Manifesto" (August). Available: www.dbmsmag.com/9708d15.html

Kimball, Ralph. 1997b. "Relocating the ODS. Moving the Operational Data Store Will Solve a Number of Problems" (December). Available: www.dbmsmag.com/9712d05.html

Kimball, Ralph. 1998a. "The Operational Data Warehouse. It Needs Both a Transaction Version of Data and a Periodic Snapshot Version of Data." Data Warehouse Architect. *DBMS* (January). Available: www.dbmsmag.com/9801d05.html

Kimball, Ralph. 1998b. "Meta Meta Data Data." Data Warehouse Architect. *DBMS* (March). Available: www.dbmsmag.com/9803d05.html

Kimball, Ralph. 2000a. "Millennium Ahead" (January 1). Available: www.intelligententerprise.com/000101/webhouse.jhtml

Kimball, Ralph. 2000b. "ERP Vendors: Bring Down Those Walls" (June 26). Available: www.intelligententerprise.com/000626/webhouse.jhtml

Kimball, Ralph, 2000c. "There are no Guaratees"; Available at: http://209.85.165.104/search?q=cache:jSyKj0NWYZIJ:www.intelligententerprise.com/000801/webhouse.jhtml+kimball+there+are+no+guarantees&hl=en&gl=us&strip=1

Kimball, Ralph. 2002a. "Divide and Conquer." Available: www.intelligententerprise.com/021030/517warehouse1_1.jhtml
(For additional information on Kimball's concept of dimensional modeling, see his white papers listed under the section "Dimensional Modeling Overview" at: www.decisionone.co.uk/resources/KimballArticles.htm)

Kimball, Ralph. 2002b. "Two Powerful Ideas" (September 17). Available: www.intelligententerprise.com/print_article_flat.jhtml?article=/020917/515warehouse1_1.jhtml

Kimball, Ralph, and Margy Ross. 2004. "Surrounding ETL Requirements" (November 13). Available: www.intelligententerprise.com/showArticle.jhtml?articleID=51201335

Laudon, Kenneth, and Jane Laudon. 2004. *Essentials of Management Information Systems*. 6th ed. Upper Saddle River, NJ: Prentice Hall.

Marakas, George M. 1999. *Decision Support Systems in the 21st Century*. Upper Saddle River, NJ: Prentice Hall.

Marakas, George M. 2003. *Modern Data Warehousing, Mining, and Visualization. Core Concepts.* Upper Saddle River, NJ: Prentice Hall.

Montgomery, Dan. 2000. "Data Warehousing Horizons: A DW Approach for the New Millennium, Part 2." *DM Review* (February). Available: www.dmreview.com/article_sub.cfm?articleID=1842

Oracle. "Unified Business Intelligence Meets the Needs of 21st Century Business." Available: www.oracle.com/solutions/business_intelligence/campaigns/searchcio_bi_wp.pdf

Poe, Vidette, Patricia Klauer, and Stephen Brobst. 1998. *Building a Data Warehouse for Decision Support.* Upper Saddle River, NJ: Prentice Hall.

Power, Daniel J. 2002. *Decision Support Systems. Concepts and Resources for Managers.* Westport, CT: Quorum Books.

Raden, Neil, and Ralph Kimball. 2003. "Real Time: Get Real, Part I and II" (June 30). Available: www.intelligententerprise.com/030630/611warehouse1_1.jhtml

SAS BI product Web site. Available: www.sas.com/technologies/bi/

Turban, E. 1995. *Decision Support and Expert Systems: Management Support Systems.* Englewood Cliffs, NJ: Prentice Hall.

Vesset, Dan. 2005. "Worldwide Data Warehousing Tools. 2005 Vendor Shares." IDC. Available: www.sas.com/news/analysts/icd_dwtools_0906.pdf.

Whitten, Jeffrey, and Lonnie Bentley. 2005. *Systems Analysis and Design Methods.* 7th ed. New York: McGraw-Hill/Irwin.

Williams, Brian, Stacey Sawyer, and Sarah Hutchinson. 2006. *Using Information Technology.* 7th ed. New York: McGraw-Hill.

6

E-mail Management

"E-mail has quickly become a substitute for telephonic and printed communications, as well as a substitute for direct oral communications. However, if e-mail has become an indispensable tool in the workplace, it has also become the 'digital smoking gun' in more and more lawsuits."

— Hewlett-Packard, 2000: 6

Not only has the volume of e-mail grown tremendously, but so too has the growing use of e-mail in critical and highly sensitive business processes and transactions, such as litigation and contract negotiations. A 2003 survey by Kahn Consultants uncovered the following types of uses by survey participants (Kahn and Blair 2003, 4):

93 percent using e-mail to answer inquiries from customers
84 percent using it to discuss business strategy
71 percent using it to negotiate contracts
69 percent using it to exchange invoices and payment information
65 percent using it to exchange confidential or sensitive information
56 percent using it to discuss human resource (HR) issues
44 percent using it to file records with official bodies
38 percent using it to respond to regulators
23 percent using it to respond to litigation

In 2005, Kahn replicated the survey and found an increase in all categories of use since the last survey, with the greatest gains in responding to litigation at 34 percent (up 42 percent) and responding to regulators 47 percent (up 24 percent). The median number of messages per day was 50, with 90 percent of that number business related (Kahn Consulting 2005, 11).

However, as e-mail has emerged as the preferred means for doing business, it has also become the "Black Hole," or the "digital smoking gun" in more and more lawsuits.

LEGAL CASES INVOLVING E-MAIL

Over the past decade there has been an astounding increase in litigation involving electronic records and particularly e-mail. For example, 69 percent of respondents to a 2004 survey by the Ferris Research User Panel stated that their organizations had been required to produce e-mail for some legal or regulatory investigation, and 42 percent responded that it was very likely that they would need to produce an e-mail message in the future for a formal court proceeding. Unfortunately, in this same Ferris Survey, 26 percent of respondents believed that it was "very likely" that their organization could not produce an e-mail in the future for a legal proceeding, and 41 percent of respondents went on to say that it was "very likely" that some e-mail had been deleted before its official retention had been completed (Ferris Research 2004, figures 10, 11, 12, 13). These survey results strongly suggest that organizations are not allocating sufficient resources into managing what they know to be a growing and vital business resource. Kahn Consulting (2005: 2) concluded: "Risk management issues and compliance failures persist, in large part due to a gap between the implementation of new technologies and organizations' management of them through formal directives and training."

Not only is e-mail becoming a target in litigation, it has also been the subject of many new government regulations and laws. These laws focus on privacy issues, records retention, oversight and monitoring for compliance, and recovery or discovery of information in response to litigation or court orders. Among public businesses this has resulted in the creation at an unprecedented level of formal policies and procedures for managing e-mail and records and for the creation of recordkeeping systems. To better understand the legal issues and the trends involving e-mail, it is instructive to review some of the court cases over the past decade involving e-mail. Because all the important record laws relate to electronic records in general and not just e-mail, the laws as they pertain to e-mail will be discussed in chapter 7.

ARMSTRONG V. EOP OR THE "PROFS" CASE, 1989–1993

The PROFS case was one of the most important early legal cases involving the management of e-mail and the status of e-mail as an official record. On January 19, 1989, a group of private citizens and public interest organizations sued the Executive Office to the President (EOP) to prevent the imminent erasure of the White House electronic mail backup tapes. The case became known as Armstrong v. EOP, after Scott Armstrong, the lead plaintiff and director of the National Security Archives. It was often also called the PROFS case, which was a reference to the White House electronic mail system called the Professional Office System (PROFS). The case ran from 1989 to 1993. However, the issues in the case can legitimately be said to extend to 1999 with the resolution of the so-called Carlin case, which is discussed next (Bearman, 1993: 118–44; Wallace, 1998).

At the heart of the PROFS case were the assertions by the plaintiffs that e-mail produced on the system could be an official government record and that the electronic e-mail record should not be considered as merely an extra and unnecessary copy of the official e-mail record preserved on paper. The plaintiffs argued that the paper copies did not necessarily capture all of the essential metadata associated with the e-mail message, such as identities of sender and recipient, date and time of receipt, and various usage statistics. They argued that the electronic version of the mail message was a record in its own right and needed to be managed according to the Federal Records Act. The defendants, on the other hand, argued that they were within their legal rights to designate the PROFS systems as a communication mechanism and not as a recordkeeping system for preserving electronic versions of e-mail. The defendants claimed that when paper copies were made, all data on the screen was reproduced and that was sufficient to describe the record.

On January 7, 1993, Judge Richey ruled that the defendants had violated the Federal Record Act by improperly destroying federal records. Richey further ruled that the electronic versions were not simply duplicates of paper printouts because they contained additional metadata not found in the paper copies. Richey went on to state that the electronic versions of mail that qualified as federal records must be retained, regardless of whether or not a paper copy was made. Finally, Richey ruled the Archivist of the United States had failed to fulfill his statutory duties as outlined in the Federal Record Act (FRA), and that the Archivist must take immediate action to preserve the electronic e-mail records and to establish guidelines for managing e-mail. On August 13, 1993, the U.S. Court of Appeals for the District of Columbia Circuit affirmed Judge Richey's January 1993 decision that the defendants' actions were in violation of FRA, and that paper printouts of electronic versions of records were not acceptable substitutes because they typically excluded essential contextual information about the e-mail message. The final rule contained the following stipulations:

- Agencies had to train staff on how to distinguish records from non-records, and on how to transfer electronic mail messages into an electronic or paper-based recordkeeping system.
- Agencies had to preserve essential transmission data (identification of sender and recipients, and essential dates) along with the e-mail message.
- Agencies were specifically instructed to ensure that e-mail be stored in a system that permitted easy retrieval of the messages in a useable format.
- The final rule also forbade the destruction of electronic versions of e-mail messages, whether they were records or not, without "prior disposition authority from NARA." This permission to destroy could be given if the e-mail message transferred to the electronic or paper-based recordkeeping system was an identical version of the original electronic record (Public Citizen, 2000a).

PUBLIC CITIZEN V. JOHN CARLIN (ARCHIVIST OF THE UNITED STATES), 1996–1999

On August 28, 1995, NARA published a notice of final rulemaking for amendments to the General Records Schedules (GRS) 20. Unlike the earlier version of GRS 20, the amended GRS 20 explicitly addressed the management of e-mail by stating that e-mail could be deleted after it had been copied to a paper or electronic recordkeeping system. The appearance of the amended version of GRS 20 resulted in a lawsuit in December 1996, initiated by roughly the same group of plaintiffs who had pursued the PROFS case. Known as Public Citizen v. John Carlin (Archivist of the United States), the plaintiffs alleged that

GRS 20 violated the Federal Records Act by authorizing the destruction of e-mail without regard to its purpose or content. They asserted that the conversion of the e-mail to paper and deleting the electronic record resulted in the loss of vital contextual and structural metadata essential to understanding and interpreting the e-mail message and in a much reduced ability to search, manipulate, and index the records.

On October 22, 1997, U.S. District Judge Paul Friedman ruled against the government and declared GRS 20 to be "null and void." In making this decision, Judge Friedman argued that in the amended GRS 20 the Archivist of the United States had illegally abdicated to the various government agencies the right to select and preserve records with administrative, legal, and research value. Friedman also agreed with the plaintiffs' argument that electronic records "do not become valueless duplicates or lose their character as 'program records' once they have been printed on paper; rather, they retain features unique to their medium" (Public Citizen v. John Carlin ruling, 2000b).

In December 1997, the government filed an appeal challenging Friedman's order. On August 6, 1999, the Court of Appeals for the District of Columbia Circuit reversed Judge Friedman's decision and upheld the Archivist's rule. The plaintiffs then filed a petition asking the Supreme Court to review the Court of Appeals decision, but the Court refused to hear the case.

LESSONS LEARNED FROM PROFS AND CARLIN CASES

1. These cases firmly established that e-mail messages can be federal records. The PROFS case was the first high profile legal case that established the record qualities of e-mail. This principle has now been widely accepted throughout society.

2. These cases led to the rejection of the government argument that electronic copies are convenience copies if the messages are maintained in paper format. The courts agreed that the ability to manipulate data in the electronic system and to maintain detailed metadata about the context of record creation is not typically available in the paper copy. The courts argued that if agencies do want to convert the electronic e-mail record to paper they must capture the essential contextual metadata along with the content.

3. These cases established the principle that e-mail cannot be appraised as a single series based on format. Instead one must determine the value of e-mail as a record by analyzing the function and content of the e-mail, just as it is done for other types of records.
4. Finally, these cases make clear that business related e-mail must be managed in a recordkeeping system. This system was not yet specifically defined, but some of its functionality was expressed. The court specified that the records must be preserved, well documented and described, and be accessible and useable.

All of these points were made by NARA in its 2006 directive 1234.24, "Standards for Managing Electronic Mail Records." In this document agencies are instructed to "consider the following criteria when developing procedures for the maintenance of electronic mail records in appropriate recordkeeping systems, regardless of format.

(1) Recordkeeping systems that include electronic mail messages must:

(i) Provide for the grouping of related records into classifications according to the nature of the business purposes the records serve;

(ii) Permit easy and timely retrieval of both individual records and files or other groupings of related records;

(iii) Retain the records in a usable format for their required retention period as specified by a NARA-approved records schedule;

(iv) Be accessible by individuals who have a business need for information in the system;

(v) Preserve the transmission and receipt data specified in agency instructions" (NARA 1234.24, 2006).

COURT CASES INVOLVING DISCOVERY AND PRESERVATION OF E-MAIL

In the last decade, the major court cases involving e-mail have revolved around the concepts of discovery and the preservation or "spoliation" of e-mail records. Legal discovery is "the act or process of finding or learning something that was previously unknown. It is the compulsory disclosure, at a party's request, of information that relates to the litigation" (Gartner Group, 2005). Forrester Research defines electronic discovery as the "process of collecting, preparing, reviewing, formatting, and producing enterprise content that may exist in either paper or digital form in response to internal, litigation, or regulatory requests" (Forrester, 2006). E-mail as a discoverable source has been an issue of debate, but as these court cases make clear, e-mail is without doubt a record that can and will be included in discovery motions.

Spoliation is another legal term that has been defined as "the destruction or significant alteration of evidence, or the failure to preserve property for another's use as evidence, in pending or future litigation" (Ballon, 1999). Spoliation of evidence can occur as a result of intentional or negligent destruction or failure to preserve records, concealment of evidence, and alteration of the record or of data.

Let us look at the more prominent legal cases involving e-mail listed and described in chronological order. (A source for brief descriptions of many of these court cases can be found at Richard Best, *Electronic Discovery of Electronic Data*, 2006.)

LINNEN V. A.H. ROBINS CO., 1999

In this case, the defendants failed to preserve e-mails and produce data as ordered by the court. Consequently, the court sanctioned the defendants for their actions and allowed spoliation inference to be given to the jury. As part of its decision, the court stated that a "discovery request aimed at the production of records retained in some electronic form is no different, in principle, from a request for documents contained in an office file cabinet. While the reality of the situation may require a different approach and more sophisticated equipment than a photocopier, there is nothing about the technological aspects involved which renders documents stored in an electronic media 'undiscoverable'" (Berkman Center, n.d.: "Linnen v. Robins").

KAUFMAN V. KINKO'S INC., 2002

In this case, the plaintiffs requested certain pertinent e-mail messages be retrieved from the defendants' computer back-up system. The defendants argued that the benefits of producing the e-mails did not justify the high costs of retrieval. The court did not agree with the defendants' argument and stated: "Upon installing a data storage system, it must be assumed that at some point in the future one may need to retrieve the information previously stored. That there may be deficiencies in the retrieval system . . . cannot be sufficient to defeat an otherwise good faith request to examine the relevant information" (LegisDiscovery, n.d.: "Case Law: Production of Data").

LANDMARK LEGAL FOUNDATION V. ENVIRONMENTAL PROTECTION AGENCY, 2003

In this case, the plaintiffs requested the court to enter a preliminary injunction prohibiting the EPA from destroying, removing, or tampering with potentially pertinent e-mails and other records. The court granted the motion and issued an injunction. Despite the court's order, the hard drives of several EPA officials were reformatted, e-mail back-up tapes were erased and reused, and e-mails were deleted. The court found the EPA in contempt and ordered them to reimburse the plaintiffs for attorney's fees and costs (a summary of this case is available at LegisDiscovery, "Case Law: Sanctions").

METROPOLITAN OPERA ASSOC., INC. V. LOCAL 100, 2003

In a labor dispute, the plaintiffs alleged that the defendants had failed to produce pertinent e-mail and other electronic documents despite multiple discovery requests. In its restatement of the facts, the court stated that it "found evidence of willful intent to withhold or conceal information. With regard to other requested documents, the court concluded that, at the very least, defense counsel's efforts to coordinate and carry out a plan to locate, review and produce relevant documents was insufficient to meet the requirements of the discovery rules." The court also provided guidance on what type of plan should have been in place to meet discovery obligations. This plan would include: "a reasonable procedure to distribute discovery requests to all employees and agents of the defendant potentially possessing responsive information, and to account for the collection and subsequent production of the information to plaintiffs; a method for explaining to their client what types of information would be relevant and responsive to discovery requests; an inquiry into the client's document retention or filing systems, and implementation of a systematic procedure for document production or for retention of documents, including electronic documents; and proper supervision of all elements of discovery that were to be carried out by non-legal personnel" (LexisNexis Applied Discovery, 2003). Consequently the court found sufficient evidence for a ruling of willful intent to withhold or conceal information, and granted the motion for severe sanctions. (For a transcription and summary of the case, see Metropolitan Opera case reference.)

THOMPSON V. UNITED STATES, 2003

In this case the plaintiffs requested that the defendants produce e-mail and other electronic records pertinent to the case. When the defendants failed to produce these records, the plaintiffs filed a motion seeking sanctions. The court ordered the defendants to produce the e-mails if they existed, but the defendants repeatedly announced that no more e-mails existed. Long after the discovery cutoff date, the defendants suddenly announced that they had discovered 80,000 e-mails, at which point the court issued a number of negative rulings against the defendants including the order that "if, at trial, the evidence revealed additional information regarding the non-production of e-mail, the plaintiffs were free to make a motion to the court that the failure to produce e-mail records as ordered by this court constituted a contempt of court" (LegisDiscovery, n.d.: "Case Law: Sanctions").

WIGINTON V. ELLIS, 2003

Two days after filing a sexual harassment class action suit, plaintiffs' counsel sent the defendants a letter requesting that all electronic materials, including e-mails, that were relevant to the lawsuit be retained. Upon receipt of this letter, the defendants sent one e-mail to their employees regarding the request, but continued to follow the company's normal document retention and destruction policies until several months later when the court entered a hold order. Because e-mail system back-up tapes were destroyed, the plaintiffs sought a motion for spoliation sanctions. The court found that the defendants had a duty to preserve relevant electronic documents that were likely to be the subject of discovery requests and had been provided with a request to retain and produce these records. However, because the extent of the lost records could not be ascertained, the court denied the plaintiffs' motion for sanctions (for summaries of the case, see the Wiginton case reference).

ZUBULAKE VS. UBS WARBURG, 2003–2005

These trials are generally considered the first definitive cases in the U.S. on a wide range of electronic discovery issues. In this case, Laura Zubulake sued her employer UBS Warburg for wrongful termination based on gender discrimination. As part of the suit, Zubulake sought the release of e-mails she sent to and received from UBS Warburg personnel. In response to this initial request for records, the defendant produced 350 pages of documents, including approximately 100 pages of e-mail. However, Zubulake claimed there was more pertinent e-mail, including hundreds of messages she had written. As result of this assertion, the court ordered the defendants to produce, at their own expense, all pertinent e-mails stored on the company's optical disks, active servers, and back-up tapes. In response to this order, UBS Warburg restored 16 back-up tapes. However, during this process it was discovered that certain back-up tapes were missing and that e-mails had been deleted. Consequently, the plaintiffs moved for evidentiary and monetary sanctions against the defendants for its failure to preserve the missing tapes and e-mails. The court did not grant the motion for sanctions, but it did assert that the defendants had a duty to preserve the missing evidence, since they should have known that the e-mails may be relevant to future litigation. The court also found that the defendants failed to comply with their own retention policy, which would have preserved the missing evidence. In the fifth and last motion, Zubulake contended that UBS Warburg had prejudiced her case by producing recovered e-mails long after the initial document requests and after two years had still not produced some of the pertinent e-mails.

Zubulake requested sanctions in the form of an adverse inference jury instruction, and this time the court agreed. Determining that the employer had willfully deleted relevant e-mails contrary to court orders, the court granted the motion for sanctions and also ordered the employer to pay costs. The jury ultimately found UBS Warburg guilty of employment discrimination and awarded Zubulake $29 million dollars in damages. In her concluding remarks Judge Shira Scheindlin stated that "counsel has a duty to effectively communicate to her client its discovery obligations so that all relevant information is discovered, retained, and produced. In other words, legal counsel (and presumably other agents involved in the management and use of records) must not play a passive role in the process but must take 'affirmative steps' to ensure that evidence is preserved." Scheindlin outlined the following "reasonable steps" that should be taken by legal counsel:

- "Becoming fully familiar with her client's document retention practices, as well as the client's data retention architecture"
- Identifying "key players" and "sources of discoverable information"
- Putting "in place a litigation hold and making that known to all relevant employees by communicating with them directly"
- Repeating the litigation hold instructions "regularly"
- "Monitoring the compliance so that all sources of discoverable information are identified and retained on a continuing basis"
- "Calling for employees to produce copies of relevant electronic evidence"
- "Arranging for the segregation and safeguarding of any archival media (e.g., back-up tapes) that [the client] has a duty to preserve."

She concluded by stating that if "a party acts contrary to counsel's instructions or to a court's order, it acts at its own peril" (Fulcrum Inquiry, 2004). (For transcriptions and summaries of the case, see Zubulake case reference.)

COLEMAN HOLDINGS VS. MORGAN STANLEY AND CO., 2003–2005

In this case, investor Ron Perelman sued Morgan Stanley in Florida for fraud in a 1998 investment deal. The company was ordered in May 2003 to produce relevant documentation, including e-mails, bearing on the deal. Morgan Stanley submitted more than 8,000 pages of documents, but Coleman asserted that these records only included a handful of the many e-mails that had been exchanged. Consequently in October 2003, Coleman served a motion to compel Morgan Stanley to produce the e-mail messages. Morgan Stanley responded that Coleman was demanding back-up system restoration efforts that would "cost at least hundreds of thousands of dollars and require several months to complete." Based upon an agreement between the parties, the court entered an order in April 2004, under which Morgan Stanley was required to search the oldest backup tapes for e-mail with certain Morgan Stanley employees and to review e-mail during a specific time period using specified search terms. In May 2004, Morgan Stanley produced an additional 1300 pages of e-mail, and in June 2004, a Morgan Stanley technology executive signed a court document certifying that he had handed over all e-mails the firm had agreed to produce. However, in November 2004, outside counsel for Morgan Stanley disclosed that Morgan Stanley had discovered additional e-mail back-up tapes. He estimated that restoration of the additional back-up tapes would be completed at the end of January and promised that the searches required in the previous order would be re-run. In a January 21, 2005, letter, Morgan Stanley's counsel explained there would again be delays in producing the e-mail because of problems in formatting documents and identifying many of the tapes. At a February 2005 hearing, Morgan Stanley officials told the judge that even more back-up tapes had been found and that software flaws were preventing complete searches of the tapes. On March 1, 2005, the court issued an adverse inference order based on discovery abuses. In outlining these abuses, the court noted that Morgan Stanley "has deliberately and contumaciously violated numerous discovery orders" (Extra LEXIS, 2005). The court instructed the jury that the defendants were in violation of federal recordkeeping requirements, and had falsely certified its compliance with the court's e-mail production directives. The plaintiffs received damages totally 1.4 billion dollars. However in 2007, Florida's 4th District Court of Appeal overturned this decision. (For the transcript and summaries of the case, see the Coleman Holdings case reference.)

INVISION MEDIA COMMUNICATIONS, INC. V. FEDERAL INS. CO., 2004

In an action for breach of an insurance contract, the defendants requested e-mail messages sent by the plaintiffs during specific time periods. The plaintiffs claimed that the e-mails could not be produced because according to company policy the e-mails were only preserved for a two week period. Eventually the plaintiffs' claim regarding deletion was proven false, and the court awarded the defendants legal costs and attorneys' fees, noting that "the plaintiff has disregarded its discovery obligations, made misleading statements regarding the existence and location of relevant evidence, and/or failed to make reasonable inquiries into matters pertinent to the pretrial discovery phase of this litigation" (LegisDiscovery, n.d.: "Case Law: Sanctions").

MASTERCARD INTERN., INC. V. MOULTON, 2004

In the case, the plaintiffs sought spoliation sanctions against the defendants for failing to produce all e-mails relating to the case. In response, the defendants admitted that they failed to retain four months' worth of e-mails sent and received after the plaintiffs filed the lawsuit. However, the defendants argued that e-mail had been automatically destroyed by the computer system in the normal course of business. The court rejected this argument and sanctioned the defendants by granting an adverse inference jury instruction. In its summation the court stated that "in this case, defendants' failure to preserve the e-mails plainly constituted at least gross negligence . . . They appear simply to have persevered in their normal document retention practices, in disregard of their discovery obligations" (Strickland, 2005: 34). (For summaries of this case, see the Mastercard case reference.)

MOSAID TECHNOLOGIES VS. SAMSUNG, 2004

In this case the plaintiff alleged that the defendants failed to preserve and disclose discoverable e-mail evidence. Challenging the plaintiffs' motion, Samsung claimed the plaintiffs did not specifically include e-mail in its definition of documents during the discovery process. Ultimately the court rejected the defendants' arguments stating that the defendants' "prejudice resulting from complete and total e-mail spoliation seems particularly obvious. . . . The fact that no technical e-mails were preserved . . . demonstrates, at the least, extremely reckless behavior." The judge issued $566,838 in sanctions against the defendants as well as an adverse inference instruction for spoliation of e-mail evidence (Arkfeld, 2004). (For another summary of this case, see the Mosaid case reference.)

UNITED STATES VS. PHILIP MORRIS, 2004

In the case of the U.S. vs. Philip Morris, the court ordered preservation of potentially relevant documents at the outset of the case, but after more than two years, the company revealed that its officials had, in fact, not complied with the court order and had instead followed a policy of deleting e-mail that was more than sixty days old. The federal district court in the District of Columbia sanctioned Philip Morris for improper deletion of e-mails after litigation began, and imposed $2,750,000 in monetary sanctions. "It is astounding," wrote Judge Gladys Kessler, that the officials failed to follow the order which, "if followed, would have ensured the preservation of e-mails which have been irretrievably lost. . . . Because we do not know what has been destroyed, it is impossible to accurately access what harm has been done to the Government and what prejudice it has suffered" (Strickland, 2005: 18). (For a transcript of this case, see the Philip Morris case reference.)

BROCCOLI V. ECHOSTAR COMMUNICATIONS CORP., 2005

In this case the plaintiffs filed a motion for sanctions against Echostar for failing to preserve e-mail and other records after notice of a potential claim was received. Based on evidence that Echostar indeed never suspended data destruction and had not preserved essential personnel documents, the court granted the plaintiffs' motion for sanctions. In its statement, the court held that "Echostar acted in bad faith in its failure to suspend its e-mail and destruction policy or preserve essential personnel documents in order to fulfill its duty to preserve the relevant documentation for purposes of potential litigation" (K&L Gates, 2005). The court further concluded that "Echostar plainly had a duty to preserve employment and termination documents when its management learned of [the plaintiff's] potential Title VII claim. . . . [Yet] none of the [e-mails] exchanged between [the plaintiff], [his] supervisors, and Echostar's upper management regarding his complaints . . . were preserved. Moreover, Echostar admits that it never issued a company-wide instruction regarding the suspension of any data destruction policy. . . . Given Echostar's status as a large public corporation with ample financial resources and personnel management know-how, the court finds it indefensible that such basic personnel procedures and related documentation were lacking" (Brownstone, 2006: 3). (For a transcript of this case, see the Broccoli case reference.)

CRANDALL V. CITY AND COUNTY OF DENVER, COLORADO, 2006

In this case the plaintiffs sought sanctions against the defendants for deleting e-mails before and during the litigation. It was discovered that the defendants' e-mail protocol automatically deleted e-mails every seven days, and that this protocol was not changed until six months after litigation started, resulting in the deletion of many relevant e-mails. However, in response to this allegation the defendants purchased data recovery software and restored 91,000 deleted e-mails. The plaintiffs still alleged relevant e-mails were destroyed and that the missing e-mails severely prejudiced their case. Consequently, the court allowed the plaintiffs to hire a computer expert to examine the defendants' e-mail system. After this review, the court concluded that the defendants had proceeded in good faith. In its summation the court stated that "only the bad faith loss or destruction of evidence will support the kind of adverse inference that Plaintiffs seek, i.e., that the supposedly deleted e-mails would in fact have been unfavorable to the Defendant. Mere negligence in losing or destroying records is not enough because it does not support an inference of consciousness of a weak case" (Strickland, 2005: 3). (For the transcript and summaries of this case, see the Crandall case reference.)

DURST V. FEDEX EXPRESS, 2006

In an employment termination dispute, the plaintiffs filed a motion seeking an adverse inference jury instruction stating that the defendants had failed to produce key accident reports, vehicle inspection records, and e-mails as demanded by the plaintiff. In response, the defendants denied having agreed to provide the requested documents and asserted the magistrate judge had never ordered production of these records. The court ultimately refused to grant the plaintiffs' motion stating the plaintiff had failed to satisfy the four essential factors required for a spoliation inference: (1) that the evidence existed; 2) that the evidence was intentionally withheld or suppressed; 3) that the evidence was relevant to the plaintiffs' case; and (4) that it was reasonably foreseeable that the evidence would later be discoverable (K&L Gates, 2006).

LESSONS LEARNED FROM THE LEGAL CASES

Many of the lessons one can learn from the court cases apply to all electronic records and not just e-mail, and these lessons will be reviewed in the next section on compliance. However, these are a few lessons that are either unique to e-mail or were prominent issues in the court cases reviewed above.

Lesson Number 1: E-mail is a potential record in the eyes of the law, and it is discoverable evidence. Discovery of e-mail is now a routine and critical aspect of many litigated cases. In the eyes of the law, e-mail messages are no different than any other form of record. As such e-mail must be managed according to the same uniform and consistently applied policies and procedures as paper records or other electronic records.

Lesson Number 2: Give special attention to e-mail. In most of the discovery cases to date, e-mail records have been prominently featured. Because e-mail is so ubiquitous and easy to use, it has become the preferred medium for mission critical communications of all types. However, as indicated earlier, e-mail is still not very well managed by most institutions. Without question e-mail is presently the highest profile, highest risk digital resource businesses must manage. E-mail is indeed the digital smoking gun of legal cases.

Lesson Number 3: Document retention, once a "sleepy backwater of the law" (McCurdy, 2005), has become a very high priority. As exhibited in the legal cases reviewed above, courts are likely to react negatively when they discover that an organization has not created polices and programs for routinely preserving and disposing of e-mail records. All the cases examined above revolved around spoliation or the willful destruction of records. Without well designed retention and disposal schedules, courts are likely to regard the deletion of relevant records as deliberate destruction of evidence. The courts have issued a clear message: willful destruction of relevant e-mails will not be tolerated.

Lesson Number 4: Once a party can reasonably anticipate litigation, it must suspend its routine document retention/destruction policies and put a litigation hold on destruction of records. Failure to suspend normal destruction routines after notice of litigation had been received was a major issue in many of the court cases examined above. Unfortunately the Ferris Research Group survey in 2004 found that 61 percent of respondents did not have a record hold mechanism in place when required for an audit, investigation, or litigation (Ferris Research,

2004: figure 32). Retention schedules are critical, but once the courts issue a hold on destruction, institutions must have well defined strategies in place to ensure no records are destroyed from that point forward.

SURVEYS ON E-MAIL MANAGEMENT

A number of recent surveys have queried institutions about how they currently manage e-mail. Let us review what these surveys tell us.

E-MAIL MANAGEMENT AS A PRIORITY

In a 2004 survey the Ferris Research User Panel asked organizations the question: Where on the IT priority list is managing the archiving and compliance issues related to e-mail? 14 percent responded that e-mail was not a priority and another 44 percent rated it as a low priority. On the other hand, 36 percent of respondents have made e-mail management a major priority, and 6 percent have made it the top priority (Ferris Research, 2004: figure 38). These results are somewhat encouraging since Ferris Research User Panel found that as recently as two years earlier, e-mail management was almost a non-issue in most organizations.

ACTIONS TAKEN TO MANAGE E-MAIL

In the 2004 Ferris survey institutions were also asked whether they had any technical systems in place to implement an e-mail strategy. To this question 75 percent of respondents stated that they did not have any technical systems in place to manage e-mail (Ferris Research, 2004: figure 40).

For those institutions that have implemented or are planning to create some type of e-mail management plan, what are the activities relating to the management of e-mail that are most important? In a 2003 survey by Kahn Consultants, 64 percent of respondents said they had taken action to make their e-mail systems more secure. A majority of the respondents believed that training was essential, and 46 percent of these organizations have offered training on policy issues during the last year. On the other hand, 67 percent believed that employees could benefit from more mail retention and storage training (Kahn and Blair, 2003: 7–8). In a 2005 follow-up survey by Kahn on e-mail, respondents rated the importance of activities related to e-mail management in this order: Create Policies 73 percent, Security 66 percent, Training 61 percent (Kahn Consulting, 2005, "Specific Actions Taken with Regards to E-mail"). In a 2006 survey on e-mail conducted by AIIM, the importance of challenges related to e-mail were ranked as "extremely important" in the following order: Retention: 39 percent, Archiving: 37 percent, Classification: 22 percent, Encryption: 22 percent, and Content Filtering and Scanning: 20 percent (AIIM, 2006: key finding 3).

E-MAIL POLICIES

Creating enterprise-wide policies is certainly the logical place to begin in creating an overall management strategy for e-mail. How are institutions doing in this area of development? Let us first look at the creation of policies for controlling the use of e-mail and the kinds of conduct that will and will not be permitted. A 1998 survey discovered that 20 percent or less of businesses responding to the survey had any rules or criteria in place outlining the proper usage of e-mail (Wallace, 1998). However, by 2006 an AIIM survey found that in large institutions (1001–10,000 employees) 90 percent of respondents had created policies on acceptable use of e-mail (AIIM, 2006: key finding 2). Clearly, institutions have gotten the message that e-mail use policies are absolutely necessary.

What about policies that relate more directly to the management of e-mail as a record, such as retention and disposal policies? Five different consulting or professional organizations have asked survey questions related to retention policies.

- AMA 2003: 34 percent have written retention and deletion policies for e-mail (American Management Association, 2003: question on "Policies and Policy Training").
- Kahn 2005: 45 percent (increase of 5 percent from 2003) have formal policies on e-mail retention (Kahn and Blair, 2003: 7; Kahn Consulting, 2005: question on "E-mail Policies").
- Cohasset 2005: 51 percent of the organizations have a retention policy for e-mail (Cohasset, 2005: question 26).
- AIIM 2006: 44 percent of the respondents have a retention policy for e-mail (AIIM, 2006: key finding 2).

- 2004 Survey by Ferris Research User Panel: 46 percent have a disposal policy for e-mail.

The Ferris Survey also discovered that organizations in the government, health-care, and educational sectors were least likely to have deletion policies for e-mail; small organizations were less likely to have a deletion policy than were medium-sized and large institutions; and non-U.S. institutions were far less likely to have a disposal policy in place than US institutions (Ferris Research, 2004: figures 27, 29, 30, 31).

These results clearly demonstrate that despite the high profile court cases and the increased awareness of the need to properly manage and store e-mail messages, a majority of organizations are still not providing written guidance to employees on how to appraise and select e-mail.

CHALLENGES IN MANAGING E-MAIL

The Ferris Research User Panel survey asked organizations to rate the challenges affecting its ability to respond to requests for the retrieval of e-mail and uncovered the following results:

> Lack of Adequate Funding Resources: Severe Challenge
> Large Volume of E-mail: Moderate Challenge
> Cost of Technology Solutions: Moderate Challenge
> Difficulty of Enforcing User Compliance: Moderate Challenge
> Lack of Adequate Employee Training: Moderate Challenge
> Lack of Adequate Executive Training: Moderate Challenge
> Inadequate Technology Solutions: Moderate Challenge
> Complexity of Regulatory Climate: Moderate Challenge

The Ferris survey also discovered that respondents from government and high-tech organizations rated "lack of adequate funding resources" as a more severe problem than respondents from other types of organizations. Respondents from educational organizations rated "difficulty of enforcing user compliance" as a more severe problem than respondents from other types of organizations. Educational and health-care organizations rated cost as a more severe problem than did other types of organizations. Finally non-U.S. organizations considered the "cost of technology solutions" to be a more severe problem than did U.S. organizations (Ferris Research, 2004: figures 52, 60). Without question, establishing e-mail management programs continues to be a challenge for all types of institutions.

STRATEGIES FOR MAKING RETENTION DECISIONS

There appear to be four distinct strategies for evaluating e-mail for retention within most institutions (general discussion of these strategies can be found in Cohasset, 2006: 8–9).

STRATEGY 1: STORAGE CONSTRAINTS BASED ON MAILBOX SIZE LIMITS

This appears to be the most popular strategy. The Kahn 2003 survey found that sixty-seven percent of respondents used maximum mailbox sizes as a de facto retention strategy (Kahn and Blair, 2003: 7). The Ferris survey in 2004 found that 71 percent of their respondents used size of inbox to limit the amount of e-mail (Ferris Research, 2004: figure 34). The AIIM 2006 survey found that 69 percent of large institutions had created policies on the maximum size of individual e-mail "mailboxes" (AIIM, 2006: key finding 2).

Advantages to This Approach

For Recordkeeping: It is easy for IT to implement, and it saves on space storage and resources to manage e-mail.

For Compliance: Some would argue it lessens legal risk by limiting the number of records according to some kind of a strategy; there is a legal line of reasoning which suggests that if a broad deletion policy is clearly defined and followed consistently, then generalized deletion of e-mail may be acceptable.

Disadvantages to This Approach

For Recordkeeping: This strategy makes no attempt to identify records with long-term value to the business, and consequently unless users are trained in appraisal, e-mail records that pertain to critical business transactions and would be of value to future historical research will be lost.

For Compliance: This strategy will destroy evidence that is required to be maintained by law, and it may be viewed by the courts as constituting spoliation of evidence.

STRATEGY 2: TIME-BASED PURGES

The 2003 survey by Kahn Consultants found that 26 percent of respondents followed a policy of retaining e-mail for less than 120 days (Kahn and Blair, 2003: 7). The 2004 Ferris survey discovered that 19 percent of respondents deleted all e-mail after 60–90 days, and 7 percent destroyed all e-mail after 30–45 days. The Ferris survey also discovered that U.S. institutions were much more likely to delete e-mail within these time frames than non-U.S. organizations, and that among the various types of institutions, large organizations employing over 2500 people and legal service organizations were most likely to purge all e-mail within a specified time frame (Ferris Research, 2004: figures 28, 29, 31). The 2006 AIIM survey found that 29 percent of end users captured and saved all e-mail regardless of content for a specific period of time (AIIM, 2006: key finding 1).

Advantages and Disadvantages: same as those outlined for strategy number 1

STRATEGY 3: ARCHIVE EVERYTHING APPROACH

According to the Kahn 2003 survey, 31 percent of respondents were keeping e-mail indefinitely (Kahn and Blair, 2003: 7). Respondents to the 2004 Ferris survey indicated a much lower percentage of 11 percent of organizations were keeping e-mail indefinitely, with health care institutions (29 percent) emerging as the type of institution that most often followed this strategy. The Ferris survey also found that this approach was followed to the same degree no matter what size the organization, and whether the organization was within or outside the United States (Ferris Research, 2004: figures 28, 29, 31).

Advantages to This Approach

For Recordkeeping: This strategy is easy for IT to implement, and no decisions are required by users on the value of records so training and other documentation on appraisal decisions are not required.

For Compliance: This strategy is built upon the premise that if all messages are stored, any potential administrative, legal, fiscal, or research need is presumably addressed.

Disadvantages to This Approach

For Recordkeeping: This strategy significantly increases the costs of storing this immense resource and of managing the retrieval, security, and preservation of this e-mail; it also complicates retrieval by creating "digital landfalls" of e-mail records where e-mails vital to the business are intermingled with e-mail of little or no importance.

For Compliance: This strategy will make it difficult for administrators to locate mission critical documents or to comply with e-discovery requests and compliance laws; it potentially creates greater liability by retaining e-mails that could normally be destroyed but which must be made available in discovery requests.

STRATEGY 4: SELECTION BASED ON CONTENT AND ACCORDING TO A RETENTION SCHEDULE

For archivists and records managers, this would be the preferred method and the strategy one would assume most organizations would follow. However, the 2003 survey by Kahn Consultants found that only 37 percent of respondents retained messages according to their content. In the 2005 Kahn survey the percentage of organizations reporting that they retained e-mail based on its ongoing business value went up to 44 percent or an increase of 26 percent (Kahn and Blair, 2003: 7; Kahn Consulting, 2005: question on "Managing Content by Its Value"). The 2004 Ferris Survey found that only 26 percent of respondents had issued content management procedures or instructions for e-mail selection, and only 12 percent followed a policy of evaluating e-mail according to content. Among types of institutions, financial services (23 percent) and government agencies (20 percent) were most likely to select e-mail by content, and health care (0 percent), legal services (4 percent), and education (5 percent) organizations were the least likely. The Ferris survey also discovered that large institutions over 2,500 employees (18 percent) were more likely to select by content and that U.S. and non-U.S. institutions selected e-mail by content at approximately the same percent (Ferris Research, 2004: figures 28, 29, 30, 31). The 2006 AIIM survey found that 47 percent of respondents apply retention periods based on the content of the e-mail (AIIM, 2006: key finding 2).

Advantages to This Approach

For Recordkeeping: This strategy is most likely to select and preserve e-mail records with value to the business and to future research; it will reduce the volume of e-mail so retrieval is more efficient and less resources are devoted to storage and management of the resource.

For Compliance: This strategy will likely retain records for periods of time designated by laws, regulations, and best practices; it does not retain e-mail that can legitimately be destroyed and thus reduces potential discovery actions uncovering information that may harm the organization.

Disadvantages to This Approach

For Recordkeeping: This strategy requires the organization to invest heavily in training sessions on how to make appraisal decisions and in creating documentation, such as disposal policies and record retention schedules.

For Compliance: There are no disadvantages; this is the best approach to meeting legal requirements relating to the management of e-mail.

STRATEGIES FOR E-MAIL MANAGEMENT

In regard to strategies for managing e-mail, there are six basic solutions that are presently being employed. Some of these may and likely will be used in unison.

No Strategy

According to the 2004 Ferris survey, 34 percent of respondents had no plans for implementing an enterprise-wide e-mail management program. Education institutions were far and away (64 percent) the most likely type of enterprise to have no plan for systematically retaining and managing e-mail at the enterprise level (Ferris Research, 2004: figures 36 and 37). In a 2006 survey on e-mail by AIIM, 35 percent of respondents reported that they "had not yet begun" to address e-mail management issues, and another 41 percent indicated that they had just begun the process. The AIIM survey also discovered that 18 percent do not "archive" e-mail at all (AIIM, 2006: key finding 1).

The Ferris survey found that many institutions (55 percent) used a system based on both paper and electronic systems to preserve e-mail. Only 15 percent exclusively used electronic systems, and 30 percent still relied on paper systems to retain e-mail (Ferris Research, 2004: figure 39).

Advantages to This Approach

This strategy is a more convenient and user friendly approach; most organizations have a paper based records management system in place, and most users feel comfortable with paper records; the printed e-mail message can be filed in folders and integrated with other related records to create a complete record of transactions; it eliminates problems associated with digital preservation, such as software and hardware obsolescence.

Disadvantages to This Approach

Essential metadata for determining context of the message may be lost thus compromising the authenticity and reliability of the record. Paper systems do not have the same ability as automated systems to link related records found anywhere in the application; paper systems cannot manipulate data as well or provide the type of access that electronic systems can. Having both paper and electronic e-mail systems complicates retention and disposition and overall management of the resource; printing to paper adds to storage and filing costs. This approach still requires policies and training on selecting e-mail to retain over time and does not allow integration of e-mail with other automated systems, such as content management systems.

USE OF BACK-UP SYSTEMS FOR LONG-TERM MANAGEMENT

Kahn Consultants found in its 2005 survey that 29 percent of respondents, an increase of 7 percent from the 2003 Kahn survey, relied on back-up systems or some type of back-end systems for e-mail retention (Kahn Consulting, 2005: question on "Use of Technologies to Manage E-mail"). The 2006 survey by AIIM found that 44 percent of respondents use the back-up process as the strategy for managing e-mail (AIIM, 2006: key finding 1).

Advantages to This Approach

This strategy is relatively easy for IT to implement since it is a strategy that IT is familiar with. This strategy will likely capture most of the important e-mail, although decisions on how long the back-up e-mail is retained will ultimately determine whether e-mail is available when needed.

Disadvantages to This Approach

Back-up tapes are excellent for disaster recovery where an entire mailbox or system needs to be quickly re-created, but they are not an effective strategy for managing a key intellectual resource, such as e-mail. Back-up systems typically do not provide effective tools for retrieving and accessing data; they are normally not subject to well designed preservation strategies, and even security of the tapes can be an issue. Eventually, a back-up strategy for e-mail will result in a massive repository (depending on how often backups are deleted) that will be costly to manage and store. In addition, e-mail in backups will not be integrated with related records stored in other data and information systems. In short, back-up systems do not meet many of the requirements for managing e-mail as a record.

MANAGING E-MAIL RECORDS WITHIN THE E-MAIL SYSTEM

This strategy is often used in conjunction with a backup system approach. Generally this strategy is a decentralized approach that requires creators of e-mail to manage their own messages at the desktop and to use the functionality within the e-mail system to manage the e-mail over time. The AIIM 2006 survey found that "62 percent of participants say that there is no definition of e-mail management and that 'users are responsible for deleting, managing, classifying, and saving e-mail on their desktops.'" Based on these results, the AIIM report concludes that "organizations largely leave the management of e-mail up to individual employees" (AIIM, 2006: key finding 1).

Advantages to This Approach

Users are familiar with the system, and it is relatively easy for them to learn how to manage, preserve, and access e-mail within the system they use on a daily basis; e-mail systems have some of the recordkeeping functionality required to manage and preserve records over time, such as the ability to classify and file messages and to sort them by various criteria; most e-mail systems capture and preserve relevant metadata related to the record.

Disadvantages to This Approach

No currently available e-mail system addresses all the requirements for managing messages as records; the functionality of e-mail systems falls far short of a recordkeeping system, particularly as it relates to the automated retention and disposal of records; this approach still requires policies and training on appraisal of e-mail and its management over time; this strategy does not allow integration of e-mail with other related records in other systems; this strategy does not offer an enterprise-wide solution for access to e-mail.

It can safely be said that the approaches outlined above have serious deficiencies as e-mail management strategies. In particular they do not meet many of the requirements for recordkeeping, and they tend to manage e-mail in isolation from records in other systems. Printing to paper and managing e-mail in the active e-mail system or with backups are not viable long-term solutions. The next three strategies are much more viable.

MANAGE WITH E-MAIL MANAGEMENT AND ARCHIVING SOFTWARE

Institutions employing this strategy can either purchase the e-mail software and manage the resource on-site, or they can opt for "hosted" services, where the e-mail is stored and managed at the vendor's location using the vendor's hardware and software systems. The Kahn Consultants' 2005 survey found 37 percent of respondents were using a software application specifically designed for e-mail. This figure was up a significant 19 percent from the results in the 2003 Kahn survey (Kahn Consulting, 2005: question on "Use of Technologies to Manage E-mail"). The 2004 Ferris survey, however, found e-mail specific software was used far less frequently than the Kahn survey. The product most used by respondents to the Ferris survey was Iron Mountain (a hosted site) at 9 percent, followed by Accutrac's e-mail management system and Legato's e-mail system at 2 percent each (Ferris Research, 2004: figure 41). The 2006 AIIM survey found that only 13 percent of respondents used a commercial e-mail application or an outsourced service (AIIM, 2006: key finding 1).

MANAGE E-MAIL WITHIN A TRADITIONAL DOCUMENT MANAGEMENT ENVIRONMENT

The Kahn Consultants' 2005 survey discovered that 29 percent of its respondents employed this approach, which was up 16 percent from responses to the same question in the 2003 Kahn survey (Kahn Consulting, 2005: question on "Use of Technologies to Manage E-mail").

MANAGE E-MAIL WITHIN A RECORDS MANAGEMENT SYSTEM OR WITHIN A DOCUMENT/CONTENT MANAGEMENT SYSTEM THAT INCLUDES ROBUST RECORDS MANAGEMENT FUNCTIONALITY

The 2005 survey by Kahn Consultants discovered that 19 percent of respondents used some type of records management software to manage e-mail. This was up 12 percent from the responses to the same question in Kahn's 2003 survey. One of the conclusions based on these results of the Kahn Consultants group was that although the use of record management software to manage e-mail was on the rise, this approach still ranked last among the preferred strategies and was well behind the use of backups to manage e-mail (Kahn Consulting, 2005: question on "Use of Technologies to Manage E-mail"). On the other hand, the 2004 Ferris survey found that a large percentage of respondents to its survey were using document/records management software to manage e-mail. The most popular products were the Documentum Enterprise Records Management software (19 percent) and Hummingbird's records management software (14 percent) (Ferris Research, 2004: figure 41). The 2006 survey by AIIM found that only 9 percent of respondents managed e-mail "as part of a records management program" (AIIM, 2006: key finding 1). However, when AIIM asked organizations what strategy would best meet future e-mail management needs, the top responses were the use of "an e-mail archiving solution that is integrated with an enterprise content management platform (28 percent), and the use of "an e-mail archiving solution that is integrated with a records management product" (27 percent). The AIIM survey further discovered that 42 percent of organizations responding to the 2006 survey planned in the future to first look at ECM vendors when seeking an e-mail management strategy. Based on this data, the AIIM report concludes that "end users clearly see the link between e-mail management and the broader question of how they manage content and documents in their organization" (AIIM, 2006: key finding 3).

Ultimately, e-mail must be managed as any other type of electronic record. This means that the system managing this resource must possess the basic recordkeeping functionality outlined in chapter 2. Effective e-mail management solutions must support the entire e-mail lifecycle including the creation, retention and disposal, documentation, auditing, security and access, retrieval, and preservation of e-mail as a record. In addition, it is extremely important that e-mail be integrated with related records stored in other information systems. In most business processes today, one or more e-mails will likely be among the records that document the transaction. Therefore, it is imperative that these e-mail records can be easily retrieved and viewed along with the correspondence, forms, and other data that were used to complete the transaction. Without question, the ability to integrate e-mail with other systems managing information and records is a critical requirement of any e-mail management system.

Among the present day e-mail management products, the choices that clearly best fulfill recordkeeping requirements are the software products especially designed for e-mail and for records management, and the content management applications that include records management functionality. The vendors of this software are aware of the need for life cycle management and are attempting to incorporate many of the recordkeeping requirements into their products. These vendors are also aware of the need to integrate their software into other applications, and many have developed strategies for achieving this.

At this point in time, I believe the systems that offer the best potential for managing e-mail are the enterprise-wide content management systems with recordkeeping functionality that were described in chapter 3. As I said in my concluding remarks on these systems, document management/content management systems have witnessed the addition of more recordkeeping functionality than any other type of application. For the foreseeable future this is the arena where discussions between IT and archivists and records managers will be occurring on how best to manage records over the entire life cycle. These are also the systems that I believe will be the primary focus of innovative strategies to develop highly integrated environments that incorporate or link with data and information from all the systems in the enterprise. For these reasons, ECM offer the best options for managing e-mail as a record and for integrating e-mail with other related business records.

REFERENCES

AIIM. 2006. "E-Mail Management: An Oxymoron?" Available: www.aiim.org/article-pr.asp?ID=32060

"American Management Association and ePolicy Institute Surveys." 2001. Available: www.messagingarchitects.com/epolicy/policy /articles/Email_Policies_Practices.pdf

Arkfield, Michael. 2004. "Judge Imposes Sanctions for Failure to Retain E-mail." Available: http://arkfield.blogs.com/ede/sanctions/ index/html

Ballon, Ian. 1999. "Spoliation of E-Mail Evidence: Proposed Intranet Policies and a Framework for Analysis." Available: http://library. findlaw.com/1999/Feb/22/131004.html

Bearman, David. 1993. "The Implication of *Armstrong v. Executive Office of the President* for the Archival Management of Electronic Records."*Electronic Evidence*: 118–144.

Berkman Center for Internet and Society at Harvard Law School. "Linnen v. Robins: The Fen/Phen Case." Available: http:// cyber.law.harvard.edu/digitaldiscovery/digdisc_library_9.html and http://cyber.law.harvard.edu/digitaldiscovery/library/preservation/ linnen.html

Best, Richard. 2006. "Electronic Discovery of Electronic Data." Available: http://californiadiscovery.findlaw.com/electronic_data_ discovery_new_developments.html

Broccoli Case: The official transcript of the case is available: http:// el.shb.com/nl_images/edisc/nov05/broccoli%20v.%20echostar.op. 080405.pdf

Brownstone, Robert D. 2006. "Preserve or Perish, Destroy or Drown – eDiscovery Morphs into Electronic Information Management." *North Carolina Journal of Law and Technology*, Vol. 8, no. 1. Available: http://mambo.ncjolt.org/content/view/77/62/1/2

Cohasset Associates, Inc. 2005. "A Renewed Call to Action, Question 26." Available: www.aiim.org/article-docrep.asp?ID=30602

Cohasset Associated, Inc. 2006. "Making the Case for E-Mail Archiving and Litigation Readiness." (pp. 8–9). Available: www.sencilo.com/ pdf/email-archive-new.pdf

Coleman Holdings Case: The official transcript of the case is available: www.vevidence.com/library/whitepages/Coleman_v_Morgan_ Stanley.pdf

(Other summaries of the case are available: www.ediscoverylaw. com/2005/03/articles/case-summaries/judge-maass-grants-adverse-inference-instruction-in-coleman-v-morgan-stanley/ OR www.post-gazette.com/pg/05136/505304.stm. For a summary of the 2007

decision, see www.iht.com/articles/2007/03/21/yourmoney/
morgan.php)
Crandall Case. The official transcript of the case is available:
www.cobar.org/opinions/opinion.cfm?OpinionID=5606
(Other summaries of the case are available: www.
ediscoverylaw.com/2006/09/articles/case-summaries/failure-to-
institute-legal-hold-does-not-warrant-sanctions-absent-some-proof-
that-potentially-relevant-evidence-was-lost-or-destroyed/)
Extra LEXIS. 2005. "Coleman 'Parent' Holdings, Inc. v. Morgan
Stanley & Co. Inc." Extra LEXIS 94 (Fla. Cir. Ct. Mar. 23). Available: www.lexisnexis.com/applieddiscovery/lawLibrary/
CaseSummaries_Articles.asp?jid=1733
Ferris Research, Inc. 2004. "Email Records Management Survey:
Guidelines, Technologies, and Trends." Available: www.ferris.com/
2004/09/25/email-records-management-survey-guidelines-
technologies-and-trends/
Forrestor. 2006. "eDiscovery Bursts onto the Scene." Available:
www.metalincs.com/solutions/
Fulcrum Inquiry. 2004. "E-mail Electronic Discovery Sanctions Continue, with New Lawyer Standards Possibly Created." Available:
www.fulcruminquiry.com/Email_Electronic_Discovery_Sanctions.
htm
Gartner Group. 2005. "E-Discovery: Definitions, Advice and Vendors."
Available: www.gartner.com/DisplayDocument?doc_cd=136366
Hewlett-Packard Company. 2000. "Managing E-mail Is Essential
in Today's Business Environment: Carrots and Stick Abound to
Ensure Companies Manage E-mail." Available: www.kahn
consultinginc.com/library/KCI%20Whitepaper-HP%20Email%
20Management.pdf
Kahn, Randolph A., and Barclay T. Blair. 2003. "Managing Email in
the New Business Reality Industry." A study conducted by AIIM
International and Kahn Consulting, Inc. Available: www.
aiimhost.com/membership/EmailSurvey1-9.pdf
Kahn Consulting, Inc. 2005. "Electronic Communication Policies and
Procedures." Available: www.kahnconsultinginc.com/library/KCI–
2005-e-communications-survey.pdf
K&L Gates. 2005. "Automatic Purging of 21-day-old Email Risky but
Defensible." Available: www.ediscoverylaw.com/2005/08/articles/
case-summaries/automatic-purging-of–21dayold-email-risky-but-
defensible-failure-to-preserve-following-notice-of-potential-
litigation-results-in-sanctions/
K&L Gates. 2006. "When It Absolutely Positively Does Not Merit an
Adverse Inference Instruction, FedEx Defeats Motion in Limine."

Available: www.ediscoverylaw.com/2006/06/articles/case-summaries/
when-it-absolutely-positively-does-not-merit-an-adverse-inference-
instruction-fedex-defeats-motion-in-limine/

LegisDiscovery. "Case Law: Production of Data." Available: www.
legisdiscovery.com/index.php?option=com_content&task=
view&id=46&Itemid=63

Legis/Discovery. "Case Law: Sanctions." Available: www.legisdiscovery
.com/index.php?option=com_content&task=view&id=57&
Itemid=63

LexisNexis Applied Discovery. 2003. "Metropolitan Opera Association
v. Local 100, Hotel Employees and Restaurant Employees International Union." U.S. Dist. LEXIS 1077 (SDNY, Jan. 28, 2003).
Available: www.lexisnexis.com/applieddiscovery/lawlibrary/
focus_03.asp

Mastercard Case: Summaries of the case are available:
www.vevidence.com/library/MastercardIntern.asp

McCurdy, Greg. 2005. "New e-Discovery Rules Would Help Businesses
Cope with the Tidal Wave of e-Documents without Affecting
Discovery."*Lawyers for Civil Justice.* Available: www.lfcj.com/
hotcases2.cfm?hotCasesID=98

Metropolitan Opera Case: The official court transcription of the case
is available: www.nysd.uscourts.gov/rulings/00CV03613_recuse_
opinion_082704.pdf
(Another summary of this case is available: www.legisdiscovery.com/
index.php?option=com_content&task=view&id=57&Itemid=63)

Mosaid Case: A summary of the case is available: www.mosaid.com/
corporate/investor-relations/litigation-samsung.php

National Archives and Records Administration (NARA). 2006. "Directive 1234.24, Standards for Managing Electronic Mail Records."
Available: www.archives.gov/about/regulations/part–1234.html

Philip Morris Case: The official transcript of the case is available:
www.usdoj.gov/civil/cases/tobacco2/ORDER%20&%20MEMO%
&20600.pdf

Public Citizen. 2000a. "Armstrong v. Executive Office of the President."
Available: www.citizen.org/litigation/briefs/ERecords/articles.cfm?
ID=617

Public Citizen. 2000b. "Public Citizen v. Carlin." Available:
www.citizen.org/litigation/briefs/ERecordsPCVCarlin/articles.
cfm?ID=685
(A summary of this case is also available: www.allbusiness.com/
professional-scientific/management-consulting-services/819714–
1.html ["The Information Management Implications of Public Citizen v. Carlin"].)

Strickland, Lee. 2005. "Electronic Data Discovery Best Practices Survey." Available: http://californiadiscovery.findlaw.com/electronic_data_discovery_new_developments.html

Wallace, David. 1998. "Recordkeeping and Electronic Mail Policy: The State of Thought and the State of Politics." Available: www.mybestdocs.com/dwallace.html

Wiginton Case: Summaries of this case are available: www.ediscoverylaw.com/2004/12/articles/case-summaries/court-denies-sanctions-for-destruction-of-certain-electronic-evidence/ OR www.discoveryresources.org/04_om_cite_0409.html

Zubulake Case: The official transcriptions of the case are available: www.vevidence.com/library/whitepapers/Zubulake_V.pdf www.vevidence.com/library/Zubulake_IV.asp www.vevidence.com/library/Zubulake_I_II_III.asp (Summaries of this case are also available: www.pss-systems.com/news/ComplianceWeek_051115.pdf www.krollontrack.co.uk/legalresources/zubulake.aspx www.lexisnexis.com/applieddiscovery/lawlibrary/focus_07.asp www.krollontrack.com/publications/ripples.pdf)

7

Laws, Regulations, and Best Practices Relating to Electronic Records Management

In the preceding chapters, we have addressed what are commonly regarded as the primary first steps in designing recordkeeping systems: articulating the functional requirements and metadata specifications and understanding how information systems in the enterprise operate and how they manage records. Perhaps ten years ago we might have ended our review with those issues. However, today one simply cannot talk about electronic records management without reviewing laws, regulations and best practices mandating or recommending how records will be managed.

There are now hundreds of laws and regulations that impact the way information is stored and managed. Financial scandals involving major corporations have prompted Congress, the Security Exchange Commission, and other government or financial agencies to issue a variety of laws and rules aimed at improving corporate governance. These laws and regulations have addressed such important issues as lack of accountability and oversight, improper disclosure of customer financial data and patient's health information, inadequate or fraudulent financial reporting and accounting practices, failure to disclose security breaches involving personal information, and the more extensive disclosure of information to investors.

Many of these laws and regulations focus on the concept of compliance. Compliance is conforming to laws, standards, and regulations applicable to the organization. From a legal and regulatory perspective, compliance has two components: 1) the policies, procedures and practices of the organization and 2) the systems and applications utilized by the organizations to address the specific regulatory, legal, and best practice requirements in an automated manner (Cohasset, 2005). As one expert has written: "Compliance is a process, not just a product" (Cohasset, 2004: 11). The compliance process is more than just products or technologies; it requires policies and procedures, training and monitoring to manage and control the process, and an ongoing effort to meet the requirements and obligations.

As shown in the section on e-mail, many corporations are discovering through court cases and the resulting penalties that there is a very close association between compliance and good recordkeeping. Records provide the documentary evidence that the legal or regulatory requirements have been met. In a white paper on compliance, consultants at Cohasset Associates define the role of records in complying with law and regulations in the following terms: "Compliance requires that business records serve two functions: Provide evidence that specific actions were taken, or processes executed . . . Demonstrate through the absence of any records or data that prohibited actions have not occurred" (Cohasset, 2005: 12). The consultants at Cohasset further define a company's compliance obligations in terms of two basic requirements: 1) "The records must provide suitable evidence of the company's history—sufficient to support all types of inquiries: audits, regulatory inspections, enforcement actions and litigation"; 2) "The records must satisfy specific rules regarding how they are created, managed and preserved. These rules are intended to assure the reliability, integrity and accessibility of the records for so long as they may be required" (Cohasset, 2005: 13). Similarly, the consultants at Kahn's advise corporations to design and implement a strategy combining compliance and good recordkeeping. They call the strategy "Information Management Compliance (IMC)," which is a process "that takes traditional compliance principles and applies them to any information management activity." IMC includes the following seven elements: "Good Policies and Procedures," "Executive Responsibility," "Proper Delegation," "Communication and Training," "Auditing and Monitoring," "Consistent Enforcement," and "Continuous Program Improvement." The Kahn consultants recommend making "compliance a part of . . . organization's information practices" (Kahn, Randolph, 2005: 3).

Unfortunately, most of the evidence from surveys on compliance reinforces the Cohasset report's finding that electronic records management programs in most corporations are underdeveloped, and, as a result, businesses are not prepared to meet compliance and legal obligations (Cohasset, 2005). The 2006 survey on compliance conducted by AIIM found that 63.3 percent of end users felt that their organizations "have not yet analyzed the risk they face from the mismanagement of electronic information," and 42.6 percent say their organization "does not yet have a clear approach toward meeting compliance" requirements (AIIM, 2006: key finding 3). The same survey discovered that organizations appear to have a very narrow definition of what compliance means. Compliance in relation to information management is typically associated with "information required by government or industry regulations" (84.2 percent), "information that could be needed in a legal action" (62.1 percent), and "paper information" (52 percent). Only a small percentage of users regarded electronic information and records in either ERP systems (21.9 percent) or content management systems (20.4 percent) as being subject to compliance scrutiny (AIIM, 2006: key finding 2). These results prompted the AIIM survey report to conclude that "contrary to popular belief, when it comes to compliance, the weakest link is electronic, not paper documentation," and that the "real compliance gap in most organizations comes when users think about how they handle ELECTRONIC information" (AIIM, 2006: key finding 5).

These attitudes toward the importance of electronic records management must change if organizations are to have any chance of consistently being compliant with laws and regulations. Records management cannot continue to be viewed as just another project to support on a short-term basis; it must become a sustainable process that has the ongoing commitment of the organization's top executives and the full support of the company's financial and technical resources.

LAWS AND ACTS

To gain a better understanding of the recordkeeping requirements outlined above, let us now review some of the primary laws, regulations, and best practices relating to compliance and how electronic records should be managed. The list is hardly exhaustive, but it does represent what most experts regard as the laws, regulations, and best practice statements that have had the most significant impact on recordkeeping practices. The emphasis is on laws, rules, and guidelines developed in the United States. However, some of the primary laws, regulations, and best practices impacting recordkeeping in Great Britain, Canada and, in one case, internationally, are also described. The laws are listed first by country and then in chronological order by date enacted.

UNITED STATES

Freedom of Information Act and the Electronic Freedom of Information Act Amendments

Enacted in 1966, the Freedom of Information Act (FOIA) established the public right to access information of the executive branch of the federal government. Thirty years later, Congress enacted the Electronic Freedom of Information Act (EFOIA)

Amendments of 1996 require that government agencies make available in electronic format public documents created on or after November 1, 1996. The EFOIA Act applies to any executive department, military department, government corporation, government controlled corporation, or other establishment in the executive branch of the government (including the Executive Office of the President), or any independent regulatory agency. In the amended Act, agencies are instructed to "provide the record in any form or format requested by the person if the record is readily reproducible by the agency in that form or format. Each agency shall make reasonable efforts to maintain its records in forms or formats that are reproducible for purposes of this section" (The Freedom of Information Act, 1996: section 3.)

Some of the challenges government agencies have faced in implementing this Act include locating information in a variety of systems and in multiple formats, ensuring that data is retained according to a defined record schedule, meeting requests in a timely fashion, and ensuring that records are not inappropriately disclosed. FOIA and the 1996 amendments require that agencies have in place records management systems for both their paper and electronic records and ensure that these documents can be inventoried, searched and retrieved in accordance with statutory mandates.

Health Insurance Portability and Accountability Act (HIPAA)

The Health Insurance Portability and Accountability Act (HIPAA) was enacted in 1996 as Public Law 104–191. Designed in part to protect healthcare information, HIPAA, among other things, outlines standards for the storage, management, and use of such information to ensure the privacy rights of healthcare customers are protected. HIPAA has three major sections, each of which outlines a series of requirements for the management of healthcare related information. HIPAA requires that regulated organizations:

- standardize the exchange of electronic data related to healthcare transactions
- protect the privacy of individual healthcare information
- protect the security of individual healthcare information (HIPPA, 1996)

In response to the Health Insurance Portability and Accountability Act (HIPAA) mandate, the United States Health and Human Services Department (HHS) published in December 2000, *Standards for Privacy of Individually Identifiable Health Information* ("Privacy Rule"). This Rule was designed to implement the requirements of HIPAA and established national standards for the protection of health information, as applied to the three types of covered entities: health plans, healthcare clearinghouses, and healthcare providers who conduct certain healthcare transactions electronically.

In March 2002, HHS proposed and released for public comment modifications to the Privacy Rule. The final modifications were published on August 14, 2002. Compliance with the Privacy Rule was required on April 14, 2003 (April 14, 2004, for small health plans). The Privacy Rule (and the Security Rule, which appeared later) protects all "individually identifiable health information" held or transmitted by a covered entity or its business associate, in any form or media, whether electronic, paper, or oral. "Individually identifiable health information" is information that "identifies the individual or for which there is a reasonable basis to believe can be used to identify the individual. Individually identifiable health information includes many common identifiers (e.g., name, address, birth date, Social Security Number)." However, there are no restrictions on the use or disclosure of what is called "de-identified" health information, which "neither identifies nor provides a reasonable basis to identify an individual" (U.S. Department of Health and Human Services, 2003: 4).

A major goal of the Privacy Rule is to define and limit the circumstances in which an individual's protected heath information may be used or disclosed. Health information on an individual must not be disclosed unless the individual, or legal representative of such, who is the subject of the information authorizes the release of the information in writing, or the HHS requests it for an investigation or enforcement action. Some data sets may be released for the purposes of research or in the interests of public health. A central aspect of the Rule is the principle of "minimum necessary" use and disclosure, i.e., reasonable efforts must be made to disclose only the minimum amount of protected health information needed to accomplish the intended purpose of the use. To protect this information healthcare organizations must develop and implement policies and procedures that restrict access and uses of protected data. This includes developing procedures for recurring disclosures and non-recurring requests for information.

Under the Rule, individuals have the right, with a few stated exceptions, to a full accounting of what was disclosed and to whom for a maximum period of six years from the point of disclosure. Individuals also have the right to request that organizations restrict use or disclosure of data in certain instances, although the healthcare organization is under no obligation to comply with the request. The Privacy Rule also makes it very clear that the healthcare organizations must "maintain reasonable and appropriate administrative, technical, and physical safeguards to prevent intentional or unintentional use or disclosure of protected health information in violation of the Privacy Rule and to limit its incidental use and disclosure pursuant to otherwise permitted or required use or disclosure." Finally the Rule states that the organization must "maintain, until six years after the later of the date of their creation or last effective date, its privacy policies and procedures, its privacy practices notices, disposition of complaints, and other actions, activities, and designations that the Privacy Rule requires to be documented" (U.S. Department of Health and Human Services, 2003: 14–15).

On August 12, 1998, HHS published a proposed rule (63 FR 43242) to establish a minimum standard for security of electronic health information. A final Security Rule became effective as of April

21, 2003. Most organizations must be in compliance by April 21, 2005; small health plans (those with annual receipts of $5 million or less) had until April 21, 2006. Administrative safeguards make up 50 percent of the Security Rule's standards. Among the most important of the administrative safeguards are the need to implement policies and procedures to prevent, detect, and correct security violations; to report and respond to security incidents; to ensure that only authorized personnel have access to restricted data and that individuals can easily access data they are authorized to view or modify; and to respond to disasters that damage information systems containing this data. In addition, organizations must develop awareness and training programs for staff, and develop strategies for evaluating the security policies and procedures.

Another set of security requirements identified by the Security Rule fall into the category of physical safeguards. These standards include requirements to create policies and procedures for protecting information systems that contain restricted data from unauthorized physical access. The Security Rule also contains technical requirements, such as access and audit controls and authentication procedures, for protecting restricted data from unauthorized modification or destruction. However, HIPAA does not mandate that organizations use any particular type of technology to comply with these requirements. Finally the Rule specifies that all documentation required by the Rule must be maintained for a "period of six years from the date of its creation or the date when it last was in effect, whichever is later" (HIPPA, Security Rule, Section "Physical Safeguards").

Organizations that do not comply with the Privacy and Security Rules are subject to a number of penalties. Civil penalties are $100 per violation, and up to $25,000 per year for each requirement violated. Criminal penalties range from $50,000 in fines and one year in prison up to $250,000 in fines and 10 years in jail.

For the past three years, the American Health Information Management Association (AHIMA) has surveyed healthcare privacy officers and others whose jobs relate to the implementing HIPAA to gain an understanding of where healthcare organizations stand with regard to implementing the privacy and security rules of the Act. The surveys by AHIMA would suggest that after three years most providers are growing accustomed to the various provisions of the privacy rule, but there are still reports of difficulties with a select few requirements, notably the requirements relating to the reporting of disclosures. The surveys would also indicate that the security regulations were much easier to achieve than the privacy rule. One year into the HIPAA security regulations, a quarter of the surveyed facilities reporting indicated compliance at the top level with another 50 percent indicating that they were close to full compliance. Finally, in regard to HIPAA enforcement, the federal government's approach has been to educate rather than fine or prosecute offenders (American Health Information Management Association, 2006).

Gramm-Leach-Bliley (GLB) Act—15 USC, Subchapter I, Sec. 6801–6809

The Gramm-Leach-Bliley Act ("GLB" Act), also known as the Financial Services Modernization Act, was signed into law in 1999. GLB generally applies to financial services organizations, such as banks, brokerages, and insurance companies. The law requires significant changes to the way that financial institutions manage their information, and requires them to take specific steps to address the privacy and security of customer financial data. In addition, GLB requires eight federal agencies to implement a regulatory framework to enforce GLB's privacy requirements.

In regard to disclosure of personal information, GLB specifies that a financial institution may not, directly or through any affiliate, disclose to a nonaffiliated third party any nonpublic personal information except under certain well defined conditions. In addition, financial institutions are required to provide customers with a notice of their information sharing policies when they first become a customer, and annually thereafter. That notice must inform the consumer of the financial institutions' policies on disclosing nonpublic personal information (NPI) to affiliates and nonaffiliated third parties, disclosing NPI after the customer relationship is terminated, and strategies for protecting NPI. As part of this disclosure the financial institution must provide the customer with copies of its policies and practices relating to disclosing NPI, the categories of NPI collected by the institution, and the policies the institution has created to protect the confidentiality and security of NPI. GLB also gives customers the right to instruct the financial institution to not share information with unaffiliated companies. Finally, the Act prohibits financial institutions from disclosing, other than to a consumer reporting agency, the access codes or account numbers to any nonaffiliated third party for use in telemarketing, direct mail marketing, or other marketing through electronic mail.

To ensure that these requirements are met, the Act instructs financial institutions to develop appropriate standards "(1) to insure the security and confidentiality of customer records and information; (2) to protect against any anticipated threats or hazards to the security or integrity of such records; and (3) to protect against unauthorized access to or use of such records or information which could result in substantial harm or inconvenience to any customer" (Gramm-Leach-Bliley Act, Title V: 1–2). To meet these requirements, financial institutions must institute sound records management practices and develop written, well designed information policies, particularly related to the security and access to records.

Electronic Signatures in Global and National Commerce Act (E-Sign)—Public Law 106–229

The Electronic Signatures in Global and National Commerce Act (E-Sign) was approved by Congress on June, 2000. E-Sign asserts that electronic signatures and electronic records have the same legal validity as their paper counterparts. The Act states that "1) a signature, contract, or other record relating to such transaction may not be denied legal effect, validity, or enforceability solely because it is an electronic document; 2) a contract relating to such transaction may not be denied legal effect, validity, or enforceability solely because an electronic signature or electronic record was used in its formation" (Electronic Signatures in Global and National Commerce Act [E-Sign], "a. In General"). One of the most significant aspects of E-Sign is that it is technology-neutral, and therefore does not promote the use of specific technologies for either e-signatures or e-records. However, the Act does specify implementers must ensure that the electronic record "a) accurately reflects the information set forth in the contract or other record and b) remains accessible to all person who are entitled to access." These points are reemphasized in section 4 of the Act where it is written that agencies must "specify performance standards to assure accuracy, record integrity, and accessibility of records that are required to be retained" (E-Sign, "d. Retention of Contracts and Records"). If these criteria are not met, the legal validity of an electronic record may be denied.

Clearly, this act places a great deal of emphasis on the proper management of the electronic records. Indicative of this is the advice provided by the National Archives of the United States to agencies implementing an electronic signature initiative. NARA tells agencies that "decisions concerning how to adequately document program functions, its risk assessment methodologies, and its records management practices are essential and interrelated aspects of an electronic signature initiative." The statement goes on to say that if the "electronically signed record needs to be preserved, whether for a finite period of time or permanently, then the agency needs to ensure its trustworthiness over time" (NARA, Records Management Guidance, 2000: "Executive Summary"). Authenticity of records is critical if this strategy is to work, and this requires the creation of trustworthy, well managed recordkeeping systems.

According to most reports on the impact of E-Sign, the goal to facilitate the use of electronic records and signatures in interstate or foreign commerce has been substantially realized. For example, the report *Electronic Signatures: A Review of the Exceptions to the Electronic Signatures in Global and National Commerce Act* found that in the last three years electronic or "e-commerce" is not only "alive and well," but is thriving and quickly becoming a well-established method of transacting business in America. The report also states that Americans with Internet access are increasingly receptive to electronic commercial transactions (U.S. Department of Commerce, 2003).

Regarding the exceptions to the use of electronic signatures outlined in the Act, a recent NTIA decision recommended that Congress retain each of the nine exceptions to the E-Sign Act to allow the further development of the electronic marketplace and the establishment of additional consumer protections in electronic transactions systems. The process for development of these policies and practices, though gradual, is occurring at an effective pace, and the acceptance of electronic signatures and electronic documents as a part of commercial transactions has developed to the extent that Congress may eventually be able to remove the exceptions (NTIA, 2003).

Uniform Electronic Transactions Act (UETA)

UETA was approved as a uniform law by the National Conference of Commissioners on Uniform State Laws in July 1999. UETA is roughly equivalent to E-Sign, but is directed towards transactions undertaken by state governments. UETA has been adopted by 48 states. Like E-Sign, UETA provides legal recognition to electronic signatures, records, and contracts. Section 7 of the Act states that: "a) A record or signature may not be denied legal effect or enforceability solely because it is in electronic form. (b) A contract may not be denied legal effect or enforceability solely because an electronic record was used in its formation. (c) If a law requires a record to be in writing, an electronic record satisfies the law. (d) If a law requires a signature, an electronic signature satisfies the law" (UETA, 1999: sec. 7). Also like E-Sign, the Uniform Electronic Transaction Act specifies in Section 12A that the electronic record that is retained must: "(1) accurately reflect the information set forth in the record after it was first generated in its final form as an electronic record or otherwise; and (2) remain accessible for later reference" (UETA, 1999: sec. 12).

Uniting and Strengthening America by Providing Appropriate Tools Required to Intercept and Obstruct Terrorism (USA PATRIOT) Act of 2001

The PATRIOT Act includes numerous requirements that impact records management practices. These include penalties for failure to collect required information, to retain information for the specified time period, to provide access to appropriate law enforcement agencies in a timely fashion, and for providing information to individuals who are not authorized to see the records. The Act applies to all institutions that conduct business in the United States, including corporations that are physically located elsewhere. The sections of the Act that most impact recordkeeping include:

Section 215—"Access to Records and Other Items Under the Foreign Intelligence Surveillance Act"—Section 215 enables the FBI to require the production of "any tangible things (including books, records, papers, documents, and other items) for an investigation to protect against international terrorism or clandestine intelligence activities" (PATRIOT Act, 2001: sec. 215). This list includes personal records, such as library, financial, phone, travel, and medical records. To obtain these materials, the FBI no longer needs a subpoena from a grand jury; they only need a search warrant from a judge.

Section 216—"Modification of authorities relating to use of pen registers and trap and trace devices"—This section extends existing telephone monitoring laws to include information relating to Internet usage, including e-mail addresses, IP addresses, and URLs for Web pages. There has been considerable opposition to sections 215 and 216 especially by the American Library Association as they relate to government access to library loan records and library computer information.

"Section 223—Civil Liability for Certain Unauthorized Disclosure"—This section states that "any willful disclosure or use by an investigative or law enforcement officer or governmental entity of information beyond the extent permitted" will result in an inquiry and potential disciplinary action (PATRIOT Act, 2001: sec. 223).

"Section A—International Counter Money Laundering and Related Measures" This section has a number of important record management implications. The primary goals of this section are to prevent individuals from disguising their identity and moving laundered money from "offshore" accounts back into the United States. To prevent this from occurring, financial institutions are required to implement procedures and systems that can detect fraud and document the identity of users. For example, in Section 311 financial institutions are instructed "to maintain records, file reports, or both, concerning the aggregate amount of transactions, or concerning each transaction." In addition, institutions must maintain data on "the identity and address of the participants in a transaction or relationship, including (i) the identity of the originator of any funds transfer; (ii) the legal capacity in which a participant in any transaction is acting; (iii) the identity of the beneficial owner of the funds involved in any transaction . . . ; and (iv) a description of any transaction" (PATRIOT Act, 2001: sec. A).

Section 312 states that each financial institution "shall establish appropriate, specific, and, where necessary, enhanced, due diligence policies, procedures, and controls that are reasonably designed to detect and report instances of money laundering through those accounts" (PATRIOT Act, 2001: sec. 312). Section 314 requires that financial institutions create systems that can efficiently search account records for information required by the government as part of an investigation and do so in an accurate and timely manner. Section 326 requires that financial institutions verify according to well defined procedures a person's identity when new accounts are created, to "maintain records of the information used to verify a person's identity, including name, address, and other identifying information"; and to consult "lists of known or suspected terrorists or terrorist organizations provided to the financial institution by any government agency to determine whether a person seeking to open an account appears on any such list" (PATRIOT Act, 2001: sec. 326).

Sarbanes-Oxley Act

On July 30, 2002, President Bush signed into law the Sarbanes-Oxley Act, named after its main architects, Senator Paul Sarbanes and Representative Michael Oxley. The Sarbanes-Oxley Act, or SOX, was passed in reaction to highly publicized corporate scandals and requires high levels of accountability from companies and their senior executives. SOX applies to public companies that are listed on the U.S. stock exchange. As such, SOX also applies to companies based outside the United States that trade their stocks in the U.S.

SOX focuses largely on corporate governance, financial reporting, and accounting practices. Prominent themes or issues include:

Accountability: SOX defines responsibilities of directors and officers and mandates that CEOs and CFOs of public companies certify the accuracy of their company's financial reports. According to the provisions of the Act, CEOs and CFOs will be held accountable if internal controls are not in place to achieve the desired results.

Enforcement: SOX establishes procedures, mechanisms, and schedules for monitoring compliance and defines severe fines and jail time for non-compliance.

Controls: SOX mandates that public companies create sound internal controls to assure financial reports are reliable.

Records Management: At its core SOX is an attempt to improve the accountability of public companies and transparency of its business processes. These qualities depend upon trustworthy and accurate records. As such, compliance with SOX is dependent upon the creation of information and records management practices that ensure the authenticity, reliability, and integrity of business records.

The Sarbanes-Oxley Act is arranged into eleven titles. The most important sections for recordkeeping are 101–107, 302, 401, 404, 409, 802 and 906 (Sarbanes-Oxley Act, 2002).

Sections 101–107

Sections 101–107 of SOX create a Public Company Accounting Oversight Board (PCAOB) to oversee the audit of public companies that are subject to the securities laws. The Board is defined as a non-profit corporation under the general oversight of the SEC. The Board is be comprised of five full-time independent members (of whom only two may be current or former certified public accountants) appointed by the SEC for five-year terms. The duties of the Board include the following:

1. "Register public accounting firms"—All accounting firms that audit public companies, including foreign accounting firms, must register with the Board.
2. Establish, or adopt, by rule, "auditing, quality control, ethics, independence, and other standards relating to the preparation of audit reports for issuers."
3. "Conduct inspections of accounting firms"—The Board is required to regularly inspect the operations of each registered public accounting firm. Firms that audit over 100 public companies must be inspected annually; all others must be inspected at least once every three years.
4. Conduct investigations and disciplinary proceedings, and impose appropriate sanctions.
5. Enforce compliance with the Act, the rules of the Board, professional standards, and the securities laws relating to the preparation and issuance of audit reports and the obligations and liabilities of accountants.

Section 302: Corporate Responsibility for Financial Reports.

Section 302 of the Act directs the SEC to adopt rules requiring the principal executive officer and principal financial officer of all companies to file periodic reports to certify that they have reviewed the company's quarterly or annual report, and that the report does not contain any false or misleading facts or statements on the financial condition of the organization. Section 302 also states that the chief officers are responsible for creating internal controls and for ensuring that these controls are effective. The chief officers must have evaluated these internal controls within a ninety-day time frame and must report on their findings. This report must include a list of all deficiencies or significant changes in the internal control systems.

Section 401: Disclosures In Periodic Reports

This section requires that financial statements be accurate and complete, and that they disclose "all material off-balance sheet transactions, arrangement, obligations . . . that may have a material current and future effect on financial condition."

Section 404: Management Assessment of Internal Controls

Section 404 requires that management provide an assessment of the effectiveness of internal controls over financial reporting. This report is required to include the following:

- A statement of management's responsibility for "establishing and maintaining adequate internal control structure and procedures over financial reporting."
- A statement identifying the framework used by management to evaluate the effectiveness of this internal control.
- An assessment of the "effectiveness of the internal control structure and procedures" over financial reporting as of the end of the company's most recent fiscal year.
- A report submitted by "each registered public accounting firm that prepares or issues the audit report for the issuer" attesting to the effectiveness of the internal control structure and procedures.

Section 404 is one of the most important sections within SOX, and it has emerged as one of the most challenging requirements for businesses to implement. Because of its importance, let us briefly review how SOX and experts on internal controls define the nature of controls. SOX defines internal control over financial reporting as "a process designed by, or under the supervision of, the registrant's principal executive and principal financial officers, or persons performing similar functions, and effected by the registrant's board of directors, management, and other personnel, to provide reasonable assurance regarding the reliability of financial reporting and the preparation of financial statements for external purposes in accordance with generally accepted accounting principles and includes policies and procedures that:

- pertain to the maintenance of records that in reasonable detail accurately and fairly reflect the transactions and dispositions of the assets of the registrant;
- provide reasonable assurance that transactions are recorded as necessary to permit preparation of financial statements in accordance with generally accepted accounting principles, and receipts and expenditures of the registrant are being made only in accordance with authorizations of management and directors of the registrant; and

- provide reasonable assurance regarding prevention or timely detection of unauthorized acquisition, use or disposition of the registrant's assets that could have a material effect on the financial statements" (Sarbanes-Oxley Act, 2002: Section 404).

Auditors describe two basic types of control deficiencies: a deficiency in design, which exists if the control was never designed into the systems, or does not meet the control objective as it was designed; and a deficiency in operation which is a control that is not functioning properly or as designed. Auditors also identify three types of internal controls: *preventive controls*, which are intended to prevent or reduce the likelihood of a negative outcome; *detective controls*, which are intended to detect and report that a negative outcome has occurred; and *corrective controls*, which are intended to remedy, and correct for a negative outcome once it has occurred. Critical elements of any strategy for internal control are the audit trails designed to provide documentation on activities that have been undertaken. Generally speaking, there are three types of controls:

- Manual controls, which are performed without the assistance of automated applications. Manual controls are subject to the inherent risk of human error and, as a result, are often considered less reliable than other types of controls.
- Automated controls, which are performed by the computer system. Generally speaking, a goal of most system designers is to reduce the number of manual controls and increase the number of automated controls.
- IT-dependent manual controls (hybrid), which is essentially a combination of manual and automated processes (Sarbanes-Oxley Act, 2002: Controls).

Section 409: Real Time Issuer Disclosures

This section requires companies to disclose information on material changes in the financial condition or operations of the company on a continuous basis and in "real-time." This represents a fundamental change in the disclosure obligations of public companies. Previously companies were permitted to defer disclosure of changes until the next quarterly or annual report. Section 409 would require companies to report these changes immediately and as they occurred.

Section 802

Section 802 amends the federal obstruction-of-justice statute by adding two new offenses. First, officials who knowingly alter, destroy, mutilate, conceal, or falsify any document with the intent to impede, obstruct or influence proceedings involving federal agencies or bankruptcy proceedings may be fined or imprisoned up to 20 years or both. Secondly, Section 802 directs accountants to maintain certain corporate audit records for a period of five years from the end of the fiscal period during which the audit or review was concluded. Those who violate these provisions can be fined or imprisoned for a maximum term of ten years or both.

Section 906

Section 906 of the Act requires that the company's chief executive officer and chief financial officer certify that their financial report complies with the requirements of Section 13(a) or 15(d) of the Securities Exchange Act of 1934, and that the information in the report accurately represents the financial condition and operations of the company. Section 906 imposes criminal penalties of up to $1 million and/or ten years in prison for knowingly filing a false certification, and up to $5 million and/or 20 years in prison for willfully filing a false certification.

Since SOX was passed into law, the SEC has convened two roundtable discussions relating to implementation. Feedback obtained from the 2005 roundtable "indicated that the internal control reporting requirements had led to increased focus by management on internal control over financial reporting . . . and identified particular implementation areas in need of further clarification to reduce unnecessary costs and burdens without jeopardizing the benefits of the new requirements" (Sarbanes-Oxley Act, Roundtable, 2005). In response, SEC staff issued new guidelines on May 16, 2005. One of the primary messages of these guidelines was that "it is the responsibility of management, not the auditor, to determine the appropriate nature and form of internal controls for the company and to scope their evaluation procedures accordingly" (Sarbanes-Oxley Act, SEC). At the 2006 roundtable, a number of participants commented that additional guidance was needed. In response to this request, the SEC issued some additional guidelines (Sarbanes-Oxley Act, Roundtable, 2006).

In the past four years, the SEC has issued a number of publications and initiated a number of activities to amend or clarify SOX requirements.

IMPACT OF SOX

Since the implementation of SOX a number of surveys have been conducted to gauge the impact of the law on businesses. A citation to relevant publications and press releases can be found at the reference Sarbanes-Oxley Act, SEC Publications.

2004 SURVEYS

A survey in 2004 by the consulting firm of PriceWaterhouseCoopers found that SOX is corporate America's number one challenge for compliance by a wide margin (49 percent to 15 percent for the second biggest challenge) (Oce, n.d.).

In July 2004, Financial Executives International (FEI), the leading professional organization serving chief financial officers and other senior financial executives, surveyed 224 public companies with average revenues of $2.5 billion to gauge Section 404 compliance cost estimates. Results showed the total cost of compliance was estimated at $3.14 million, or 62 percent more than the $1.93 million estimate identified in FEI's January 2004 survey. The increase in Section 404 compliance costs resulted from a 109 percent rise in internal costs, a 42 percent jump in external costs, and a 40 percent increase in the fees charged by external auditors (Financial Executives International, 2004).

A 2004 report published by the American Electronics Association (AEA) found that implementation costs for Section 404 were 20 times greater than the SEC originally estimated. The report went on to say that the "Section 404's guidance has not differentiated between large and small companies, and as a result, auditors have been applying a one-size-fits-all approach to implementation. This is having a devastating effect on smaller business" (AEA, 2004: 3). The study estimated that for small companies the cost per employee to comply with Section 404 was 10 times the amount spent by large firms. The report also suggested that cost burdens had resulted in some foreign companies withdrawing from the U.S. public securities market, or at least postponing their entry (AEA, 2004).

A 2006 CRA International survey showed that the costs of complying with Section 404 fell substantially in year 2, as shown in figures 7.1 and 7.2. Auditors consulted by CRA attributed this decline in implementation costs to increased efficiencies in testing controls, reductions in the amount of documentation, and to the less frequent use of outside consultants (CRA, 2006). The CRA 2006 survey data also discovered that the number of significant system deficiencies identified by the company or the auditor declined from year one to year two (CRA, 2006). For smaller companies, the number of deficiencies fell from an average of 5.3 in year one to 1.3 in the second year. For larger companies, the number of deficiencies declined from 5.0 on average in year one to 2.5 on average in year two. It appears that SOX is having a positive effect on the management of information systems.

In its 2003 and 2005 surveys, Cohasset Associates Inc. explored the impact of Sarbanes Oxley on records management programs. In 2005, 8 percent of respondents stated that SOX had had a significant impact on their organization's records management programs, and 19

Figure 7.1
Smaller Company Cost Summary

	Year 2	Year 1	% change
404 Cost Summary:	in 000s ($)	in 000s ($)	
Internal Issuer 404 Costs	301	355	-15.2%
Third Party Costs for 404	223	463	-51.8%
Total 404 Issuer Costs	**524**	**818**	**-36.0%**
404 Audit Fees	336	423	-20.6%
Total 404 Costs	**860**	**1,241**	**-30.7%**
Proxy Audit Fee Component Summary:			
404 Audit Fees	336	423	-20.6%
Other (non-404) Audit Fees	477	423	12.8%
Total Proxy Audit Fees	**813**	**846**	**-3.9%**

Based on data from CRA International, 2006. Permission provided by CRA International. Available: www.s-oxinternalcontrolinfo.com/pdfs/CRA_III.pdf, p. 3.

Figure 7.2
Larger Company Cost Summary

	Year 2	Year 1	% change
404 Cost Summary:	in 000s ($)	in 000s ($)	
Internal Issuer 404 Costs	2,220	4,260	-47.9%
Third Party Costs for 404	980	2,230	-56.1%
Total 404 Issuer Costs	**3,200**	**6,490**	**-50.7%**
404 Audit Fees	1,570	2,020	-22.3%
Total 404 Costs	**4,770**	**8,510**	**-43.9%**
Proxy Audit Fee Component Summary:			
404 Audit Fees	1,570	2,020	-22.3%
Other (non-404) Audit Fees	3,540	3,080	14.9%
Total Proxy Audit Fees	**5,110**	**5,100**	**0.2%**

Based on data from CRA International, 2006. Permission provided by CRA International. Available: www.s-oxinternalcontrolinfo.com/pdfs/CRA_III.pdf, p. 3.

percent claimed that it had had a meaningful impact. Thirty-nine percent stated that SOX had had no impact on its records management program. When the percentages for the 2005 survey were compared to those in 2003, the number of responses in the significant impact category increased by 100 percent and in the meaningful impact by 58 percent, and the no impact response decreased by 36 percent. Clearly SOX was having a greater impact in how organizations managed records, and it was the opinion of Cohasset staff that the impact of SOX and litigation on records management programs would continue to grow (Cohasset, 2003: Question 21; Cohasset, 2005: Question 28).

Cohasset staff also asked in the 2003 and 2005 surveys: "to what extent has Sarbanes-Oxley resulted in your organization increasing its budget for records management?" In 2003 only 1 percent responded that it led to a large increase (a more than 35 percent increase), which grew to 4 percent in 2005. In 2003 87 percent stated it resulted in no increase, and this percentage decreased to 72 percent in 2005. Clearly, records management budgets had not increased to the extent one would have anticipated and expected (Cohasset, 2003: Question 22; Cohasset, 2005: Question 29).

The survey's results indicate that SOX implementation, particularly Section 404, continues to be a major challenge for organizations. However, for a number of reasons costs associated with implementation have decreased significantly in the last three years. Unfortunately, the Cohasset survey would suggest that the additional resources committed to implementing SOX have not resulted in significant increases in records management budgets.

Government Paperwork Elimination Act (GPEA)

The Government Paperwork Elimination Act (GPEA, Pub. L. 105–277) requires that, when appropriate, Federal agencies use electronic forms, electronic filing, and electronic signatures to conduct official business with the public. The objectives of the Act were to make it easier and more efficient for the public to transact business and to minimize the paperwork burden for individuals and institutions that collect data and information by or for the Federal government. Like E-Sign, the purpose of GPEA is to "preclude agencies or courts from systematically treating electronic documents and signatures less favorably than their paper counterparts" (GPEA: "Purpose"). Also like E-Sign, the Act is technology neutral and does not recommend or endorse a specific type of technology for implementing the act. GPEA also goes to great lengths to describe the various responsibilities of the director and the various agencies in overseeing or managing the electronic records produced by the Act.

Heads of agencies are responsible for managing a number of records management activities including "carrying out the agency's information resources management activities to improve agency productivity, efficiency, and effectiveness; maintaining a current and complete inventory of the agency's information resources; improving the integrity, quality, and utility of information to all users within and outside the agency, including capabilities for ensuring dissemination of public information, public access to government information, and protections for privacy and security; conducting formal training programs to educate agency program and management officials about information resources management; ensuring that the public has timely and equitable access to the agency's public information; and implementing and enforcing applicable policies, procedures, standards, and guidelines on privacy, confidentiality, security, disclosure and sharing of information collected or maintained by or for the agency" (GPEA: "Federal Agencies Responsibilities").

The California Database Protection Act of 2003 (CDPA)

This act requires any person, agency, or company doing business in California to disclose security breaches to each affected California customer whose personal information has been compromised. Failure to comply may result in lawsuits and damages. Personal information is defined as an unencrypted first name and last name or initials and last name in combination with a social security number or driver's license number, or an account number or credit or debit card number in combination with any required security code, access code, or password that would permit access to an individual's financial account. The name of the person in and of itself does not constitute a breach of security according to the Act. A "breach of the security system" includes unauthorized access, data theft, data manipulation, the introduction and use of viruses, or theft of systems that store personal information. The Act requires that disclosure be made "in the most expedient time possible and without unreasonable delay" (CDPA, 2003: section 1798.82). It is generally agreed that compliance with this law will require that companies conduct a comprehensive analysis of the company's information security system, including reviews of technical controls such as firewalls and access controls, physical security, data back up and storage procedures, procedures for security breaches, and use of intrusion detection technologies. It will also require a review of how companies implement incident response policies and procedures that lead to quick and effective internal investigations of security breaches.

CANADA

Access to Information Act

This 1985 Act sought to "extend the present laws of Canada to provide a right of access to information in records under the control of a government institution in accordance with the principles that government information should be available to the public, that necessary exceptions to the right of access should be limited and specific and that decisions on the disclosure of government information should be reviewed independently of government" (Canadian Access to Information Act, 1985, "Purpose"). The first section of the Act states that Canadian citizens have the right of access to government records, including documents in electronic format. In regard to access to records, the Act states that written requests will normally be fulfilled in thirty days, except under certain conditions outlined in the Act. Under the provisions of the Act, citizens denied access to records may submit written complaints, and procedures for reviewing the complaint are outlined in the law. In sum, like all information access laws, the Canadian Act certainly requires that federal agencies develop records management procedures for preserving the records they create and for making them readily accessible to those who have a need and right to review them.

Privacy Act

This Act was passed in 1985, and its purpose was "to extend the present laws of Canada that protect the privacy of individuals with respect to personal information about themselves held by a government institution and that provide individuals with a right of access to that information" (Canadian Privacy Act, 1985: "Purpose"). Within the section of the Act related to the "collection, retention and disposal of personal information, it is stated that only personal information that "relates directly to an operating program or activity of the institution" will be collected, and that government agencies will inform individuals regarding the purpose for which the information is being collected. The Act further states that the agency "shall take all reasonable steps to ensure that personal information that is used for an administrative purpose by the institution is as accurate, up-to-date and complete as possible" (Canadian Privacy Act, 1985: "Collection, Retention, and Disposal of Personal Information"). The Act also clearly states that the agency collecting the data will systematically dispose of the data in accordance with established retention and disposal policies and procedures. In the section on protection of personal information, the Act specifies that this data will not be used or disclosed without the consent of the individual to whom it relates, except under certain well defined conditions. Finally, in the section on access to personal information, the Act states every Canadian citizen has the right of access to his/her personal data, and is entitled to request corrections to personal data that may contain errors or omissions. These responsibilities to protect, to systematically retain and destroy, and to keep accurate the personal or information of its citizens clearly demands that Canadian government agencies develop recordkeeping systems that manage this personal data over the life cycle.

Personal Information Protection and Electronic Documents Act

This Act was approved in 2000 and was created for two reasons: 1) "to support and promote electronic commerce by protecting personal information that is collected, used or disclosed in certain circumstances" (Personal Information Protection and Electronic Documents Act, 2000: Definition of Act); in essence, the Act updates the protection of personal information by defining conditions of use and management for electronic records; and 2) to authorize the use of electronic documents to communicate or record information or transactions.

The Act begins by reiterating that the collection, use, and disclosure of personal information in electronic format without the knowledge or consent of the individuals who are the subjects of the data is prohibited except under certain well defined conditions. Significantly, the Act includes a section on the use of audits if the Commissioner overseeing the implementation of the Act has discovered evidence that an agency is not fulfilling the requirements of the Act.

The second part of the Act authorizes the use of electronic documents to record and communicate information and transactions, as long as certain conditions are met. In the section on collection and storage of records, the Act states that government agencies "may use electronic means to create, collect, receive, store, transfer, distribute, publish or otherwise deal with documents or information whenever a federal law does not specify the manner of doing so" (Personal Information Protection and Electronic Documents Act, 2000: 33). In addition, the Act specifies that payments to government agencies may be made electronically.

The Act then goes on to discuss issues involved in the proper management of these electronic records, including authentication procedures and activities designed to preserve the evidence within the record. Authentication of electronic records is directly addressed in the section on "original documents," where the Act specifies that the requirement for documents to be in their original form is satisfied if the electronic document "contains a secure electronic signature that was added when the electronic document was first generated in its final form and that can be used to verify that the electronic document has not been changed since that time" (Personal Information Protection and Electronic Documents Act, 2000: 42). The message is very clear: electronic records can be used in the transaction of business, but only if the records are properly managed.

The Data Protection Act (DPA)

The DPA was passed in 1998 and gives citizens certain rights regarding information held about them. It also clearly delineates the responsibilities of organizations for managing this data, particularly as it relates to the access and use of the data. The primary purpose of the Act is to protect the individual rights and freedoms of persons and especially their right to privacy with respect to the processing of personal data. The Act contains eight Data Protection Principles. These state that personal data shall be:

1) "processed fairly and lawfully" and in accordance with the conditions of this Act.
2) "obtained only for one or more specified and lawful purposes, and shall not be further processed in any manner incompatible with that purpose or those purposes."
3) "adequate, relevant and not excessive in relation to the purpose or purposes for which they are processed."
4) "accurate and, where necessary, kept up to date."
5) "kept for no longer than is necessary for that purpose or those purposes."
6) "processed in accordance with the rights of data subjects under this Act."
7) kept secure "against unauthorised or unlawful processing of personal data and against accidental loss or destruction of, or damage to, personal data."
8) transferred only to a "country or territory [that] ensures an adequate level of protection for the rights and freedoms of data subjects in relation to the processing of personal data" (Data Protection Act, 1998: Schedule 1).

The Data Protection Act defines conditions under which personal data may be made available.
These include:

1) data subject has given his consent to the processing;
2) the process is necessary because the data subject is entering into or involved in a contract;

3) to comply with a legal obligation or other functions of a public nature; and
4) to protect the vital interests of the data subject" (Data Protection Act, 1998: Schedule 2). Unless the request falls into one of these categories the personal information may not be disclosed.

In order to meet the requirements of this Act an organization must have in place well designed and effective recordkeeping systems. The system must maintain authentic records, and should have a disposition plan so that data is stored only as long as necessary. In addition, the data must be readily accessible to those who have the rights to access, but the data must also be protected against unauthorized users and from modification and corruption.

The U.K. Freedom of Information Act

The Freedom of Information Act (FOI) was passed on November 30, 2000, and became fully implemented in January 2005. The Freedom of Information Act gives anyone the right to request information from a government organization, about any subject of interest to them. According to the Act, any citizen who makes a request to a public authority for information must be informed in writing whether that agency has that information. The Act outlines conditions under which information may be withheld because "the public interest in maintaining the exclusion of the duty to confirm or deny outweighs the public interest in disclosing whether the public authority holds the information" (FOIA [U.K.], 2000: 3). Without question, complying with the Freedom of Information Act requires that government agencies maintain authentic records within systems that manage these records over the life cycle.

RULES AND REGULATIONS

United States

Securities and Exchange Act

In 1934, Congress passed the Securities and Exchange Act to regulate the securities industry. The Act required the creation and maintenance of records of securities transactions for the purpose of review and audit in order to better protect investors and the U.S. economy. 17 CFR § 240.17a–4 (SEC 17a–4 Rule) is a rule created by the SEC under the Exchange Act that stipulates specific recordkeeping requirements for certain exchange members, brokers, and dealers in the securities industry. Rule 17a–4 applies to any financial institution whose business units trade securities are regulated by the Securities and Exchange Commission (SEC) and the National Association of Securities Dealers (NASD).

The rule was updated in 1997 to expressly allow for the storage, retention, and reproduction of records by means of "electronic storage media." Compliance with Rule 17a–4 as revised requires that members, brokers, and dealers carefully evaluate their information management processes and systems to ensure that authentic and reliable electronic records are captured, preserved, and accessible for as long as required by the Act.

Specific requirements of the 1997 Rule as they relate to recordkeeping include:

- Members, brokers and dealers must "preserve for a period of not less than three years, the first two years in an easily accessible place . . . originals of all communications received and copies of all communications sent" related to their business as broker-dealers, including electronic communications such as e-mail and instant messaging.
- The electronic storage media must preserve the records "in a non-rewriteable, non-erasable format," verify the "quality and accuracy of the storage media recording process," be able "to download indexes and records preserved on the electronic storage media to any medium acceptable under this paragraph."
- If a member, broker, or dealer uses micrographic media or electronic storage media, it shall "at all times have available, for examination by the staffs of the Commission and self-regulatory organizations of which it is a member, facilities for immediate, easily readable projection or production of micrographic media or electronic storage media images and for producing easily readable images."
- "The member, broker, or dealer must have in place an audit system providing for accountability regarding inputting of records required to be maintained and preserved" (SEC 17a–4 Rule, sections b and f).

In 2002, the SEC made some revisions to the Act. The most important change for recordkeeping related to requirements on the use of third parties in managing an organization's records. The so-called "Designated Third Party (D3P)" requirement states that "every member, broker, or dealer exclusively using electronic storage media for some or all of its records preservation" shall designate a third party that can independently provide the SEC with access to the third party broker-dealer's records upon request if the organization cannot or will not meet its recordkeeping obligations (SEC 17a–4 Rule, section f). The third party's responsibilities are to notify the SEC in writing they intend to fulfill the access requirements for the organization, and to provide regulators with access to the information and with instructions on how to download the records. Generally speaking, D3P is designed to ensure that a broker-dealer's records are always accessible to regulators.

Impact of SEC Rules

In a 2004 report, experts estimated that the cumulative organizational penalties for SEC 17a–4 infractions would grow from $500 million to $1 billion (SunGard Availability Services, 2004: 3). In the past few years, the SEC has fined several companies particularly large amounts of money. In the most high-profile case, in December 2002, the Securities and Exchange Commission, the New York Stock Exchange, and NASD announced joint actions against five companies for violations of recordkeeping requirements concerning e-mail communications. The three regulatory agencies found the companies had "violated Section 17(a) of the Securities Exchange Act of 1934, Rule 17a–4 under the Exchange Act, NYSE Rule 440 and NASD Rule 3110 by failing to preserve for a period of three years, and/or preserve in an accessible place for two years, electronic communications relating to the business of the firm, including interoffice memoranda and communications." They also charged the five brokerage houses with violating "NYSE Rule 342 and NASD Rule 3010 by failing to establish, maintain and enforce a supervisory system to assure compliance with NASD and NYSE rules and the federal securities laws relating to retention of electronic communications" (U.S. Securities and Exchange Commission, 2002). The firms agreed to a penalty of a censure and fines totaling $8.25 million, and to review their procedures for complying with recordkeeping statutes and rules.

Federal Rules of Evidence (FRE)

The Federal Rules of Evidence are the rules that govern the admissibility of evidence in the United States federal court system. While the Federal Rules of Evidence apply only in federal courts, a large majority of states have adopted similar (and sometimes identical) rules for use in their respective courts. The United States Supreme Court created drafts of the FRE in 1969, 1971, and 1972, but Congress did not allow the FRE to become federal law until 1975, and only after enacting a series of modifications to the rules.

Since 2006, the FRE are divided into eleven articles, with each article containing one or more rules. Not all of the articles have passed Congressional approval.

I.	General Provisions
II.	Judicial Notice
III.	Presumptions in Civil Actions and Proceedings
IV.	Relevancy and its Limits
V.	Privileges
VI.	Witnesses
VII.	Opinions and Expert Testimony
VIII.	Hearsay
IX.	Authentication and Identification
X.	Contents of Writings, Recordings, and Photographs
XI.	Miscellaneous Rules

Within these Articles, there are 84 total rules (Federal Rules of Evidence, 2006). A number of the rules deal with the admissibility of electronic records as evidence. In the Federal Rules, the admission of electronic records as evidence is dependent upon two factors.

First, the government must demonstrate that human statements are not inadmissible hearsay. To do this the records must fall within the business records exception (Federal Rules of Evidence, 2006: 803–806) or be classified as records of regularly conducted activities. The 803 (6) exceptions define a business record as a "memorandum, report, record, or data compilation, in any form, of acts, events, conditions, opinions, or diagnoses, made at or near the time by, or from information transmitted by, a person with knowledge, if kept in the course of a regularly conducted business activity, and if it was the regular practice of that business activity to make the memorandum, report, record, or data compilation, all as shown by the testimony of the custodian or other qualified witness, unless the source of information or the method or circumstances of preparation indicate lack of trustworthiness" (Federal Rules of Evidence, 2006: sec. 803).

As indicated in the definition of a business record, the government must also establish the authenticity of all computer records by providing "evidence sufficient to support a finding that the matter in question is what its proponent claims" (Federal Rules of Evidence, 2006: sec. 901). Without some strategy for authenticating the author of a record, the courts may question the document's validity. Decisions in many court cases have focused on the authenticity of the electronic evidence. For example, in *Pettiford v. N.C HHS*, in *Sea-Land Serv. v. Lozen Int'l*, and in *Gamber-Johnson v. Trans Data Net Corp*, the inability to properly authenticate records resulted in the court refusing to consider them as evidence (Kahn Consultants, 2005: 8).

Challenges to the authenticity of computer records often take one of three forms. First, parties may challenge the authenticity of electronic records by questioning whether the records were altered, manipulated, or damaged after they were created. However, in most cases to date the courts have not favored unsupported claims that computer records have been altered. Second, parties may question the authenticity of computer-generated records by challenging the reliability of the information system that managed and preserved the records or the computer program that generated the records. The Federal Rules of Evidence clearly states that electronic evidence can be authenticated by demonstrating that the systems or processes that produced and managed the record are trustworthy. Conversely, if the trustworthiness of the system is called into question, then all records produced by that system are tainted. This issue points out how important it is for organizations to have trustworthy recordkeeping systems that capture and maintain authentic records. Third, parties may challenge the authenticity of computer-stored records by questioning the identity of their author.

Food and Drug Administration (FDA), 21 CFR Part 11

In 1997, the Food and Drug Administration (FDA) released 21 CFR Part 11, which allowed FDA-regulated industries, such as the pharmaceutical, biotechnology and medical devices and food processing industries, to use electronic records and electronic signatures for business purposes. The final rule provides criteria under which FDA will consider electronic records to be equivalent to paper records, and electronic signatures equivalent to traditional handwritten signatures. In order for these electronic records to be accepted, the rule outlines detailed requirements for the management of the electronic records to ensure that they are trustworthy, authentic, and reliable.

Section 11.10 of the regulation identifies activities that must be implemented to ensure the integrity of information within the information system. These measures include: "1) Validation" of the computer systems and software used to process, manage and store electronic records; "(2) the ability to generate accurate and complete copies of records; (3) archival protection of records; (4) use of computer-generated, time-stamped audit trails; (5) use of appropriate controls over systems documentation; and (6) a determination that persons who develop, maintain, or use electronic records and signature systems have the education, training, and experience to perform their assigned tasks." Section 11.10 also addresses the security of systems and requires that: "(1) System access be limited to authorized individuals; (2) operational system checks be used to enforce permitted sequencing of steps and events as appropriate; (3) authority checks be used to ensure that only authorized individuals can use the system, electronically sign a record, access the operation or computer system input or output device, alter a record, or perform operations; (4) device (e.g., terminal) checks be used to determine the validity of the source of data input or operation instruction; and (5) written policies be established and adhered to holding individuals accountable and responsible for actions initiated under their electronic signatures, so as to deter record and signature falsification" (U.S. Food and Drug Administration Act, 1997: sec. 11.10). In order to validate the signature the Act specifies that electronic signatures must include metadata with the printed name of the signer, dates and time when completed, and a designation of the nature of the transaction. The signature must also be logically linked to the records they are part of so that signatures cannot illegally be transferred to another record. Finally, Section 11.20 of the Act "provides that electronic signatures not based on biometrics must employ at least two distinct identification components such as an identification code and password" (U.S. Food and Drug Administration Act, 1997: sec. 11.20).

National Association of Security Dealers (NASD) and New York Stock Exchange (NYSE) Rules

On May 10, 2002, the Securities and Exchange Commission (SEC) approved new NASD Rule 2711, Research Analysts and Research Reports. The rule is intended to address potential conflicts of interest in the issuance of research reports by members, improve the objectivity of research, and provide investors with more useful and reliable information when making investment decisions. The SEC also approved on that day similar amendments to New York Stock Exchange (NYSE) Rule 472. The NASD and NYSE rules and interpretations are virtually identical.

The new rules incorporate a number of requirements for more extensive disclosure of information. They require disclosure of financial interests in companies covered by the analyst and the firm, disclosure of existing and potential investment banking relationships with subject companies, disclosure in research reports of data and price charts that assist investors, and disclosure in research reports of the distribution of buy/hold/sell ratings and the percentage of investment banking clients in each category. The Round 1 Amendments were phased-in incrementally during the period from July 9, 2002, to November 6, 2002, to provide members time to implement necessary policies, procedures, systems, and other measures to comply with the new rules (U.S. Securities and Exchange Commission, 2003).

On July 29, 2003, the SEC approved a second set of amendments to the rules. In its description of its changes, the NYSE wrote that these amendments were necessary in order to comply with the mandates of SOX, which required the creation of "rules reasonably designed to address conflicts of interest that can arise when securities analysts recommend equity securities in research reports and public appearances, in order to improve the objectivity of research and provide investors with more useful and reliable information." As with the Round 1 Amendments, the Round 2 Amendments were phased-in incrementally (NYSE, Amendments).

As a consequence of all these disclosure requirements, financial organizations were forced to review their records management and establish better recordkeeping practices to identify and protect regulated data, to prevent unauthorized data access and usage, and to provide audit trails that documented how data is managed.

As of November 30, 2005, NASD Enforcement has settled 29 cases involving Rule 2711 violations. The vast majority of these actions have involved violations of the disclosure requirements involving over 265 research reports. From 2002 to 2005, the NYSE also conducted a number of investigations involving improper disclosure of information. Sanctions in the settled cases have included fines ranging from

$10,000 to $50,000, and other penalties. In addition, on April 28, 2003, the SEC, NYSE, NASD, NASAA and the New York Attorney General's Office announced that they had reached an agreement (the "Global Settlement") with ten investment banking firms settling actions alleging fraudulent or misleading research. Provisions of the agreement relating to recordkeeping included improving disclosure practices and more transparency in regard to potential and actual conflicts of interests involving research analysts (NASD and NYSE, 2005).

The Federal Rules of Civil Procedure

In December 6, 2006, new rules relating to the Federal Rules of Civil Procedure went into effect. These new rules were created to accommodate electronic records and will have a major impact on e-discovery and on how electronic records are managed. One can view these changes as attempts to address many of the electronic discovery issues outlined in the Zubulake decisions (discussed in chapter 6) and in other high profile court cases involving e-discovery. The amendments cover five important topics related to the management of records for e-discovery.

Definition of Discoverable Material

The amendments introduce the phrase "electronically stored information" to Rules 26(a)(1), 33, and 34, to acknowledge that electronically stored information is discoverable and can be subpoenaed. The new rules broaden the definition of what must be disclosed to include "any designated documents or electronically stored information—including writings, drawings, graphs, charts, photographs, sound recordings, images, and other data or data complications stored in any medium from which information can be obtained or translated, if necessary, by the respondent into reasonably usable form" (Federal Rule of Civil Procedure, 2006: rule 34[a]). E-mail certainly qualifies under this definition.

Early Attention to Electronic Discovery Issues

The new rule requires that legal counsel, IT personnel, and records managers be proactive in how they manage data and records. For example, Rule 26 (f) states that the parties in the court case should convene early in the process to discuss and resolve any issues relating to disclosure or discovery of electronic records. The rule states that this meeting should include a discussion relating to the format of the electronic records and to any issues regarding preservation or restrictions on access to discoverable information. Implied in this rule is the requirement that legal counsel, IT, and records managers know where electronic records are stored, how they are managed and preserved, and how they can be retrieved (Federal Rule of Civil Procedure, 2006: rule 26[f]).

Usability—Arrangement and Format of Records

The new rule allows the requesting party in a discovery motion or in a subpoena to "specify the form or forms in which electronically stored information is to be produced." If the form is not specified, the responding party is instructed to "produce them as they are kept in the usual course of business" or in a form that is "reasonably useable." The rule also provides a framework for resolving disputes over the form of production, in the event that the responding party objects to the requested formats (Federal Rule of Civil Procedure, 2006: rule 34[b]).

Electronically Stored Information from Sources that Are Not Reasonably Accessible

Under the new rule, a responding party to a discovery motion or subpoena "need not provide discovery of electronically stored information from sources that the party identifies as not reasonably accessible because of undue burden or cost" (Federal Rule of Civil Procedure, 2006: rule 26[2,b]). However, this amendment does not relieve corporations of the duty to preserve evidence. Even if the electronic information is not reasonably accessible, "the court may nonetheless order discovery from such sources if the requesting party shows good cause" (Federal Rule of Civil Procedure, 2006: rule 26[2,b]). In determining whether the burden or expense of the discovery action outweighs the benefits, the courts will consider "1) the specificity of the discovery request; 2) the quantity of information available from other and more easily accessible sources; 3) the failure to produce relevant information that seems likely to have existed but is no longer available on more easily accessed sources; 4) the likelihood of finding relevant, responsive information that cannot be obtained from other, more easily accessed sources; 5) predictions as to the importance and usefulness of further information; 6) the importance of the issues at stake in the litigation; and 7) the parties' resources" (Federal Rule of Civil Procedure, 2006: rule 26[2,b]).

Loss of Information as a Result of Routine Operations

This was the most controversial new rule. This rule states that "absent exceptional circumstances, a court may not impose sanctions under these rules on a party for failing to provide electronically stored information lost as a result of the routine, good-faith operation of an electronic information system" (Federal Rule of Civil Procedure, 2006: 37[f]). This rule acknowledges the fact that a party may lose potentially discoverable information "without culpable conduct on its part" (Federal Rule of Civil Procedure, 2006: 37[f]). Because of this protection, this rule has come to be referred to as the "Safe Harbor" rule. The rule also notes, however, that the good faith requirement "means that a party is not permitted to exploit the routine operation of an information system to thwart discovery obligations . . . in order to destroy specific stored information that it is required to preserve" (Federal Rule of Civil Procedure, 2006: 37[f]). In other words, once legal holds on destruction can be anticipated or have been received, the organization must suspend the normal disposal activities of its information system.

INTERNATIONAL

Basel II

In June 2004, the Basel Committee on Banking Supervision released its report, *International Convergence of Capital Measurement and Capital Standards: A Revised Framework*, widely known as Basel II. Basel II is based on a risk management strategy that rewards banks for controlling credit risk and ensuring adequate capital reserves. However, in order to successfully implement this strategy, financial institutions must have access to large quantities of high quality data, and this requires a well designed record management program to capture, manage, and preserve data. As one commentator has stated, "A successful Basel II implementation requires the ability to take an enterprise-wide view of business events across multiple systems and quickly deliver accurate and verifiable data" (Omni RIM, 2005: 9). Most of the literature on Basel II compliance recommends that banks develop retention and disposal strategies and tighten access and security procedures. Experts also recommend that regular and frequent internal audits be implemented to review the accuracy and completeness of data. Without question, Basel II has the potential to improve and tighten policies and procedures for managing records within the international banking community (Bank for International Settlements, 2006).

Implementation of Basel II began at the end of 2006, but the extent to which it will be implemented will not be the same in all countries. For example, regulators in the United States have stated "that only a small number of large, internationally active US banking organizations . . . will be required to use the Revised Framework and that only the advanced approaches may be adopted." By contrast, the EU has indicated that all lenders will comply with all aspects of the Basel II framework (Omni RIM, 2005: 7).

GUIDELINES AND BEST PRACTICES

In chapter 2, we reviewed some of the guidelines for recordkeeping, such as the DOD 5015.2 and the Australian metadata standard. In this chapter, we will review guidelines for information management established by other professional groups, such as IT personnel, auditors, and lawyers.

Why would archivists and records managers be interested in these documents? There are two reasons: 1) they represent tools our potential partners are using and include objectives they consider important; understanding their tools will make us better able to communicate with them and to work with them in the implementation of a records management strategy; and 2) they provide the archivist and records manager with a useful framework for reviewing issues relating to recordkeeping, including such important requirements as the need for audit controls, documentation and policies, and the importance of evaluating risk in developing strategies for recordkeeping.

UNITED STATES

Committee of Sponsoring Organizations of the Treadway Commission (COSO): Internal Control—Integrated Framework and Enterprise Risk Management—Integrated Framework

COSO is a voluntary private-sector organization formed in 1985 and dedicated to improving the quality of financial reporting through better business ethics and more effective internal controls and corporate governance. The publication *Internal Control—Integrated Framework* was issued in 1992 and became the most commonly used control framework in the United States, and has been adopted by most auditing organizations. It has become such an important tool that the SEC recently stated that the COSO framework can and should be used to satisfy the control requirements outlined in SOX.

In this publication, COSO defined the internal control process as follows: "Internal control is broadly defined as a process, affected by an entity's Board of Directors, management and other personnel, designed to provide reasonable assurance regarding the achievement of objectives in the following categories: effectiveness and efficiency of operations, reliability of financial reporting, and compliance with laws and regulations" (COSO, "Internal Controls"). In 2004, COSO added the creation of "high-level goals, aligned with and supporting its mission" to its definition of internal controls (COSO, 2004: 3).

The *Enterprise Risk Management—Integrated Framework* report was issued in 2004 and emphasized the importance of identifying and managing risks across the enterprise. COSO defined enterprise risk management as:

> a process, effected by an entity's board of directors, management and other personnel, applied in a strategy setting and across the enterprise, designed to identify potential events that may affect the entity, and manage risk to be within its risk appetite, to provide reasonable assurance regarding the achievement of entity objectives (COSO, 2004: 2).

The original COSO framework *Internal Control—Integrated Framework* contained five control components: internal control environment, risk assessment, control activities, information and communication, and monitoring. The most recent control framework outlined in *Enterprise Risk Management—Integrated Framework* added three new components: objective setting, event identification, and risk response.

Internal Control Environment

The control environment creates the foundation for effective internal controls and establishes a structure of accountability at the executive level. Control environment factors include "the integrity, ethical values and competence of the entity's people; management's philosophy and operating style; the way management assigns authority and responsibility, and organizes and develops its people; and the attention and direction provided by the board of directors" (COSO: "Internal Controls").

Objective Setting

The goal here is to ensure that objectives are in place and that these objectives support the enterprise's mission.

Event Identification

In this process internal and external events that impact upon the objectives of the business are identified and assessed as to whether they represent risks or opportunities.

Risk Assessment

Risk assessment involves analysis by management of relevant risks and a determination of how these risks will be managed. Risk assessment may occur at the organizational level or at the business unit or even at the specific process level. Because economic, industry, regulatory, and operating conditions will continue to change, the risk assessment process will also identify and assess the special risks associated with change.

Risk Response

In this process management selects an appropriate risk response—avoiding, accepting, reducing, or sharing the risk—and implements an appropriate strategy.

Control Activities

Control activities are the policies, procedures, and practices that are put into place to achieve business objectives and to implement risk mitigation strategies. Control activities occur throughout the organization, at all levels and for all functions. "They include a range of activities as diverse as approvals, authorizations, verifications, reconciliations, reviews of operating performance, security of assets and segregation of duties" (COSO: "Internal Control").

Information and Communication

COSO stresses that "pertinent information must be identified, captured and communicated in a form and timeframe that enable people to carry out their responsibilities." This information should not only include operational guidelines but also data about external events and activities that will impact upon decision making, such as how management communicates with customers, suppliers, regulators and shareholders (COSO: "Internal Control").

Monitoring

According to COSO, monitoring is the "process that assesses the quality of the system's performance over time." There are two types of monitoring activities: continuous or ongoing monitoring, and ad hoc and as needed evaluations of systems, particularly those systems that include high risk processes (COSO: "Internal Control").

Relationship of Objectives and Components

COSO states that the relationships between the categories and components of its review structure can best be depicted in a three-dimensional matrix in the form of a cube, such as the one shown in Figure 7.3. "The four objective categories—strategic, operations, reporting, and compliance—are represented by the vertical columns, the eight components by horizontal rows, and an entity's units by the third dimension" (COSO, 2004: 4–5).

Figure 7.4 shows a broader view of the relationships between COSO and other prominent laws, regulations, and guidelines.

Figure 7.3
Relationships in COSO

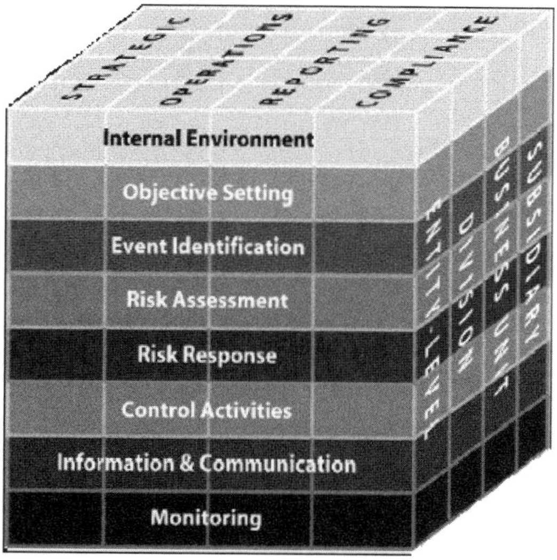

Reproduced with permission from www.sox-online.com.

Figure 7.4
Relationships between SOX, SEC, COSO, and CobiT

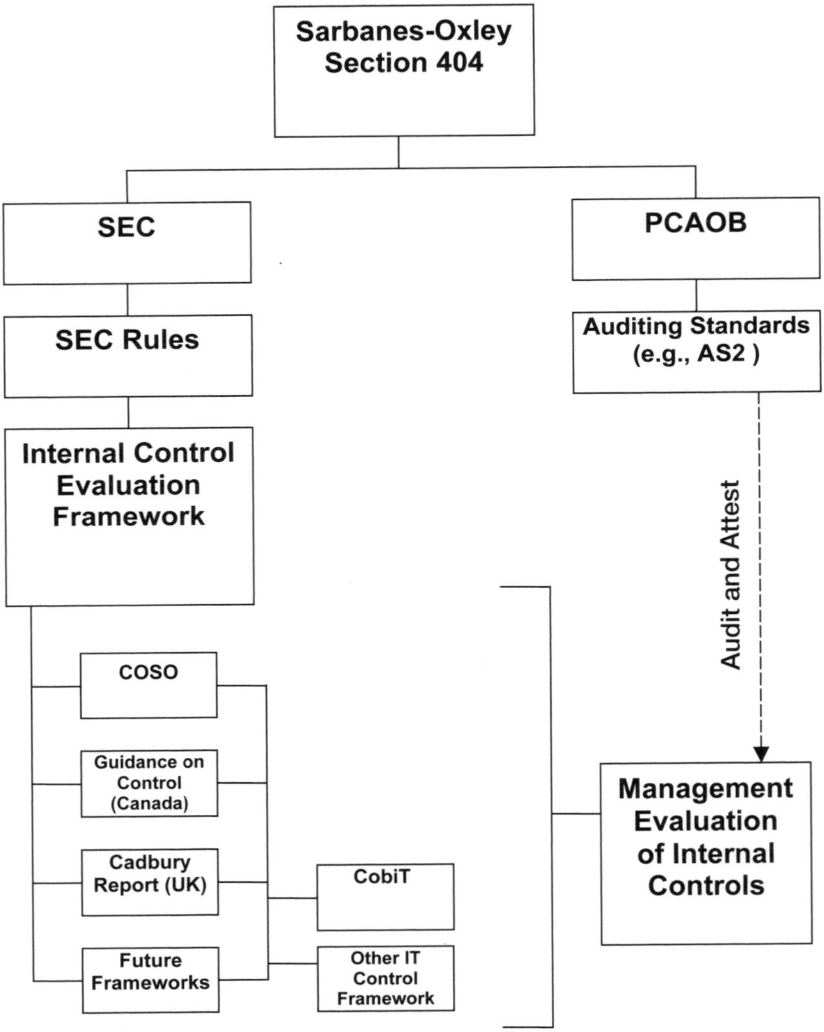

```
                    ┌─────────────────────┐
                    │   Sarbanes-Oxley    │
                    │    Section 404      │
                    └─────────────────────┘
          ┌───────────────────────┴───────────────────────┐
    ┌───────────┐                                   ┌───────────┐
    │    SEC    │                                   │   PCAOB   │
    └───────────┘                                   └───────────┘
    ┌───────────┐                              ┌──────────────────┐
    │ SEC Rules │                              │ Auditing Standards│
    └───────────┘                              │   (e.g., AS2 )   │
                                               └──────────────────┘
┌──────────────────┐                                      │
│ Internal Control │                                      │
│   Evaluation     │                              Audit and Attest
│   Framework      │                                      │
└──────────────────┘                                      │
        │                                                 │
    ┌────────┐                              ┌──────────────────┐
    │  COSO  │───┐                          │   Management     │
    └────────┘   │                          │   Evaluation     │
    ┌────────┐   │                          │  of Internal     │
    │Guidance│   │                          │   Controls       │
    │on      │   │                          └──────────────────┘
    │Control │───┤
    │(Canada)│   │
    └────────┘   │
    ┌────────┐   │   ┌────────┐
    │Cadbury │   │   │ CobiT  │
    │Report  │───┼───┤        │
    │(UK)    │   │   └────────┘
    └────────┘   │
    ┌────────┐   │   ┌────────┐
    │Future  │   │   │Other IT│
    │Frame-  │───┴───┤Control │
    │works   │       │Framework│
    └────────┘       └────────┘
```

The Information Systems Audit and Control Association, Control of Business Information Technology (CobiT)

CobiT is a framework of IT control objectives and practices that was first published by the Information Systems Audit and Control Association (ISACA) in 1996. The fourth edition was published in December 2005. ISACA's objectives in developing CobiT were to provide "a framework and supporting toolset that allow managers to bridge the gap with respect to control requirements, technical issues and business risks, and communicate that level of control to stakeholders," and to enable "the development of clear policy and good practice for IT control throughout enterprises" (ISACA, "CobiT Guidelines": 8). CobiT is based on the assumption that in order to achieve business objectives managers must understand the status of their IT systems and be able to determine what types of controls are in place. CobiT provides a tool for analyzing IT systems and processes in terms of six overlapping categories: efficiency, security, integrity, reliability, accessibility, and compliance. These categories form the foundation for CobiT's control objectives.

In its 4th edition, CobiT has 34 high level objectives that cover 215 control objectives organized into four domains: Plan and Organize, Acquire and Implement, Deliver and Support, and Monitor and Evaluate (ISACA, "CobiT Guidelines").

The following table lists the high-level processes included in each of the CobiT domains:

PLANNING AND ORGANIZATION	ACQUISITION AND IMPLE- MENTATION	DELIVERY AND SUPPORT	MONITORING
Define a strategic IT plan	Identify automated solutions	Define and manage service levels	Monitor the processes
Define the information architecture	Acquire and maintain application software	Manage third-party services	Assess internal control adequacy
Determine technological direction	Acquire and maintain technology infrastructure	Manage performance and capacity	Obtain independent assurance
Define the IT organization and relationships	Develop and maintain procedures	Ensure contin-uous service	Provide for independent audit
Manage the IT investment	Install and accredit systems	Ensure systems security	
Communicate management aims and direction	Manage changes	Identify and allocate costs	
Manage human resources		Educate and train users	
Ensure compli-ance with external requirements		Assist and advise customers	
Assess risks		Manage the configuration	
Manage projects		Manage problems and incidents	
Manage quality		Manage data	
		Manage facilities	
		Manage operations	

For each high-level process, CobiT provides a set of control objectives. For instance, the "manage change" process within the category of Acquisition and Implementation includes the following detailed control objectives:

- Change Request Initiation and Control
- Impact Assessment
- Control of Changes
- Emergency Changes
- Documentation and Procedures
- Authorized Maintenance
- Software Release Policy
- Distribution of Software

For each of these control objectives, CobiT defines a set of practices designed to mitigate risk related to the efficiency, security, integrity, reliablility, accessibility, and compliance of IT systems and processes.

CobiT and Sarbanes-Oxley and Other Regulatory Laws

CobiT has gained favor and attention as a framework for addressing compliance with Sarbanes-Oxley and other regulatory laws. Recent surveys conducted in conjunction with CobiT's creator (the Information Systems Audit and Control Association) strongly suggest that a growing number of organizations are adopting CobiT-based control frameworks and auditing processes. A 2005 survey by PriceWaterhouseCooper discovered that awareness of CobiT has increased among CIOs and CEOs by 50 percent (from 18 percent to 27 percent) in the period from 2003 to 2005. In addition, one out of six respondents who know of CobiT claimed they understood the contents to a great extent. The survey discovered that the control objectives and audit guidelines were the most widely used portions of CobiT. 41 percent of CobiT users regarded the tool to be very valuable in the IT governance effort, up 50 percent from 2003. 38 percent of CobiT users indicated that Sarbanes-Oxley legislation or other new laws or regulations was a reason to introduce CobiT into their organization (PriceWaterhouseCoopers, 2006).

Those who have used CobiT as a tool for meeting compliance requirements have discovered that CobiT goes well beyond the scope of what is required for Sarbanes-Oxley compliance. In most cases,

Sarbanes-Oxley compliance requires significantly less than half of the CobiT control objectives. In response to the expressed need for a CobiT document that specifically addresses the requirements in Sarbanes-Oxley, the IT Governance Institute has issued *IT Control Objectives for Sarbanes-Oxley*. The document identifies a subset of CobiT requirements for use in Sarbanes-Oxley IT compliance initiatives. This subset includes the following high-level processes:

- acquire or develop application software
- acquire technology infrastructure
- develop and maintain policies and procedures
- install and test application software and technology infrastructure
- manage changes
- define and manage service levels (ISACA, 2006).

Public Company Accounting Oversight Board (PCAOB), Auditing Standard No. 2, entitled An Audit of Internal Control Over Financial Reporting Performed in Conjunction with an Audit of Financial Statements

The Sarbanes-Oxley Act requires public accounting firms that audit public companies to register with the Public Company Accounting Oversight Board (PCAOB) and to adhere to professional standards established by the Board for audits of public companies. In March 2004, the PCAOB approved Auditing Standard No. 2, entitled *An Audit of Internal Control Over Financial Reporting Performed in Conjunction with an Audit of Financial Statements*. Auditing Standard No. 2 became effective in June 2004, upon approval by the SEC. In over 200 pages, Standard 2 delineates the PCAOB's expectations for an internal control audit and imposes many new responsibilities on public companies' auditors and, by extension, on the public companies themselves.

In the PCAOB Auditing Standard No. 2, information technology is described as having a "pervasive" effect on internal control over financial reporting. Consequently, the auditing standard requires companies to understand how IT is used in the financial reporting process and how IT controls are designed and implemented to manage risks. The auditing standard highlights four IT controls that need to be reviewed in relation to Sarbanes-Oxley requirements: program development, program changes, computer operations, and access to programs and data. Standard 2 also defines management's responsibilities regarding controls. According to the Standard, managers must do the following:

- Accept responsibility for the effectiveness of the company's internal controls over financial reporting.
- Evaluate the effectiveness of internal controls over financial reporting using suitable control criteria such as the COSO framework or an alternative recognized framework developed by a body of experts following due process.
- Support the evaluation with sufficient documented evidence.
- Present a written assessment about the effectiveness of the company's internal control as of the end of the most recent fiscal year.

Once a deficiency has been reported, the company has until the next audit to correct the problem. In Auditing Standard No. 4, *Reporting on Whether a Previously Reported Material Weakness Continues to Exist*, the PCAOB describes the steps to be used by auditors when a company voluntarily engages them to report on whether a deficiency has been corrected (PCAOB, 2004).

Sedona Conference Documents

The Sedona Conference is a research and educational institute comprised of academics, industry experts, lawyers, and judges dedicated to the advancement of law and policy in the areas of antitrust law, intellectual property rights, and complex litigation. Since its establishment in 1997, the Sedona Conference has concentrated on the development of principles, guidelines, and best practices in new and emerging litigation practices.

The Conference has produced two key documents that bear on electronic document discovery and electronic records management: *The Sedona Guidelines for Managing Information and Records in the Information Age* (September 2005) and *The Sedona Principles: Best Practices Recommendations and Principles for Addressing Electronic Document Production* (issued, 2003; revised, 2005). The *Guidelines* provide advice on organizing and maintaining a viable records management program. The underlying assumption is that without records management an organization will not likely be able to manage discovery motions and/or any litigation involving access to record systems. The *Guidelines* outline five basic principles in developing an information management strategy. For each guideline there is detailed advice on implementation.

"**1. An organization should have reasonable policies and procedures for managing its information and records.**" As part of this process, the Conference stresses that the policies should not mandate the retention of all information, but should selectively retain records.

"**2. An organization's information and records management policies and procedures should be realistic, practical and tailored to the circumstances of the organization.**" In this guideline they stress the need for practical, flexible, and scalable solutions; for retention and destruction policies and procedures that account for legal requirements; and for strategies designed to assess the operational and strategic value of its information. Finally they remind businesses that "no single standard or model can fully meet an organization's unique needs."

"**3. An organization need not retain all electronic information ever generated or received.**" In this guideline businesses are reminded that destruction of records is an acceptable, indeed, necessary action to eliminate information with no continuing value. More specifically they tell organizations that "systematic deletion of electronic information," including metadata and electronic mail, "is not synonymous with evidence spoliation," unless of course there is a court order or other legal requirement that prohibits this destruction.

"**4. An organization adopting an information and records management policy should also develop procedures that address the creation, identification, retention, retrieval, and ultimate disposition or destruction of information and records.**" To satisfy this requirement businesses are told they must train employees in the appraisal of records, particularly information with legal value, and in the overall management of records. They also remind managers that they should consider the impact of technology on the creation and disposition of records. Finally they suggest that organizations implement periodic compliance reviews of its policies and procedures and revise these documents as necessary in response to legal and regulatory requirements and to changes in workflow and business practices.

"**5. An organization's policies and procedures must mandate the suspension of ordinary destruction practices and procedures as necessary to comply with preservation obligations related to actual or reasonably anticipated litigation, government investigation or audit.**" In this guideline the Conference reminds organizations that they must have a strategy and mechanisms in place to communicate a notice of a legal hold and to suspend normal destruction procedures if so ordered by the courts. (See Sedona Conference Guidelines IV and V.)

The *Principles* set forth criteria and guidelines for use by attorneys and the courts when dealing with discovery in litigation. The document sets forth 14 principles briefly summarized below:

1. Electronic data and documents are potentially discoverable and, therefore, organizations should preserve electronic documents that can reasonably be expected to be relevant to litigation.
2. In evaluating discovery motions, courts need to balance cost, burden, and need for electronic data and documents as well as the nature of the litigation and the amount at stake.
3. Parties should confer early in the litigation process to define the scope of the discovery action and each party's obligations regarding the preservation and production of electronic documents.
4. Discovery requests should make as clear as possible what documents are being requested, and responses to discovery should precisely disclose what has been produced.
5. Parties need to make reasonable, good faith efforts to preserve relevant documents. However, this statement is qualified by asserting it is unreasonable to expect businesses to preserve all potentially relevant data.
6. Responding parties to discovery actions are in the best position to evaluate procedures, methodologies, and technologies appropriate for producing their own electronic documents.
7. The requesting party on a motion to compel needs to demonstrate precisely that the responding party's actions to preserve and produce relevant data were inadequate.
8. The primary source of electronic data in a discovery motion "should be active data and information purposefully stored in a manner that anticipates future business use and permits efficient searching and retrieval." Resorting to disaster recovery back-up tapes and other sources of data requires the requesting party to demonstrate the "need and relevance that outweigh the cost, burden, and disruption of retrieving and processing from such sources."
9. Except under special conditions, a responding party should not be required to preserve or produce "deleted, shadowed, fragmented, or residual data or documents."

10. "A responding party should follow reasonable procedures to protect privileges and objections to production of electronic document data and documents."

11. A responding party may satisfy its obligations to preserve and produce electronic data through the use of data sampling, searching, or use of selection criteria.

12. Unless it is relevant to resolving the dispute, or it is covered by agreement between the parties or order of the court, there is no obligation to produce metadata.

13. Costs of retrieving and producing data should in most cases be borne by the responding party, unless the data "is not reasonably available to the responding party in the ordinary course of business," in which case costs should be borne by the requesting party.

14. Sanctions, including spoliation findings, should be imposed only if the "court finds there was an intentional or reckless failure to preserve and produce relevant electronic data and that there is a reasonable probability that the loss of the evidence has materially prejudiced the adverse party" (Sedona Conferences Principles: 1).

CANADA

Guidance on Control (CoCo)

The Canadian Institute of Chartered Accountants issued the report, *Guidance on Control* (CoCo) in 1995. CoCo defines control as comprising "those elements of an organization (including its resources, systems, processes, culture and tasks) that, taken together, support people in the achievement of the organization's objectives" (AMANS, 2005: 13). The CoCo model identifies four interrelated elements of internal control: purpose, commitment, capability, and monitoring and learning. Within those four elements, CoCo specifies that an assessment of the effectiveness of control be made against twenty specific criteria.

The element "purpose" provides a sense of the organization's direction. It addresses objectives, risk and opportunities, policies, planning tools, and performance target and indicators. The element "commitment" provides a sense of the organization's identity and addresses its ethical values, and its means of establishing authority, responsibility, and accountability. "Capability" criteria provide a sense of the organization's competence. They deal with knowledge, skills and tools, communication processes, information, co-ordination and control activities. As part of the communication process, CoCo emphasizes that for "control to be effective, a municipality should have a communication process capable of supporting open communication of timely, relevant, and reliable information" (AMANS, 2005: 11). Finally, the "monitoring and learning" element provides a sense of the organization's processes of review and assessment. More specifically, this component involves reviewing internal and external environments, monitoring performance against targets, challenging assumptions, reassessing information needs and systems, establishing follow-up procedures, and assessing the effectiveness of control. Taken together these criteria form an interrelated framework for reviewing and evaluating the organization from an internal controls perspective. However, as the authors make clear, the document is intended as a guide for making decisions for designing and assessing controls; it is not intended as a set of prescriptive requirements.

CoCo should be viewed as a set of guidelines of an internal control framework that complements the COSO and Turnbull guidelines (discussed below). Though there are some significant differences in definition and scope and in some of the underlying concepts, all three sets of guidelines share much in common. Included in this set of common assumptions is the importance placed on developing strong and effective records management programs and audit procedures to ensure that reliable and trustworthy records are accessible to those who have need of them.

UNITED KINGDOM

Cadbury Report

The Cadbury Report, formally entitled "The Report of the Committee on the Financial Aspects of Corporate Governance," was published in December 1992, based on the recommendations of the Committee chaired by Sir Adrian Cadbury. The Committee was formed in 1991 by the London Stock Exchange in response to various financial scandals in the 1980s involving United Kingdom companies. The Cadbury Report has been the starting point for the development of corporate governance codes in the United Kingdom, and recommendations from the Report have been adopted in varying degrees by the European Union, the United States, the World Bank, and others.

In the preface to the Report the authors state that the "Committee's recommendations are focused on the control and reporting functions of boards, and on the role of auditors. This reflects the committee's purpose, which was to review those aspects of corporate governance specifically related to financial reporting and accountability." Later in the introduction the authors write that the "principles on which the Code is based are those of openness, integrity and accountability" (Cadbury Report: "Preface").

Recommendations in the Report related to recordkeeping include:

- the importance of the annual audit as one of the "cornerstones of corporate governance" that provides an "external and objective check on the way in which the financial statements have been prepared and presented." For the authors of the Report the "question is not whether there should be an audit, but how to ensure its objectivity and effectiveness" (Cadbury Report: "Introduction"). The Committee therefore recommends that all listed companies should establish an audit committee.
- the "need in practice to maintain a system of internal control over the financial management of the company, including procedures designed to minimize the risk of fraud." Therefore the authors of the Report recommend "that directors should report on the effectiveness of their system of internal control, and that the auditors should report on their statement."
- the need for open disclosure by means of more frequent and detailed reports "to include balance sheet information." In the words of the authors of the Cadbury Report, the "most direct method of ensuring that companies are accountable for their actions is through open disclosure by boards and through audits carried out against strict accounting standards" (Cadbury Report: "Reporting and Auditing").

Combined Code on Corporate Governance

This Code applies to reporting years beginning on or after November 1, 2006, and it supersedes and replaces the Combined Code issued in 2003. The Code applies to all companies incorporated in the UK and listed on the Main Market of the London Stock Exchange. Overseas companies listed on the Main Market are required to disclose the significant ways in which their corporate governance practices differ from those outlined in the Code.

The Combined Code on Corporate Governance sets out standards of good practice in relation to issues such as board composition and development, remuneration, accountability and audit, and relations with shareholders. It should be noted that many of the recommendations relating to the roles and responsibilities of non-executive directors were taken from the 2002 Higgs Reports, and that recommendations on the responsibilities of audit committees were taken from the 2003 Smith Report. In regard to recordkeeping the Code makes several important recommendations in regard to the responsibilities of the board of directors and the auditors. In regard to the board of directors, the Code recommends that the non-executive directors have several important responsibilities which include:

- Monitoring the integrity of financial information and ensuring that "that financial controls and systems of risk management are robust and defensible." These activities would include the creation of annual or more frequent reviews that describe the "effectiveness of the group's system of internal controls and should report to shareholders that they have done so. The review should cover all material controls, including financial, operational and compliance controls and risk management systems."
- Establishing "formal and transparent arrangements for considering how they should apply the financial reporting and internal control principles and for maintaining an appropriate relationship with the company's auditors."

The code outlines the responsibilities of an audit committee, which are to monitor the integrity of the financial statements of the company, to review the company's internal financial controls, and to assess the effectiveness of the company's internal audit function.

Overall, the Code emphasizes the need for well designed and effective records management and audit programs which will ensure that authentic and reliable records and reports are available to shareholders and regulators (Financial Services Authority, 2003, sec. 1.C).

Internal Control: Guidance for Directors on the Combined Code, commonly referred to as the Turnbull Guidance

The Turnbull guidance statement was issued in October 2005 by the Institute of Chartered Accountants of England and Wales (ICAEW) at the request of the London Stock Exchange. The guidance was written to provide advice to directors of listed companies in implementing the requirements in the Combined Code relating to internal control. In the introduction to the statement, the authors state that the objectives of the guidance are to "reflect sound business practice whereby internal control is embedded in the business processes by which a company pursues its objectives; remain relevant over time in the continually evolving business environment; and enable each company to apply it in a manner which takes account of its particular circumstances" (Financial Reporting Council, 2005: 9). In the section on "Maintaining a sound system of internal control," the authors outline the responsibilities of directors in regard to internal control and identify the elements of a well designed system of internal control. Their definition of a well designed internal control system "encompasses the policies, processes, tasks, behaviours and other aspects of a company that, taken together... facilitate its effective and efficient operation. ... This includes the safeguarding of assets from inappropriate use or from loss and fraud and ensuring that liabilities are identified and managed" (Financial Reporting Council, 2005: 13). It also includes controls to "ensure the quality of internal and external reporting," and "requires the maintenance of proper records and processes that generate a flow of timely, relevant and reliable information from within and outside the organization" (Financial Reporting Council, 2005: 13).

In another section of the document the authors discuss activities designed to assess the effectiveness of the internal control system. In this section they state that "effective monitoring on a continuous basis is an essential component of a sound system of internal control. The board cannot, however, rely solely on the embedded monitoring processes within the company to discharge its responsibilities. It should regularly receive and review reports on internal control. In addition, the board should undertake an annual assessment for the purposes of making its public statement on internal control" (Financial Reporting Council, 2005: 15).

Finally the authors outline the types of information the board's statements or reports on internal controls should include. As part of these instructions, they state that in "its narrative statement of how the company has applied Code Principle C.2, the board should, as a minimum, disclose that there is an ongoing process for identifying, evaluating and managing the significant risks faced by the company, that it has been in place for the year under review and up to the date of approval of the annual report and accounts, that it is regularly reviewed by the board and accords with the guidance in this document" (Financial Reporting Council, 2005: 18).

The Turnbull guidance statement clearly emphasizes the importance of internal controls within the enterprise, and with equal vigor states that an effective system of internal controls is not possible without a sound records management program.

LESSONS LEARNED FROM THE LAWS, REGULATIONS, AND BEST PRACTICES

What has been the impact on recordkeeping of the laws, rules, and guidelines passed or promulgated in the last decade? There are at least seven primary messages related to records management.

Lesson: To be compliant, organizations must develop effective records management programs that manage records throughout the life cycle

The laws, regulations, and best practices that were reviewed in this chapter outlined a wide variety of requirements. However, every one of them explicitly or implicitly states that sound records management practices are essential for meeting compliance requirements and for avoiding legal risks. For example, though the Sarbanes-Oxley Act (SOX) is fundamentally about the accountability of public companies and the transparency of its business processes, the law states quite clearly that compliance with SOX is dependent upon the creation of information and records management practices that ensure the authenticity, reliability, and integrity of business records.

In the area of regulations and rules, the message is the same. For example, the Food and Drug Administration (FDA) Rule 21 CFR Part 11 is primarily concerned with establishing criteria under which FDA will consider electronic records to be equivalent to paper records, and electronic signatures equivalent to traditional handwritten signatures.

However, in order for these electronic records to be accepted, the rule outlines detailed requirements for the management of the electronic records. In essence, the FDA establishes requirements to ensure that electronic records and electronic signatures are trustworthy, authentic, and reliable.

International laws and regulations on compliance provide similar advice. The United Kingdom's Data Protection Act was passed to protect individual rights and freedoms and especially the right to privacy with respect to the processing of personal data. However, the Act clearly states that in order to meet the requirements of this Act an organization must have in place well designed and effective recordkeeping systems. Canada's Privacy Act was created to protect the personal information of its citizens, but to achieve this, Canadian government agencies are advised to develop recordkeeping systems that manage this personal data over the life cycle. The message of these laws and acts is very clear: effective records management programs are essential to being and remaining compliant.

Lesson: Records retention and disposition policies and procedures are key elements of a compliance strategy

In virtually every law, regulation, or best practice statement, the importance of establishing record retention and disposal policies is emphasized as a primary factor in an organization's ability to remain compliant. For example, the Health Insurance Portability and Accountability Act (HIPAA) states that the organization must "maintain, until six years after the later of the date of their creation or last effective date, its privacy policies and procedures, its privacy practices notices, disposition of complaints, and other actions, activities, and designations that the Privacy Rule requires to be documented" (U.S. Department of Health and Human Services, Summary: 15).

The Security and Exchange Commission (SEC) Rule 17a–4 states that members, brokers, and dealers must "preserve for a period of not less than three years, the first two years in an easily accessible place . . . originals of all communications received and copies of all communications sent" related to their business as broker-dealers, including electronic communications such as e-mail and instant messaging (SEC 17a-4 Rule: "Section b").

The laws and regulations make it quite clear that legal and regulatory compliance cannot consistently be achieved without the development of enterprise-wide retention and disposition schedules, and without well-designed strategies for suspending destruction of records when court imposed hold orders are issued.

Lesson: Internal controls are critical to meeting compliance requirements

An internal control is "a process, effected by an entity's board of directors, management and other personnel, designed to provide reasonable assurance regarding the achievement of objectives in the following categories: Effectiveness and efficiency of operations, reliability of financial reporting, compliance with applicable laws and regulations" (COSO: "Internal Control"). A common theme of virtually all the laws, regulations, and best practices is the need to identify these internal controls and to standardize these controls across business units.

For example, within SOX creating and monitoring internal controls over financial reporting is a major requirement. Similarly, the United Kingdom's Combined Code on Corporate Governance recommends that corporations monitor the integrity of financial information and conduct reviews that describe the "effectiveness of the group's system of internal controls and should report to shareholders that they have done so. The review should cover all material controls, including financial, operational and compliance controls and risk management systems" (Federal Services Authority, 2003: sec.1.C).

Because of this emphasis on the creation of controls, guidelines and procedures for implementing internal control systems have become widely used by corporations. In the United States these tools include the COSO publication *Internal Control—Integrated Framework;* CobiT; and the PCAOB Auditing Standard No. 2. In Canada the primary tool on internal controls is CoCo, and in the United Kindom the primary publication is the Turnbull Guidance. The message is clear: automated internal controls are essential to creating trustworthy records that document compliance with laws and regulations, and businesses are getting the message. It is estimated that by 2008 more than 75 percent of large and midsize companies will purchase controls automation and monitoring solutions, and that by 2011 "companies that pursue an integrated strategy of a risk-oriented approach to compliance, standardization of controls and automation will reduce the scope of manual process controls by 70 percent" (Gartner Group, 2006: section on "Predictions").

Lesson: Systematic auditing of business processes is essential for meeting compliance requirements

Auditing of internal controls and business processes is a key element of all the compliance laws and regulations, and again business has gotten the message. A survey found that for companies complying with SOX, auditors' fees in year two implementation accounted for 39 percent of total Section 404 costs for smaller companies and 33 percent for larger companies (CRA International, 2006: 4). Although resources devoted to auditors' fees for SOX compliance are decreasing, there remains a strong emphasis within businesses on the need for developing more robust auditing and monitoring strategies.

In fact the demands by executives for assurances that the company is meeting compliance requirements are motivating organizations to accelerate the frequency of internal audit cycles. "Continuous" or more frequent audits for monitoring controls and processes have become more common in the last few years. For example, the PriceWaterhouseCoopers' 2006 survey on the internal audit profession found that 81 percent of 392 companies reported that they either had a continuous auditing or monitoring process in place or were planning to develop one. From 2005 to 2006, this same survey discovered that the percentage of survey respondents claiming they had some form of continuous auditing or monitoring process within their internal audit functions increased from 35 percent to 50 percent. The PriceWaterhouseCooper survey also found that the most common continuous auditing "cycle" is quarterly, with 57 percent of respondents falling into this category. Another 34 percent performed monthly audits, while only 9 percent focused on daily applications of their continuous auditing processes (PriceWaterhouseCoopers, 2006: 3). Continuous auditing is still considered an emerging phenomenon, but evidence suggests that it will continue to grow in response to managements' demand for faster and higher-quality real-time information on compliance. Since audit trails are such an integral component of a recordkeeping system, this trend of more frequent audits of systems is a positive development for archivists and records managers.

Lesson: Partnerships between professional groups responsible for managing information are essential to meeting compliance demands

One of the prominent messages of the laws, regulations, and guidelines concerning compliance is that partnerships between professional groups involved in information management are absolutely necessary for any strategy to succeed. Typically, the partners that are listed include information technologists/information managers, auditors, lawyers, records managers, and high level administrators. Unfortunately, evidence would strongly indicate that in many environments these groups do not collaborate effectively on information management and compliance issues. A Cohasset survey discovered that at present, strategies for managing "electronic records operate in an independent 'silo' context." Cohasset consultants argue that these "traditional communications barriers must be broken down and a newfound understanding of the complementary roles of all the stakeholders must take their place" (Cohasset, 2005: 51).

Many of the regulations and guidelines identify various types of committees and teams that should be created to implement compliance and electronic document discovery strategies. Foremost among these is a records management oversight and policy group comprised of representatives from the legal department, IT, audit, records management, and administration. This group would be responsible for creating integrated, coordinated, and well supported records management and compliance programs. They would identify recordkeeping issues, develop action plans to mitigate or eliminate the risks associated with poor recordkeeping, develop and update an audit process by which compliance with the records management program directives can be assessed and measured, and communicate to senior management the ongoing need for records management program support. Because of the importance of records retention in complying with many of the laws and regulations, many experts also recommend the creation of a separate records-retention committee comprised of members from the same five professional groups.

Another prominently mentioned team is a litigation response team that manages and responds to court ordered hold orders to preserve documents. Finally many experts recommend forming a disclosure assessment committee consisting of individuals responsible for reviewing and evaluating disclosure reports in order to assess their accuracy and completeness. Clearly, the management of records to meet compliance cannot be achieved by one group of professionals. It requires a team of people working together and contributing their own unique knowledge and skills to the process.

Lesson: Managers of the compliance process must be proactive agents of change

All the laws and regulations make it quite clear that those individuals responsible for managing the compliance process must be proactive and not reactive participants. For example, the Federal Laws of Civil Procedure strongly recommends that legal counsel, IT personnel, and records managers be proactive in how they manage data and records, and warn that if this type of systematic and diligent management is not implemented the corporation can be subject to serious fines and penalties. Laws such as SOX require that executives assume responsibility for financial reporting, which means they must become more involved in ensuring that certain requirements are achieved.

Similarly, legal departments are advised to take a much more active role in records management and to become more knowledgeable about where data and information is located, how it is managed, and how it can be retrieved. Lawyers can no longer assume that records are being properly managed or that hold orders are being obeyed; they must take an active role in ensuring that these strategies are being effectively implemented. Some experts go so far as to say that in any compliance issue, the legal department must emerge as the primary "enabler," who coordinates the activities of IT, records management and business units in meeting compliance obligations.

Most experts on compliance also recommend a more active role for IT in managing the compliance process. IT staff are advised to become more knowledgeable about records management and the life cycle management concept. In particular, compliance guidelines recommend that IT be more proactive in addressing the issue of records retention and digital preservation.

Finally, most experts on compliance requirements advise that records managers and archivists become a more integral part of the teams that are managing the process. Presently it appears that in many businesses records managers play a supporting but not a lead role in determining compliance strategies. The 2006 compliance survey by AIIM asked who would be involved in compliance discussions, and the top three choices were IT (81.6 percent), Legal Department (64.4 percent), and Records Management (56.7 percent). When asked to name the groups who would have the most influence in driving compliance decisions, the top choices were executive staff (25.1 percent), legal (22.4 percent), and IT (17.7 percent) (AIIM, 2006: key finding 4). If records managers and archivists are to assume a leading role in the creation of compliance strategies, they must become more proactive in promoting awareness of life cycle management and of the requirements of recordkeeping systems. It will also require that record managers and archivists more aggressively inform the information management community regarding the skills they possess and the contributions they can make to the development of a strategy for legal compliance.

Lesson: Assessing and evaluating risk is critical to an effective compliance strategy

A lesson or challenge identified in many surveys or studies on the implementation of compliance requirements is the need to base decisions on an assessment of the highest risk areas of the business. According to most experts, a top-down, risk-based approach should form the basis not only for determining what internal controls to evaluate, but also for determining the nature, timing, and extent of the evaluation procedures. The implementation of a risk approach was described in COSO's *Enterprise Risk Management—Integrated Framework*.

According to SEC reports, organizations continue to experience difficulty applying a top-down, risk-based approach in their individual assessments. One of the reasons cited most frequently by businesses for the higher than anticipated costs in their first year of compliance with the Section 404 requirements was that too much work was done to test and document low-risk areas. Many of the discussions on risk management strategies emphasize that a strong records management program can help identify and detect risks or the potential for adverse events occurring. Records are often the first sign or signal that something is wrong and needs to be corrected. In essence records provide the evidence required to conduct effective assessments and evaluation of business risk.

REFERENCES

AIIM. 2006. "Compliance: It's Real, It's Relevant, and It's More Than Just Records." Available: www.aiim.org/viewpdfa.asp?ID=31842

AMANS, NSMFC, and FMCBC. 2005. "Enhancing Management Involvement with Internal Control." Available: www.gov.ns.ca/nsmfc/documents/EnhancingManagementInvolvementwithInternalControl.pdf

American Electronics Association (AeA). 2004. "NASDAQ and American Electronics Association Sarbanes-Oxley Act Cost and Compliance Survey." Available: www.aeanet.org/governmentaffairs/AeANASDAQSurvey.asp

American Health Information Management Association (AHIMA). 2006. "The State of HIPAA Security and Privacy Compliance." Available: www.ahima.org/emerging_issues/2006StateofHIPAA Compliance.pdf

Bank for International Settlements. 2006. "Base II: International Convergence of Capital Measurement and Capital Standards: A Revised Framework – Comprehensive Version." Available: www.bis.org/publ/bcbs128.htm

Cadbury Report. 1992. "The Report of the Committee on the Financial Aspects of Corporate Governance." Available: www.ecgi.org/codes/documents/cadbury.pdf

The California Database Protection Act of 2003 (CDPA). 2003. "Civil Code Section 1798.80–1798.84." Available: www.leginfo.ca.gov/cgi-bin/displaycode?section=civ&group=01001–02000&file=1798.80–1798.84

"Canadian Access to Information Act." 1985. Available: http://laws.justice.gc.ca/en/A–1/index.html

"Canadian Privacy Act." 1985. Available: http://laws.justice.gc.ca/en/P–21/index.html

Cohasset Associates, Inc. 2003. "A Call to Action." Available: www.aiimhost.com/membership/Call_To_Action_ES.pdf

Cohasset Associates, Inc. 2004. "IBM DB2 Records Manager and Record-Enabled Solutions." Available: www.merresource.com/pdf/ibm-wp–1.8.pdf

Cohasset Associates, Inc. 2005. "A Renewed Call to Action." Available: www.aiimhost.com/whitepapers/rmsurvey05.pdf

Committee of Sponsoring Organizations of the Treadway Commission (COSO). "Internal Control-Integrated Framework. Executive Summary." Available: www.coso.org/publications/executive_summary_integrated_framework.htm

Committee of Sponsoring Organizations of the Treadway Commission (COSO). 2004. "Enterprise Risk Management-Integrated Framework. Executive Summary." Available: www.coso.org/Publications/ERM/COSO_ERM_ExecutiveSummary.pdf

CRA International. 2006. "Sarbanes-Oxley Section 404 Costs and Implementation Issues: Spring 2006 Survey Update." Available: www.s-oxinternalcontrolinfo.com/pdfs/CRA_III.pdf

"Data Protection Act (DPA)." 1998. Available: www.opsi.gov.uk/ACTS/acts1998/19980029.htm

"Electronic Signatures in Global and National Commerce." 2000. Available: http://frwebgate.access.gpo.gov/cgi-bin/getdoc.cgi?dbname= 106_cong_public_laws&docid=f:publ229.106.pdf
(A good summary of the E-Sign Act is available: www.emc.com/ news/analyst/kahn_consulting/pdf/2005_10_11_KCI_EMC_ ESIGN_Compliance_Brief.pdf)

"Federal Rule of Civil Procedure." 2006. Available: www.law. cornell.edu/rules/frcp
(A good summary of the Federal Rules is available: www.emc.com/ news/analyst/kahn_consulting/pdf/2005_10_11_KCI_EMC_ FRCP_Compliance_Brief.pdf)

"The Federal Rules of Evidence (FRE)." Available: www.law.cornell.edu/ rules/fre/rules/htm

Financial Executives International (FEI). 2004. "FEI Survey on Sarbanes-Oxley Section 404 Implementation." Available: www.fei.org/download/section404_summary.pdf

Financial Reporting Council. 2005. "Revised Guidance for Directors on the Combined Code [Turnbull Guidance]." Available: www.apb.org.uk/documents/pagemanager/frc/Revised% 20Turnbull%20Guidance%20October%202005.pdf

"The Freedom of Information Act (FOIA) 5 U.S.C. 552, As Amended By Public Law No. 104–231, 110 Stat. 3048. 1996." Available: www.usdoj.gov/oip/foia_updates/Vol_XVII_4/page2.htm

"The Freedom of Information Act (FOIA) 2000 [UK]." 2000. Available: www.opsi.gov.uk/ACTS/acts2000/20000036.htm

Gartner Group. 2006. *The 2006 Planning Guide for Compliance: Risk-Orientation, Standardization and Automation.*

"Gramm-Leach-Bliley Act (GLB Act) Title V, 1–2. 1999." Available: http://banking.senate.gov/conf/fintl5.pdf OR www.omnirim.com/ PDFs/OmniRIMwhitePaper_RM_GLB.pdf
(Good summaries of the GLB Act are available: www. kahnconsultinginc.com/library/compliancebrief/KCI-GLB-Brief.pdf www.emc.com/news/analyst/kahn_consulting/pdf/2005_10_11_KCI_ EMC_GLB_Compliance_Brief.pdf)

"Government Paperwork Reduction Act (GPRA) (44 U.S.C. 3501 et seq.)" Available: www.archives.gov/federal-register/laws/paperwork-reduction/

"Health Insurance Portability and Accountability Act (HIPAA) of 1996. Public Law 104–191." 104th Congress. Available: http:// aspe.hhs.gov/adminsimp/pl104191.htm

"Health Insurance Portability and Accountability Act (HIPAA), Security Rule, Section on 'Physical Safeguards.'" Available: www.hipaadvisory.com/regs/finalsecurity/index.htm

ISACA. "Cobit Guidelines, version 4." Available: www.isaca.org/
Template.cfm?Section=COBIT6&Template=/MembersOnly.
cfm&ContentID=23325
ISACA. Cobit. 2006. "IT Control Objectives for Sarbanes-Oxley." Available: www.isaca.org Template.cfm?Section=Home&CONTENTID=
17003&TEMPLATE=/ContentManagementContentDisplay.cfm
Kahn Consultants. 2005. "The New Compliance Mandate." Available:
www.emc.com/pdf/products/centera/kahn_the_new_compliance_
mandate_wp_ldv.pdf
Kahn, Randolph. 2005. "When Information Management Compliance
Became a D&B Problem." Available: www.kahnconsultinginc.com/
library/KCI%20Report-IMC%20a%20D&B%20Problem.pdf
NASD and NYSE. 2005. "Joint Report by NASD and the NYSE on the
Operation and Effectiveness of the Research Analyst Conflict of
Interest Rules." Available: www.nasd.com/web/groups/rules_regs/
documents/rules_regs/nasdw_015803.pdf
National Archives and Records Administration (NARA). 2000.
"Records Management Guidance for Agencies Implementing Elec-
tronic Signature Technologies." Available: www.archives.gov/
records-mgmt/faqs/pdf/electronic-signature-technology.pdf
NTIA. 2003. Available: www.ntia.doc.gov/ntiahome/frnotices/2002/
esign/report2003/coverack.htm
NYSE, Amendments: The 2003 Amendments to the Rules are avail-
able: www.nasd.com/web/groups/rules_regs/documents/
notice_to_members/nasdw_003202.pdf
Oce. "Effective Records Management in Today's Business Environment." Available: www.oceusa.com/main/product_group.jsp?
WebLogicSession=FZzfMTppyJb50Y4kLfnbQd3J4MpMVMrzy2Y12nd
WfqvG3NWhCgRd!-1891987685&FOLDER%3C%3Efolder_id=
2534374302161354&bmUID=1163506656718
Omni RIM. 2005. "Records Management and Basel II." Available:
www.omnirim.com/PDFs/OmniRIMWhitePaper_RM_BaselII.pdf
PATRIOT Act of 2001. Public Law 107–56. Available: http://
fl1.findlaw.com/news.findlaw.com/cnn/docs/terrorism/hr3162.pdf
Personal Information Protection and Electronic Documents Act. 2000.
Available: http://laws.justice.gc.ca/en/P–8.6/
PriceWaterhouseCoopers. 2006. "State of the Internal Audit Profession
Study: Continuous Auditing Gains Momentum." Available:
www.pwc.com/images/gx/eng/about/svcs/grms/06_IAState_
Profession_Study.pdf
Public Company Accounting Oversight Board (PCAOB). 2004. "Bylaws
and Rules"– Standards – AS2." Available: www.pcaobus.org/Rules/
Rules_of_the_Board/Auditing_Standard_2.pdf

Sarbanes-Oxley Act of 2002. Available: www.sarbanes-oxley.com/
section.php?level=1&pub_id=Sarbanes-Oxley
(Good summaries of Sarbanes-Oxley are available: www.omnirim.
com/PDFs/OmniRIMwhitePaper_RM_SOX.pdf
http://thecaq.aicpa.org/Resources/Sarbanes+Oxley/Summary+of+
the+Provisions+of+the+Sarbanes-Oxley+Act+of+2002.htm
www.emc.com/news/analyst/kahn_consulting/pdf/2005_10_11_
KCI_EMC_SOX_Compliance_Brief.pdf
www.kahnconsultinginc.com/library/KCISOXReport.pdf)
Sarbanes-Oxley Act, Controls: Good discussions of auditors' definitions
of internal control can be found at:
    Protiviti, Independent Risk Consulting. "Guide to the Sarbanes-
    Oxley Act: Managing Application Risks and Controls." Available:
    http://protiviti.com/portal/site/pro-us/menuitem.b005e436366907
    3bdd22d10f5ffbfa0/
    Quest Software. 2005. "Taking Control of Your IT Environment."
    Available: http://secureitalliance.org/blogs/quest_software/archive/
    2006/02/08/469.aspx
Sarbanes-Oxley Act, Roundtable 2005. Available: www.sec.gov/spotlight/
soxcomp.htm
    (Another source of information on these findings of the
    Roundtable is available: www.winston.com/siteFiles/publications/
    SECRoundtableonSOX404all4–2005.pdf)
Sarbanes-Oxley Act, Roundtable 2006. Available: www.sec.gov/spotlight/
soxcomp.htm OR www.jeffersonwells.com/Knowledge/Internal/
sec_pcaob.pdf
Sarbanes-Oxley Act, SEC. Available: www.sec.gov/rules/concept/2006/
34–54122.pdf
Sarbanes-Oxley Act, SEC Publications. Available: www.sec.gov/spotlight/
sarbanes-oxley.htm
Sarbanes-Oxley Act, Section 404. Available: www.sec.gov/news/press/
2003–66.htm
SEC 17a–4 Rule. Available: www.law.us.edu/CCL/34ActRIs/rule17a–
4.html
    (Good summaries of SEC 17a–4 are available:
    www.omnirim.com/PDFs/OmniRIMwhitePaper_RM_SEC_
    Rule17a.pdf
    www.kahnconsultinginc.com/library/compliancebrief/KCI–17a–4-
    Brief.pdf
    www.kahnconsultinginc.com/library/KCI-SEC-ThirdParty.pdf)
Sedona Conference. 2005. "The Sedona Guidelines for Managing Information and Records in the Information Age." Available:
www.thesedonaconference.org/publications.html

Sedona Conference. 2003. "The Sedona Principles: Best Practices Recommendations and Principles for Addressing Electronic Document Production (Revised, 2005)." Available: www.thesedonaconference.org/publications.html

SunGard Availability Services. 2004. "Building Best Practices in Records Management Compliance: ILM Strategies for Security, Protection, Recovery and Availability." Available: www.availability.sungard.com/NR/rdonlyres/527C9098–1C0F–4C3B–968F-FF339E3CCF94/0/RecordsManagementEBfinal.pdf

Uniform Electronic Transactions Act (UETA). 1999. Available: www.law.upenn.edu.bll/ulc/fnact99/1990s/ueta99.htm

U.S. Department of Commerce. 2003. "Electronic Signatures: A Review of the Exceptions." Available: www.ntia.doc.gov/ntiahome/frnotices/2002/esign/report2003/esignfinal.pdf

U.S. Department of Health and Human Services. 2003. "Summary of the HIPAA Rule." Available: www.hhs.gov/ocr/privacysummary.pdf (Good summaries of HIPAA Privacy Rule are available: www.omnirim.com/PDFs/OmniRIMWhitePaperHIPAA.pdf OR www.emc.com/news/analyst/kahn_consulting/pdf/2005_10_11_KCI_EMC_HIPAA_Compliance_Brief.pdf)

U.S. Food and Drug Administration. 1997. "Title 21. The FDA Act." Available: www.fda.gov/ora/compliance_ref/part11/frs/background/11cfr-fr.htm
(Good summaries of the FDA Act are available: www.omnirim.com/PDFs/OmniRIMwhitePaper_RM_21CFRPart11.pdf OR www.emc.com/news/analyst/kahn_consulting/pdf/2005–11–09_KCI_EMC_Part_11_Compliance_Brief.pdf)

U.S. Securities and Exchange Commission. 2002. "SEC, NYSE, NASD Fine Five Firms Total of $8.25 Million for Failure to Preserve E-Mail Communications." Available: www.sec.gov/news/press/2002–173.htm

U.S. Securities and Exchange Commission. 2003. "NASD and NYSE Rulemaking. Release No. 34–47912; File Nos. SR-NYSE–2002–49; SR-NASD–2002–154." Available: www.sec.gov/rules/sro/34–47912.htm

8

Conclusion

As we look at results of the preceding review of information systems, I think one can accurately state that there is both good news and bad news regarding the future of electronic records management. Let us start with the good news. There are many legitimate reasons to be optimistic about the future of electronic recordkeeping.

PROGRESS

1) Records management programs in businesses appear to be steadily improving. Cohasset Associates have concluded that their surveys would indicate that the tide is turning and businesses are getting the message that they must improve their programs for managing records (Williams and Ashley, 2005). Most experts attribute this improvement primarily to new regulations, court cases, technology solutions, and the realization that sound records management is the keystone to compliance and effective governance.

2) Recordkeeping functionality is definitely being integrated into most of the electronic information systems, with the most progress occurring within enterprise content management systems. The recordkeeping functionality of the new document management/content management applications is better in almost every respect than that found in systems a decade ago. The new systems have more controls and audit trails to maintain and document authenticity, far more metadata to enhance the quality of the evidence, more effective reten-

tion and disposal functionality, and overall superior strategies for managing records over the life cycle. In large part, this trend is a result of requests or demands from users. Survey results indicate that records management and archiving functionality is near the top of most users' lists of desirable requirements.

3) Issues related to compliance will continue to motivate businesses to improve their recordkeeping systems. The message from the courts is quite clear: institutions cannot systematically meet compliance requirements without a strong records management program. Every law, regulation, and best practice stresses the need to create more detailed and frequent audits, develop better internal control systems, and design and implement more effective retention and disposal programs. Meeting compliance requirements is the archivist and records manager's strongest argument for better recordkeeping. Presently, compliance issues are primarily the problem of public businesses. However, in the near future, I think we will witness the emergence of these issues at other types of institutions, including academic institutions.

4) The software tools to manage digital objects and records are improving every year, which potentially will make it easier to implement the functional requirements for a recordkeeping system. I feel certain that much of the sophisticated software now being developed for decision support systems will eventually be applied to recordkeeping systems as well.

5) The emergence of enterprise-wide architecture provides archivists and records managers with a more realistic and cost effective strategy for managing all types of records in one environment. Clearly we are not as close as vendors would have us believe to the one unified system that will manage all our information. However, in the last ten years tremendous progress has been made in developing more effective enterprise-wide strategies for managing all types of information, and this is a very positive development for electronic recordkeeping.

6) Emphasis on standards in building information systems is a very positive development for records managers and archivists. The use of standards in creating access and preservation strategies has always been an important component in an electronic records management strategy. It is very encouraging to see that other information professionals are also advocating this approach.

7) Capturing more metadata documenting a wider variety of activities is becoming a more standard strategy for designers of all types

of systems. As I reviewed metadata requirements for each of the types of information systems, I was struck by how these specifications are beginning to look more and more like the lists of recordkeeping metadata elements developed by archivists and records managers. In the future I think it will be less difficult for our professions to convince our IT partners to include additional recordkeeping metadata.

Unfortunately there are also many reasons to be pessimistic about the short-term and long-term future of electronic records management.

CHALLENGES

1) Sufficient resources still are not being allocated to developing strong programs for managing electronic records. According to a 2005 survey, 35 percent of the institutions do not include electronic records in their records management program, and 43 percent do not have comprehensive records retention schedules for electronic records. In this same survey, 49 percent said that if legally challenged they were slightly confident or not at all confident (the two lowest categories) that their business organization could successfully demonstrate that its electronic records were accurate, reliable, and trustworthy. Finally in regard to such a basic management requirement as preservation of records, 68 percent responded that their business does not have in place a formal plan to migrate older records, and 82 percent responded they do not have a specific budget in the organization for record migration (Williams and Ashley, 2005).

Awareness of the need to improve electronic records systems is certainly growing, but this has not yet translated into the allocation of sufficient resources to improve the performance of these systems. Although satisfying compliance requirements is having a positive impact on recordkeeping practices, most of the surveys on compliance would strongly suggest that most managers continue to view records management as just another project to support on a short-term basis. This has to change if organizations are to have any chance of consistently being compliant with laws and regulations. Ultimately, the goal according to most experts must be to make electronic records management a high priority business initiative that has the full support of corporate leadership. In other words, records management cannot continue to be viewed as a temporary remedy to problems. It must become a sustainable process that has the ongoing commitment of the organization's top executives and the full support of the company's financial and technical resources.

2) Partnerships between IT, audit, legal counsel, and archives and records management have not developed to the point that is needed to create an effective electronic records management program. Evidence would strongly indicate that in many environments these professional groups do not collaborate effectively on information management and compliance issues. Evidence would indicate that in many instances IT is not actively working with records professionals in solving and managing the problems relating to the life cycle management of electronic records. Conversely, one might also conclude from this evidence that archivists and records managers are doing a poor job reaching out and forming effective partnerships with IT professionals and other potential allies. This is a major problem that will essentially derail any attempts to develop effective electronic records management programs. The tasks at hand are far too varied and complex for one professional group to tackle by itself. Effective records management programs will be created only as a result of the contributions of many information professionals, and certainly one of the most critical members of this team are IT personnel (Williams and Ashley, 2005).

3) Evidence from surveys would also indicate that IT still has a long way to go in understanding some of the issues associated with recordkeeping. For example, surveys strongly suggest that IT personnel are not familiar with strategies for managing records over the life cycle, nor does IT view electronic records management as a high priority (Williams, 2002). Conversely (although there is no survey data available), I strongly believe that archivists and records managers still do not have enough technical knowledge on how information systems work nor do they possess the understanding of the concepts and vocabulary to communicate effectively with IT personnel.

4) Much progress still is required in developing automated strategies for implementing many of the functional requirements for recordkeeping systems. In particular, there is a need to automate more fully the capture of record content and metadata as part of an automated workflow or business process model. As an archivist it is encouraging to witness the development of more robust business process management applications; this software has the potential to provide an effective strategy for capturing records as they are created and used.

However, it seems to me that we are still a long way from implementing such a strategy within most information and transaction processing systems. In particular, I am most pessimistic about the development of strategies for capturing transactional records and moving them to a recordkeeping system. Automating retention and disposal decisions are also still a problem. In many cases, businesses are unsuccessfully attempting to match up retention schedules created for paper records to digital objects or data in tables. In my opinion, the failure of these endeavors can be traced primarily to the absence in most systems of a classification scheme that can efficiently implement the disposition strategy. I am strongly of the opinion that retention and disposal decisions within automated systems can only effectively be implemented by means of associating records with the business processes that created them. Until these business process models are fully integrated into information systems, I believe we will continue to struggle to automate the retention and disposal process.

5) Unfortunately, many data and information systems still do not include well designed strategies for preserving records over time. Designers and managers of these systems are aware that they must keep the data alive for a period of time, but most strategies still focus on back-up systems and do not articulate a clear strategy for preserving records according to a well-defined schedule. For example, advice on "archiving" and preservation within the data warehouse environment typically focuses on strategies for transferring older, less useful data, or the more detailed and voluminous transaction level data to off-line storage. Nothing is said on how to manage and preserve that data after it is moved to that off-line environment. Without doubt, archivists and records managers must make the creation of a strategy for preservation and not just data recovery a major priority in system design and modification. It is important to remember in planning this strategy that the problem demands administrative planning as well as technology solutions. Technological solutions certainly get most of the attention and undoubtedly there will be quite a number of decisions to be made about how to implement specific preservation strategies. However, these decisions on technology must be accompanied by the creation of a management regime for implanting the technological solutions.

6) The management of e-mail is still a major problem for most institutions. On the positive side, more and more software and technology solutions are appearing every year. Unfortunately, most insti-

tutions have not developed strategies and methodologies for evaluating and classifying e-mail so that they can make use of this technology. Most significantly, surveys would indicate most institutions do not evaluate and appraise e-mail according to the content or based on the value of the business process that created the records. Until institutions develop better methodologies for determining what e-mail to keep and for how long, any strategy for managing this resource is bound to fail.

7) Most managers of electronic records and information have not yet made the transition from reactive participants to proactive "change agents." All the laws and regulations make it quite clear that those individuals responsible for managing the compliance process must be proactive and not reactive participants. They must be "change agents," or "enablers" in the process of improving the way the organization manages its records to meet the requirements of the laws and regulations. For example, SOX requires that executives assume responsibility for financial reporting, which means they must become more involved in ensuring that certain requirements are achieved. Similarly, legal departments are advised to take a much more active role in records management and to become more knowledgeable about where data and information is located, how it is managed, and how it can be retrieved. Most experts on compliance also recommend a more active role for IT in managing the compliance process. IT staff are advised to become more knowledgeable about life cycle management concepts and particularly records retention and digital preservation. Finally, most experts on compliance requirements advise that records managers/archivists become a more integral part of the teams that are managing the process. One of the keys to achieving this goal is for records managers to become more proactive in promoting awareness of life cycle management and of the requirements of recordkeeping systems. It also requires that records managers and archivists more aggressively inform the information management community regarding the skills they possess and the contributions they can make to the development of a strategy for legal compliance. Unfortunately, this transition of information managers to proactive change agents is happening very slowly, and from my perspective much too slowly. My message to my colleagues is clear: to be an effective records manager in the age of automation, you must begin the journey to proactively influence how electronic information systems are designed and modified.

When all is said and done, however, I am more optimistic than pessimistic about the future of electronic records management. After decades of technology implementation, it is increasingly understood that "technology used to enable these information processes is considerably less important than the information that systems hold. Information is dynamic, capable of creating great value, and is the glue that holds enterprises together" (McGee and Prusak, 1993: 3). However we are all beginning to realize that just creating and storing the information is not enough. This information only becomes an asset if it is properly managed. In fact, as organizations are discovering, these records, if neglected, can do harm to an institution. Consequently, I believe we are entering a decade when more emphasis will be placed on developing better recordkeeping systems. I think there is a strong sense that society has lost control of its information resource, and that we need to step back and rethink how we manage it. For archivists and records managers, this is a period of great opportunities, but also great risks. If we properly train ourselves and confidently and aggressively form partnerships and define what we can contribute to the management of information, we can emerge as important and recognized contributors to the management of information within the institution. However, if we sit back and wait for IT personnel to come to us and do not obtain the necessary skills to manage electronic information, we could easily be left out of the process. At this point we control our own fate, and our actions will define the future of the profession.

REFERENCES

McGee, James V., and Lawrence Prusak. 1993. *Managing Information Strategically*. Hoboken, NJ: Wiley.

Williams, Robert F. 2002. *Realizing the Need and Putting the Key Components in Place to "Getting it Right" in Records Management*. AIIM/ Cohasset. Available: www.merresource.com/pdf/getting_it_right.pdf

Williams, Robert, and Lori Ashley. 2005. *2005 Electronic Records Management Survey. A Renewed Call to Action*. Cohasset Associates. Available: www.cohasset.com/whitepaper_survey2005.html

Index

About the Author

Philip Bantin is presently Director of the Indiana University Office of University Archives and Records Management. Bantin has been actively involved in electronic records management since 1995. He has received two NHPRC grants to develop strategies for managing electronic records, has authored numerous articles on the subject, and in the last 12 years has given over 50 presentations on various aspects of electronic records management to professional organizations in the United States, Europe, and Africa. Bantin is Associate Adjunct Professor at the Indiana University School of Library and Information Science, where he is Director of the Specialization in Archives and Records Management. In 2003, Bantin was elected a fellow of the Society of American Archivists.